The Real God Code

The Real God Code:
The Ten Commandments In The Leningrad Codex

Robert M. Pill

The Real God Code: The Ten Commandments In The Leningrad Codex
Copyright © 2021-2023 by Robert M. Pill.

For Jewish Scripture quotations:
Hebrew font based Scripture taken from digitized Westminster Leningrad Codex (WLC), © 2004 Christopher V. Kimball,
https://www.tanach.us/License.html version number 26.2;
English Text taken from Jewish Publication Society version of 1917 (JPS 1917), in the public domain;
Verse ordering structure for both have been modified by the author to conform to the actual Leningrad Codex for The Ten Commandments. Additionally, for the English Text, certain names have been changed to reflect a transliteration closer to their Hebrew pronunciations.

For New Testament quotations:
Scriptures marked ESV are taken from the THE HOLY BIBLE, ENGLISH STANDARD VERSION (ESV): Scriptures taken from THE HOLY BIBLE, ENGLISH STANDARD VERSION ® Copyright© 2001 by Crossway, a publishing ministry of Good News Publishers. Used by permission.

Definitions of Hebrew words, unless otherwise noted, are from Ernest Klein, "A Comprehensive Etymological Dictionary of the Hebrew Language for Readers of English" (Carta, Jerusalem);
Copyright © 1987 by The Beatrice & Arthur Minden Foundation & The University of Haifa.

Digitized version of Klein Dictionary:
Ernest Klein, 'Klein Dictionary', Sefaria, accessed 13 May 2021,
https://www.sefaria.org/Klein_Dictionary.

All rights reserved. No part of this publication may be reproduced, distributed or transmitted in any form or by any means, including photocopying, recording, or other electronic or mechanical methods, without the prior written permission of the publisher, except in the case of brief quotations embodied in critical reviews and certain other noncommercial uses permitted by copyright law.

Book and Cover design by Robert M. Pill

ISBN: 978-1-7373435-0-9 (Soft Cover)
ISBN: 978-1-7373435-1-6 (eBook)
ISBN: 978-1-7373435-2-3 (Hard Cover)

First Edition: Year 2021 Month

10 9 8 7 **6** 5 4 3 2 1

Psalms 19:15

יִהְיוּ לְרָצוֹן ׀ אִמְרֵי־פִי וְהֶגְיוֹן לִבִּי לְפָנֶיךָ יְהֹוָה צוּרִי וְגֹאֲלִי׃

Let the words of my mouth and the meditation of my heart be acceptable before Thee, Yehovah, my Rock, and my Redeemer.

Table of Contents

Preface .... *iii*

Introduction *1*

   The Two Tablets of Stone 3
   A Source Document of Ancient Biblical Hebrew? 6
   The Source Has The Intended Verse Separations! 6
   Exodus 20 Has 21 verses In *The Leningrad Codex* 7
   Does verse ordered structure make any difference to the meaning? 8
   Judeo-Christian Tradition — "the Law" Based Upon Holy Scripture 9
   A Basic Sense of Justice 10
   "Supreme Law" — The Ten Commandments 10
   The Sermon on the Mount 11
   What If The Christian Source *Is Not* The *de facto* Jewish–Hebrew Source? 12
   The Christian Doctrine of *"The Curse Of The Law?"* 13
   A Word Of Warning 13
   An Idolatry of the Heart 13
   But, Isn't "The Word of God" Supposed To Be "Without Error?" 14
   ... for it is written, *"Cursed is everyone who is hanged on a tree"* 14
   A *"Hebrew Of The Hebrews,"* Or An Abject Liar, *A Purposeful Deceiver?* 15
   Thus, Paul's "God" Should NOT Be Confused with יְהֹוָה [Yehovah] –The אֱלֹהִים [Elohim] of Abraham, Isaac and Jacob! 16
   The *Curse: Only When A Body Remains Hung After The Sun Sets!* 16
   <u>Jesus's Body *DID NOT REMAIN* "Hung On The Cross" — After Sunset!</u> 18

- The New Testament Supersedes The Tanakh? 19
- *"He makes the first one obsolete"* 20
- In my opinion, Jesus is merely the proxy to Paul! 20
- Is Paul the de facto Christian Messiah? 21
- But Are There "Non-Redeemable" Sins? 21
- "Sex" With A Beast (Animal); Taking A Bribe To Murder An Innocent Person 22
- Get-Out-Of-Hell-Free — "Merely by How One Thinks/Believes" 22
- Do The Ten Commandments Apply To Everyone? 22
- Except For The Seventh Day Sabbath (the Fourth Commandment)! 23
- The Ten Commandments: The *Real* God Code! 23
- Biblical Hebrew — An Ancient Language 24
- What Is Modern Hebrew? 25

Exodus 20:1–12 29

Getting The Third Commandment Right 35

How Many Commandments? 41
- Why I Promote Exodus 20 Over Deuteronomy 5 43

The Commandments With Comments 45
- The Idea of Ten In Idiomatic Phrasing 59

Root Definitions For Exodus 20:1-12 63
- Common Prepositions / Prefixes / Suffixes (Klein Dictionary) 64
- Common Suffixes 67
- Verses 1-12 And Root Definitions Of Each Word 69

Epilogue 145

Acknowledgements 149

Preface

I began writing this book because I wanted the knowledge of the Ten Commandments to be known and understood by more people than just those who were visiting my website, https://www.the-iconoclast.org, where I have much to say regarding the subject.

To me, The Ten Commandments represent the very best expression of a focus which must be turned towards the Creator, rather than on man's infatuation with satisfying his own desires, focusing on self.

Left to his own devices, man seems to be "hell-bent" on self destruction. There also appears to be a general lack of knowledge and understanding of the presence of The Almighty God, even though many people express that they have "faith" or "religion."

From my way of thinking, if more people really had faith and a true expression of their religion, society would benefit, generally, in a positive way more so than it does currently.

Can a good understanding of **The Ten Commandments** bring greater civility to humanity, even that we might then come to consider it normal to 'love our neighbor as ourselves?' I certainly hope so!

During the course of writing this book, a couple of incidents occurred, which I will now use just to further show a general lack of knowledge and understanding of any supreme and "Holy Law," and the results of a casual disregarding of it.

My apologies, in advance, if my telling of the circumstances of these events is too detailed and long; but, I want to use them to drive home the point, really, of a base depravity of mankind in society (essentially a lack of any real knowledge and fear of a Holy Creator-God!).

The first incident was where I heard of the sudden death of someone my family had known in the last several years.

The initial report came that "B" was said to have been driving his pickup truck and rolled the vehicle into a ditch, killing him in the process.

As time went by I found out more details of the incident.

The woman "B" had been engaged to and had been living with for several years, who had also acted as the office manager for his small business, had recently left "B" to move in with one of his older brothers!

"B" did not just have an accident of chance. As it turns out, he was initially stopped by police officers, but he "took off" when they got out of their vehicle to approach him! He fled at over 100 miles per hour when he lost control and immediately died from the violent impact.

Clearly, "B" was responsible for his own actions. However, could it also be said that the actions which led to his untimely death were a direct result of his mental state after his now ex-fiancé left him so abruptly?

To me, this tragedy is a result of a **general acceptance of sin** within our society. This is evident in the casual attitude that people take with each other's lives without considering that their actions can have unforeseen and tragic consequences, such as in the death of "B."

A second incident involved someone I have known for a long time.

I will begin this discussion by giving a little background.

"L" has Asperger's Syndrome (he is a high functioning autistic); he is non-observing Jewish (this information will help to understand later details regarding a "Muslim daughter-in-law"). Although "L" believes in God, he has no religious affiliation. In fact, he has little tolerance for *religion* per se. Most of the events herein are from his perspective.

"L" had had what was then **thought to be a stroke** a little over a year previous to the "incident;" it took him about six months to recover enough to where he could speak clearly. Also, even though he had held down a contract programming job for many years, in his condition the stress proved to be too great, and he just quit about a month prior to the "incident."

"L" had been living with the family of a then 86 year old woman ("P") for most of the last 30 years; after deaths and family members leaving, it was just the two of them living together at that point.

"P" was taking a newly prescribed anti-depression medicine in addition to having been on Warfarin, blood thinning medicine, for some time. It should be noted that any person on Warfarin blood thinning medicine typically bruises, and can bleed, easily.

At the time of this particular incident, "L" had been sick and had gone on a "<u>self-medicated alcoholic binge</u>," so much so that his body was most likely in a toxic state. "P" was clearly not herself either. She had been having a bad reaction from her newly prescribed anti-depression medicine where mood swings affected her behavior.

In her own "condition," the chain of events began after she became angry and actually threw hot food directly out of a skillet upon "L!"

Suffice it to say, anyone familiar with an ***autistic person*** knows that they can be easily agitated even under "normal" conditions.

"L" reacted by grabbing his friend, pushing her to the ground, and bruising her. She later stated that he had threatened to kill her.

Ok, here's the "rub."

In the state of Texas there is a law which makes it a ***felony*** if it can be reasonably shown that a person over the age of 65 has been injured by another person!

That law makes it so that the only real "evidence" needed to be seen to make a charge is for law enforcement personnel, along with the testimony of the victim, to determine that the elderly person has been harmed. Apparently, the law does not need to take into account a domestic living situation, even in the time of "COVID," or any mitigating circumstances, including any potential provocation by the said "victim!"

In this particular case, merely the word of the elderly woman or her spokesperson (her "Muslim daughter-in-law," in this case), merited calls for "L," the "offender," to be arrested and charged with **felony abuse of an elderly person.**

No investigation, no circumstantial evidence, no questions to the "assailant", no consideration that there may have been a provocation, or that he may have Asperger's Syndrome and had also had significant signs of a stroke were important or necessary in **law enforcement's supposed "investigation" leading to arrest.**

Such an offense automatically becomes a **"crime against the state of Texas,"** not longer a personal crime as with someone under the age of 65. All a District Attorney has to do is **prove** that the elderly person was injured (**even just bruised up as in this case**).

The result is a **_two_ to _ten_ year prison sentence** upon conviction in a court of law!

In the judicial milieu in which we find ourselves today, murderers, thieves, illegal "migrants" etc. all seem to receive lesser punishment; and they are typically treated with greater respect!

Moreover, apparently the **"Muslim daughter-in-law" had previously made threats to "L."** She had left at least one message on his cell phone, threatening that she was going to have her **law enforcement friends** set him up to be arrested, so that he would be "killed" from the resulting process!

On the day of this particular incident, afterwards the elderly woman drove, **on her own,** to the house where her son and daughter-in-law live. Her daughter-in-law apparently was then able to get emergency services to come. In this process, **a charge was brought against "L" for felony abuse of an elderly person.**

Needless to say, it was reported that two officers went to the house, opened the back door, went upstairs to where "L" was laying in bed with only basic clothing on, having no socks or shoes on his feet.

"L" says that the officers beat him up, kicked him in the back so hard that he could not walk, hand-cuffed and dragged him down the stairs and into their vehicle. Subsequently, the tops of his feet and toes were heavily cut and bruised.

"L" said that these officers also dragged him from their vehicle into the Granbury jail where **he spent Christmas week sleeping on the bare, cold concrete floor.** As I understand it, he was given no covering for his feet such as socks or shoes; he was not provided even a bunk or mattress to sleep on!

It should be mentioned that **these law enforcement officers,** in addition to charging "L" with felony abuse of an elderly person, **also charged him with a misdemeanor crime of interfering with a 911 call!**

Would there ever be a time when that kind of treatment upon an elderly autistic person should also be considered a crime, in the least for a violation of basic civil rights, not to mention basic human dignity in mistreatment of a handicapped person?

Moreover, since "L" had extremely high blood pressure (again, he may have had a stroke around November 2019), "P" took "L's" blood pressure medicine to the jail for him the day following his arrest. Unfortunately, **the jailhouse M.D. refused to allow "L" to take his prescribed blood pressure medicine while in the jail!**

When I first saw "L" a week after his arrest, he was heavily bruised in his upper body and his feet and toes still had open wounds! He could barely walk. He was still so agitated over the events of his arrest that he was not able to focus on many other things easily.

It appears to me, in at least some cases, in the city of Granbury, law enforcement and its jailing facilities do not behave as if a person is to be considered <u>**innocent until proven guilty**</u>; **it seems punishment for a "crime" starts with an arrest just after an *<u>uninvestigated accusation</u>*!**

Of course, if a person has been "set up," where small town *powers-that-be* control all, a charge alone is enough to bring the weight of the city's **"good-old-boy" justice system** upon an individual, and they have no trouble justifying that any civility can be easily disregarded.

It certainly appears that their attitude is that there is no need to be subject to any supreme law or to even determine that the punishment should be anywhere equivalent to having been considered as "an eye for an eye or a tooth for a tooth," that is, as in ***Biblical justice!***

Rather, this **"set up"** could essentially result in a death sentence for an autistic man over the age of 60 who may have had a stroke; to go to prison for up to ten years for what could otherwise be seen as a **domestic *scuffle* perhaps instigated by the "victim!"**

Any basic investigation might show that 'P," the Eighty-Six year old woman, had had a bad reaction from her own newly prescribed anti-depression medicine. By provoking a response from the 63 year old autistic man by throwing hot food directly from a skillet on him; having been on Warfarin blood thinning medicine, and by being easily bruised, **a felony charge was brought upon "L!"**

Again, **"P" was not so "injured"** that she could not drive herself to her son's house, nor was she injured enough to require more than minimal treatment; and she was able to return home that same day!

So, who should be considered as responsible in this particular case?

No doubt, "L," who responded to the provocation from the elderly woman he was living with these many years, is responsible for his own actions. Losing one's temper, though perhaps understandable, is not warranted to injure an elderly friend you know and love!

Again, anyone who knows even a high functioning autistic person is well aware of how easy it is to **"get them riled up"** even under otherwise "normal" circumstances. However, as mentioned earlier, "L" was also "self-medicated," under the influence of excess alcohol at the time of the incident!

At some level, should not this elderly woman's provocation of having thrown hot food from a skillet on "L" bear some consideration before such a severe charge and subsequent punishment is brought about? No doubt but the new anti-depressant drugs she was on influenced her own behavior **bringing about "L's" predictable response.**

How about the "Muslim daughter-in-law," who had previously threatened "L" that she was planning this particular event with her law enforcement "friends?" Would a fair and honest discovery investigation yield some complicity or even conspiracy by any or all of these parties?

Should not consideration be given about the possibility of an over-zealous District Attorney, who chose to pursue the charges for this case without any regard to any potentially mitigating circumstances?

"L's" attorney also indicated that the District Attorney merely has to *prove* that the elderly lady was harmed in order to get a conviction!

This, despite the elderly woman having written and signed a letter of non-prosecution, and any evidence of any manner of provocation, or the autistic man, the "offender," having had a stroke, or even that there may have been a "set up" between the "Muslim Daughter-in-Law" and her law enforcement friends, would not be considered important to the District Attorney in her decision to try this case!

Has "L's" <u>attorney</u> done all that he can, except to tell "L" his <u>only</u> <u>choice</u> <u>is</u> <u>to</u> <u>plead</u> <u>guilty</u> in a plea agreement "deal," as it would be a "slam–dunk" case for the District Attorney to prove guilt in a court, because all the prosecutor has to do is show that the elderly woman had been harmed; again, no accounting being needed for the extent of injury nor circumstances surrounding it?

Perhaps, "L" would have been better served by a **court-appointed attorney.** It turned out that **"L" was coached by his friend** "P's" lawyer in her recommending him to seek the services of a different lawyer. Incidentally, her recommendation was for one **who had previously been the District Attorney** in that very same county!

No doubt but **"lawfare"** extends to the family of an accused person in such cases. To give him even "half of a fighting chance," they had to immediately outlay about $11,000 to pay for bail and attorney fees. Needless to say, both **bail and attorney fees were increased substantially** due to the <u>added</u> <u>misdemeanor</u> <u>charge</u> <u>of</u> <u>interfering</u> <u>with</u> <u>a</u> <u>911</u> <u>call</u>, which was "thrown-out" in pre-trial hearings!

Further, should the jail itself, in its treatment of "L," be subject to scrutiny? How about some sort of medical board attention to be given regarding the "jailhouse physician," because of his refusal to allow a man with extremely high blood pressure access to his potentially life-saving medicine? Should medical mispractice even be entertained?

I have to ask, do justice and mercy have any place within our judicial system? Is this the accepted norm in Granbury, Texas? Could there actually be an **overarching 'secret handshake' of justice there?**

If it somehow turns out that the "Muslim daughter-in-law" had signed off that she claimed she was an eyewitness, that could certainly be considered fraud and lying to law enforcement. She clearly was not present to witness the "incident."

No doubt but if she was complicit in working with her law enforcement friends to set "L" up for this felony charge, shouldn't some sort of investigation be given consideration in the ensuing judicial process?

Further, the 86 year old woman had later sent an email regarding Granbury law enforcement harassment. Here's a snippet, just for information purposes (I have preserved spelling, punctuation):

> *I need to tell you why I was wondering about the trail. A Inspector for the Sheriffs department was very rude to me and told me I had to talk with him that it was urgent we didn't have anytime to waste. I called your Lawyer and he told me I didn't have to talk with him. I knew he was going to pump and twist my words crucify "L" and get his brownie points so blocked his calls and refused to talk to him. That was about 3 weeks ago, must not have been the urgent.*

Again, it appears that no higher, universal law merits any consideration to **the-powers-that-be** in the city of Granbury, Texas!

Moreover, the Sheriff's department seems to have no compunction in harassing an 86 year old woman after they have clearly **"man-handled"** her 63 year old autistic friend and brought felony charges against him!

> *"One witness shall not rise up against a man for any iniquity, or for any sin, in any sin that he sinneth; at the mouth of two witnesses, or at the mouth of three witnesses, shall a matter be established." [Deuteronomy 19:15 JPS 1917]*

Postscript

On Saturday, September 18, 2021, the above mentioned "L" passed away in a Granbury, TX hospital. He had been an inmate in the Granbury jail and succumbed to what was determined to be an acute liver disease.

Not long thereafter, the 86-year old lady, **"P,"** **asked the family for a copy of the death certificate,** so that she could collect on the **life insurance policy** she had previously taken out on "L," her long-time friend and companion!

I have mentioned this account as a means to illustrate the state of mind and the similar conditions easily repeated elsewhere; e.g. the abject depravity of man even within the criminal justice system!

Essentially, there appears to be no basic sense of a higher law or really any **"fear of God"** in the laws and in those that are supposed to carry them out in the real world.

My sense is that if people would regularly meditate and focus upon the very heart of the base for the laws of Western Civilization, **the Ten Commandments,** greater civility could, in the least, be a result.

It is my sincere desire that those who read this book come to appreciate the profound greatness and love that the Almighty, Creator – God has **for those who seek Him with their whole heart.**

Robert M. Pill (September 2023)

Introduction

In this present day and age, there are many disparate voices that present themselves to be *the de facto* **source of truth** for all things related to "God."

I certainly hope that I do not appear to be that way. Moreover, I do not want to imply that I claim to be a spokesman, a prophet or in any way hold a special position in the realm of the Almighty; but, rather just to being a simple messenger, as "one crying in the wilderness," of that greater voice — the exclusive Author of Truth, (יְהֹוָה [1][Yehovah[2]]) — the one and only *Creator of the Universe.*

To wit, I whole–heartedly consider that the *Creator of the Universe* has given *the license* to the knowledge of what He has determined to be as His representative voice, namely the Tanakh,[3] the Jewish,

---

[1] The name of God, in Hebrew, with vowel pointers indicating the correct pronunciation.

יְהֹוָה, יְהוָֹה m.n. the proper name of God in the Bible, Tetragrammaton. [It prob. derives from הוה (= to be). The usual transliteration 'Jehovah' is based on the supposition that the Tetragrammaton is the imperfect Qal or Hiph'il of הוה and lit. means 'the one who is', 'the existing', resp. 'who calls into existence'. In reality, however, the pronunciation and literal meaning of the Tetragrammaton is unknown. cp. יָהּ [1].]
Ernest Klein, A Comprehensive Etymological Dictionary of the Hebrew Language for Readers of English" (CARTA, Jerusalem), p 255 (right column).
Ernest Klein, 'A Comprehensive Etymological Dictionary of the Hebrew Language for Readers of English', Sefaria, accessed 9 Mar 2021, https://www.sefaria.org/Klein_Dictionary

[2] Yehovah. The English transliteration of the name of God in Hebrew (יְהֹוָה).
For more information, see Hebrew Voices #47 - A Disastrous Misunderstanding of the Name Yehovah (Posted on March 11, 2020 by Nehemia Gordon): "In Hebrew Voices, A Disastrous Understanding of the Name Yehovah, Nehemia Gordon explains the meaning of Yehovah, the mistake people make thinking it has to do with "destruction," and how Yahweh in Gnostic sources is the god of chaos. Listen to the short podcast, and then check out the detailed grammatical explanation below, of how we know Yehovah has nothing to do with the Hebrew word for "destruction."
Suzette wrote: "Forgive me, I was one of those people who knew just enough Hebrew to be dangerous… Thanks for the article!".''
Nehemia Gordon, 'Hebrew Voices #47 – A Disastrous Misunderstanding of the Name Yehovah', Nehemia's Wall, last modified 11 Mar 2020, https://www.nehemiaswall.com/disastrous-misunderstanding-yehovah

[3] Tanakh. "Though the word "Bible" is commonly used by non-Jews -- as are the terms "Old Testament" and "New Testament" -- the appropriate term to use for the Hebrew scriptures ("scripture" is a synonym used by both Jews and non-Jews) is Tanakh. This word is derived from the Hebrew letters of its three components:

Torah: The Books of Genesis (Bereshit), Exodus (Shemot), Leviticus (Vayikrah), Numbers (Bamidbar) and Deuteronomy (Devarim).

Hebrew-language based Scriptures, to those whom He has chosen to reveal it.

More particularly, the specific reference within the Hebrew Scriptures that consists of the essence of what I am calling "The *Real* God Code," are the well known **TEN COMMANDMENTS** of Exodus 20!

In my opinion, it is only by a regular, disciplined meditation on those *Ten Commandments* sourced directly from *the Leningrad Codex* that one can truly become *open* to ascertaining "**The *Real* God Code,**" in fact, to knowing אֱלֹהִים [Elohim] (aka God)![4]

That statement infers that a disciplined meditation (or study) is the key to knowing אֱלֹהִים [Elohim] (God). Two passages readily come to my mind that support that position: Joshua 1:8 and Psalms 1:1-2:

Nevi'im (Prophets): The Books of Joshua, Judges, I Samuel, II Samuel, I Kings, II Kings, Isaiah, Jeremiah, Ezekiel, Hosea, Joel, Amos, Obadiah, Jonah, Micah, Nahum, Habukkuk, Zephaniah, Haggai, Zechariah, and Malachi. (The last twelve are sometimes grouped together as "Trei Asar" ["Twelve"].)

Ketuvim (Writings): The Books of Psalms, Proverbs, Job, Song of Songs, Ruth, Lamentations, Ecclesiastes, Esther, Daniel (although not all that is included in the Christian Canon), Ezra and Nehemiah, I Chronicles, and II Chronicles."
Shamash Hadash, 'The Tanakh', Jewish Virtual Library, accessed 25 Apr 2021,
https://www.jewishvirtuallibrary.org/the-tanakh

[4] אֱלֹהִים Elohim.

אֱלָהוּת, אֱלָהוּת f.n. divinity. [Formed from אֱלֹהַּ with suff. וּת. cp. Aram. אֱלָהוּתָא, Syr. אֱלָהוּתָא, Arab. 'ilâha, 'ulūha, 'ulūhiyya (= divinity).]

אֱלֹהִי, אֱלֹהִי adj. MH Godlike, divine. [Formed from אֱלֹהַּ with suff. י.] cp. Syr. אֱלָהָיָא, Arab. 'ilāhiyy (= divine).]

אֱלֹהִים, אֱלֹהִים m.n. pl. 1 gods. 2 God (pl. of majesty). 3 supernatural beings. 4 judges. [According to some scholars אֱלֹהִים is the pl. of אֱלוֹהַּ, according to others it is the pl. of אֵל I.]

אֵל I m.n. 1 god. 2 God. [Of uncertain etymology. Formerly most scholars derived the word from the base אול (= to be strong). Nöldeke connected it with base אול (= to be in front), which is probably identical orig. with אול (= to be strong); see אול I. According to Lagarde it is a derivative of אלה (= to strive or reach after a person), hence lit. means 'He whom everyone strives to reach'. Ewald and König derive it from base אלה (= to be strong). None of these etymologies, nor any others suggested, is convincing. Related to Phoen. אל, אלן, Samaritan אל, Ugar. 'l (= the mightiest god. 'El', 'lt (= name of the wife of 'El'), Akka. ilu (= god), Arab. al-ilāt (= goddess). cp. אֵל II, אֱלָה II. cp. also the second element in יִשְׂרָאֵל.]

אֵל II m.n. power. [Prob. derived from אול (= to be strong), and possibly to אֵל I.]
Ernest Klein, 'Klein Dictionary', Sefaria, accessed 2 May 2021,
https://www.sefaria.org/Klein_Dictionary.

Joshua 1:8

ח לֹא־יָמוּשׁ סֵפֶר הַתּוֹרָה הַזֶּה מִפִּיךָ וְהָגִיתָ בּוֹ יוֹמָם וָלַיְלָה לְמַעַן תִּשְׁמֹר לַעֲשׂוֹת כְּכָל־הַכָּתוּב בּוֹ כִּי־אָז תַּצְלִיחַ אֶת־דְּרָכֶךָ וְאָז תַּשְׂכִּיל:

8 This book of the Torah shall not depart out of thy mouth, but thou shalt meditate therein day and night, that thou mayest observe to do according to all that is written therein; for then thou shalt make thy ways prosperous, and then thou shalt have good success.

Psalms 1:1-2

א אַשְׁרֵי־הָאִישׁ אֲשֶׁר ׀ לֹא הָלַךְ בַּעֲצַת רְשָׁעִים וּבְדֶרֶךְ חַטָּאִים לֹא עָמָד וּבְמוֹשַׁב לֵצִים לֹא יָשָׁב:

1 Happy is the man that hath not walked in the counsel of the wicked, nor stood in the way of sinners, nor sat in the seat of the scornful.

ב כִּי אִם בְּתוֹרַת יְהֹוָה חֶפְצוֹ וּבְתוֹרָתוֹ יֶהְגֶּה יוֹמָם וָלָיְלָה:

2 But his delight is in the Torah of Yehovah; and in His Torah doth he meditate day and night.

Necessarily, there are **certain ground-rules** which I believe should be entertained for the purpose of getting the most out of this book:

1) believing that there is a **Supreme Creator** is advantageous;
2) believing that **He**, the Supreme Creator, has provided a preserved reference about **Himself** in the Hebrew-language based Jewish Scriptures is likewise opportune;
3) having a **healthy belief system** that can allow itself to be questioned and challenged is always essential to intellectual integrity and honesty!

The Two Tablets of Stone

יְהֹוָה [Yehovah] considered that the **two tablets of stone**,[5] on which **He** personally wrote the **Ten Commandments**, were of such

---

[5] Two tables of stone.

Exodus 24:12 "And Yehovah said unto Moses: 'Come up to Me into the mount and be there; and I will give thee the tables of stone, and the Torah and the commandment, which I have written, that thou mayest teach them."

Exodus 31:18 "And He gave unto Moses, when He had made an end of speaking with him upon mount Sinai, the two tables of the testimony, tables of stone, written with the finger of God."

Exodus 32:15, 16, 19. "15 And Moses turned, and went down from the mount, with the two tables of the testimony in his hand; tables that were written on both their sides; on the one side and on the other were they written. 16 And the tables were the work of God, and the writing was the writing of God, graven upon the tables. 19 And it came to pass, as soon as he came nigh unto the camp, that he saw the calf and the dancing; and Moses' anger waxed hot, and he cast the tables out of his hands, and broke them beneath the mount."

Exodus 34:1, 4, 28, 29. "1 And Yehovah said unto Moses: 'Hew thee two tables of stone like unto the first; and I will write upon the tables the words that were on the first tables, which thou didst break. 4 And he hewed two tables of stone like unto the first; and Moses rose up early in the morning, and went up unto mount Sinai, as Yehovah had commanded him, and took in his hand two tables of stone. 28 And he was there with Yehovah forty days and forty nights; he did neither eat bread, nor drink water. And he wrote upon the tables the words of the covenant, the ten words. 29 And it came to pass, when Moses came down from mount Sinai with the two tables of the testimony in Moses' hand, when he came down from the mount, that Moses knew not that the skin of his face sent forth beams while He talked with him."

Deuteronomy 4:13 "And He declared unto you His covenant, which He commanded you to perform, even the ten words; and He wrote them upon two tables of stone."

Deuteronomy 5:20 "These words Yehovah spoke unto all your assembly in the mount out of the midst of the fire, of the cloud, and of the thick darkness, with a great voice, and it went on no more. And He wrote them upon two tables of stone, and gave them unto me."

Deuteronomy 9:9, 10, 11, 15, 17. "9 When I was gone up into the mount to receive the tables of stone, even the tables of the covenant which Yehovah made with you, then I abode in the mount forty days and forty nights; I did neither eat bread nor drink water. 10 And Yehovah delivered unto me the two tables of stone written with the finger of God; and on them was written according to all the words, which Yehovah spoke with you in the mount out of the midst of the fire in the day of the assembly. 11 And it came to pass at the end of forty days and forty nights, that Yehovah gave me the two tables of stone, even the tables of the covenant. 15 So I turned and came down from the mount, and the mount burned with fire; and the two tables of the covenant were in my two hands. 17 And I took hold of the two tables, and cast them out of my two hands, and broke them before your eyes."

Deuteronomy 10:1-5. "1 At that time Yehovah said unto me: 'Hew thee two tables of stone like unto the first, and come up unto Me into the mount; and make thee an ark of wood. 2 And I will write on the tables the words that were on the first tables which thou didst break, and thou shalt put them in the ark.' 3 So I made an ark of acacia-wood, and hewed two tables of stone like unto the first, and went up into the mount, having the two tables in my hand. 4 And He wrote on the tables according to the first writing, the ten words, which Yehovah spoke unto you in the mount out of the midst of the fire in the day of the assembly; and Yehovah gave them unto me. 5 And I turned and came down from the mount, and put the tables in the ark which I had made; and there they are, as Yehovah commanded me.--"

importance that **He** commanded Moses to make a box of acacia wood and place them into it. That ***box*** is better known as the **Ark of the Testimony, the Ark of the Covenant.** Thus, the place where the *"written by the finger of Elohim"* Ten Commandments[6] were located was known among the ancient Israelites as the earthly dwelling place of the ***Creator of the Universe***, יְהֹוָה [Yehovah] (i.e. God)!

If יְהֹוָה [Yehovah] held His Ten Commandments to be in such esteem, is it too much a stretch to think that, likewise, we should hold them in high regard ourselves?

Might we consider that, in studying them, we may come to learn to comprehend that our own reason for being could be discerned by knowing the אֱלֹהִים [Elohim] (God) of Abraham, Isaac and Jacob *personally*?

[It should be noted that in our day, many people are confused in just who wrote the Ten Commandments on the tablets of stone. Clearly, from the above passages, it is shown that it was Yehovah himself who wrote on the tablets (i.e. *with the finger of God*).]

[6] Written by the finger of God.
Exodus 31:18 "And He gave unto Moses, when He had made an end of speaking with him upon mount Sinai, the two tables of the testimony, tables of stone, written with the finger of God."

Exodus 32:15, 16. "15 And Moses turned, and went down from the mount, with the two tables of the testimony in his hand; tables that were written on both their sides; on the one side and on the other were they written. 16 And the tables were the work of God, and the writing was the writing of God, graven upon the tables."

Deuteronomy 9:10, 11. 10 And Yehovah delivered unto me the two tables of stone written with the finger of God; and on them was written according to all the words, which Yehovah spoke with you in the mount out of the midst of the fire in the day of the assembly. 11 And it came to pass at the end of forty days and forty nights, that Yehovah gave me the two tables of stone, even the tables of the covenant.

Deuteronomy 10:1-5. 1 At that time Yehovah said unto me: 'Hew thee two tables of stone like unto the first, and come up unto Me into the mount; and make thee an ark of wood. 2 And I will write on the tables the words that were on the first tables which thou didst break, and thou shalt put them in the ark.' 3 So I made an ark of acacia-wood, and hewed two tables of stone like unto the first, and went up into the mount, having the two tables in my hand. 4 And He wrote on the tables according to the first writing, the ten words, which Yehovah spoke unto you in the mount out of the midst of the fire in the day of the assembly; and Yehovah gave them unto me. 5 And I turned and came down from the mount, and put the tables in the ark which I had made; and there they are, as Yehovah commanded me.--

A Source Document of Ancient Biblical Hebrew?

Leningrad Codex (Cover page E, folio 474a)

Of all known sources of the ancient Hebrew Scriptures, the definitive, authoritative source is the **Leningrad Codex**.[7] **The Leningrad Codex** dates from the year 1009. It is the oldest, **complete** manuscript of the Hebrew–language based Jewish Scriptures.

The Source Has The Intended Verse Separations!

There are some surprising details relating to the verse separations that the Masoretes[8] used in putting together **The Leningrad Codex,**

---

[7] Let us say on the outset that the Leningrad Codex is one of the most important Hebrew documents extant, with ramifications and influence that is immeasurable. It is -- along with the other famous biblical codex, the Aleppo Codex -- one of the sources for biblical tradition, for the study of Hebrew Scriptures, and for providing an accurate text for the reading and writing of the Torah and the other books of the Bible.

The Leningrad Codex is the oldest complete manuscript of the Tanakh, the 39 books of the Bible. Written in Cairo on parchment in the year 1009 (the date appears on the manuscript), it is inextricably bound up with the Aleppo Codex, which is about a century older but undated. Moreover, the Aleppo Codex, housed for many years in the Aleppo Synagogue in Syria, was badly damaged in a fire during anti-Jewish riots in Syria in 1947, and so it is incomplete. The Aleppo Codex, now safely stored at the National Hebrew Library in Jerusalem, along with the Leningrad Codex, set the standard for the correct text of the Tanakh, including its vocalization and the musical accents (trop or te'amim) that accompany every word. Although the spelling of a word may be consistent in Hebrew, in the absence of vocalization (more commonly called the vowel "dots"), there can be variations as to how the letters are pronounced.
Curt Leviant, 'Jewish Holy Scriptures: The Leningrad Codex', Jewish Virtual Library, accessed 13 Dec 2020, https://www.jewishvirtuallibrary.org/the-leningrad-codex

[8] The Masoretic text refers to the authoritative version of the Hebrew Bible used universally by Jews today. This version was codified around the ninth century by a group of Jewish scholars known as the Masoretes, whose name derives from the Hebrew word mesorah, meaning tradition. The text defines not only the Jewish biblical cannon, but also specific vocalizations and anomalous textual elements in the written Torah scroll.

In traditional Jewish thought, every single letter of the Torah is believed to be the direct word of God, so great care was taken by early copyists to preserve the text perfectly. Nevertheless,

particularly for the Ten Commandments, but not published elsewhere, at least as of September 2019, when I first published an online Hebrew–English Tanakh on my website![9]

It is notable that most modern Bibles lay claim to using **the Leningrad Codex** as their source for the Hebrew–language based Jewish Scriptures.

I find it fascinating that **_none of them actually adhere to the exact verse separations of the source document itself_**, in both references, in the Torah,[10] for the Ten Commandments found in Exodus 20 and Deuteronomy 5!

Exodus 20 Has 21 verses
In *The Leningrad Codex*

Where the **"Ten Commandments"** first appear in **the Leningrad Codex,** Exodus Chapter 20 contains **21 verses.**

It should be noted that the **Masoretes** used a trop (pronounced trope with a long "o") mark to indicate the end of a verse, which looks very similar to our colon symbol (:); it is called a סוֹף פָּסוּק [Sof Pasuq[11]].

---

certain errors in transmission crept in over time, as evidenced by variations among several early texts of the Bible.

The establishment of the Masoretic text was therefore considered an enormous accomplishment by establishing an authoritative version of Jewish scripture. Today, making any changes to the text, regardless of how scholarly sound they might seem, would be considered sacrilegious.
MJL, 'The Masoretic Text', My Jewish Learning, accessed 13 Jan 2021,
https://www.myjewishlearning.com/article/the-masoretic-text/

[9] https://www.the-iconoclast.org/resources/tanakh/; see publication notes at bottom. In September, 2022, I published my 3 volume book, The Pill Tanakh: Hebrew-English Jewish Scriptures (Tanakh: Torah, Neviim, Ketuvim (Torah-Prophets-Writings)).

[10] "For Jews, the concept of "Torah " is much broader than the books themselves, the delimited concept of the Torah. "Torah" can refer to all of traditional Jewish learning, but "the Torah" usually refers to the Torah she'bi'ktav, the written Torah, also known as the chumash (the five volumes or Pentateuch, sometimes referred to as the Five Books of Moses)."
MJL, 'The Torah', My Jewish Learning, accessed 13 Dec 2020,
https://www.myjewishlearning.com/article/the-torah/.

[11] Sof pasuq / Silluq Hebrew: סוֹף פָּסוּק/סִלּוּק or Sof pasuk / Siluk ׃ is a trope (from Yiddish טראָפּ trop) in the Jewish liturgy and is one of the biblical sentence, stress and cantillation symbols Teamim that appear in the Tanach. Translated, Sof Pasuq means 'end of the verse'. The sign is at the end of each verse in the Tanach and thus roughly corresponds to a point in German.
Sof pasuq, Wikimedia Foundation, 1 Dec 2019, https://de.zxc.wiki/wiki/Sof_pasuq

For the entire chapter of Exodus 20:
the King James Bible (KJV) and the English Standard Bible (ESV) each has **26** verses;
the Jewish Publication Society of 1917 (JPS 1917) has **22** verses;
the New International Version (NIV) has **24** verses;
the Stone Edition Tanakh, the Koren Publishing Tanakh and the Complete Jewish Bible (CJB) each has **23** verses;
again, the Leningrad Codex has 21 verses!

However, it is not just the number of verses that has Exodus 20 in the *Leningrad Codex* stand out, but also the individual verse separations unique to it.

Notably, **no modern Bible** adheres to the verse separations found in the source *Leningrad Codex* for the Ten Commandments.

The Ten Commandments actually appear in the **first twelve verses of Exodus 20** in the definitive source: *the Leningrad Codex!*

Compared to Exodus 20:1-12 in the Leningrad Codex:
Exodus 20:1-17 accounts for the Ten Commandments in:
    the King James Version (KJV),
    the English Standard Version (ESV),
    the New International Version (NIV);
Exodus 20:1-14 accounts for the Ten Commandments in:
    the Complete Jewish Bible (CJB),
    the Stone Edition Tanakh,
    the Koren Tanakh.

Does verse ordered structure make any difference to the meaning?

I doubt that I am alone for those who believe that changing the structured ordering of sentences (or verses) can alter the meaning and interpretation of a whole section! That is easy to understand when someone "quotes" a work out of its original context! However, when verse order is changed from an original, it is sometimes less easy to discern that there might be a discrepancy in meanings as a result, especially when the words themselves are unchanged.

As I previously mentioned, **no modern Bible** actually adheres to the **Masoretic text** of the **Leningrad Codex** Hebrew source in its verse structured order!

Moreover, I find it quite telling that in the reference relating to the **Masoretes**,[12] a snippet from the last sentence, *."..making any changes to the text...,"* would actually *condemn* me in what I have done with my online Tanakh (and 3 volume book, The Pill Tanakh) for the Hebrew and corresponding English texts!

This is because I have altered the Westminster Leningrad Codex derived Hebrew and the JPS 1917 English to correspond to the actual **Leningrad Codex**.[13] As I mentioned earlier, as of September 2019 I am not aware of any other publication of the Ten Commandments which corresponds to actual verse ordering of the **Leningrad Codex**!

— Judeo-Christian Tradition — "the Law" Based Upon Holy Scripture

At least up until recent times, there has been a prevailing assumption that Western Civilization is rooted in *the **Judeo-Christian tradition***, providing a reference for the knowledge of a scriptural basis for law and order.

Understandably, the term ***Judeo-Christian Tradition*** should connote the idea of the inclusion of the tradition of both **Jewish** and **Christian** religions. However, I believe that *the **Judeo–Christian tradition*** is actually just the influence of **Christianity** in Western nations like Great Britain and in the foundation of the United States of America, but not so much from a **Jewish** tradition itself!

Moreover, among those ***"Christian"*** denominations that identify themselves as a ***"people of the book,"*** they have included a 39 book prefix to their "Bible" which they call **The Old Testament**, aka the **Jewish Scriptures.**

Yet, surprisingly, otherwise than claimed, **they have not necessarily gathered their text from the definitive Jewish, Hebrew–language based source!** For that matter, the order of books is a bit different than the Jewish rendering. Also, verse numbering is often off by one or two verses in comparison throughout the Christian "Bible" in relation to the Jewish, Hebrew–language based Scriptures.

---

[12] See note #8.
[13] Robert Pill, 'Leningrad Codex Hebrew JPS 1917 English Tanakh', The-Iconoclast, last modified 17 May 2021, https://www.the-iconoclast.org/resources/tanakh/

Nonetheless, I believe it is the inclusion of the "Old Testament" into the Christian Bible that forms the basis for the term *"**Judeo**"* within **Judeo–Christian tradition.**

A Basic Sense of Justice

OK, I'm going to assume that you also ascribe to the idea of Christian influence on Western Civilization as I have suggested.

That said, what is that influence on your life?

I propose that it is related to **a basic sense of justice.**

To provide a clear example, I believe that most people have a sense that if someone **murders** another person that the penalty should be, as in *an eye for an eye*,[14] that the murderer should be judged and executed as a fitting punishment for his or her crime.

— "Supreme Law" — The Ten Commandments

Interestingly, among *Westerners*, it appears that, at some level, that sense of justice can be tied to a typical understanding that *the Ten Commandments* bring forth the idea of a codified supreme law, the correct way to behave, etc.

Yet, just about everyone who identifies with that idea *acts* as if they innately keep those commandments themselves. If that is

---

[14] "Eye for an eye"
Exodus 21:23-26.
23 But if any harm follow, then thou shalt give life for life, 24 eye for eye, tooth for tooth, hand for hand, foot for foot, 25 burning for burning, wound for wound, stripe for stripe. 26 And if a man smite the eye of his bondman, or the eye of his bondwoman, and destroy it, he shall let him go free for his eye's sake.

Leviticus 24:16-22.
16 And he that blasphemeth the name of Yehovah, he shall surely be put to death; all the congregation shall certainly stone him; as well the stranger, as the home-born, when he blasphemeth the Name, shall be put to death. 17 And he that smiteth any man mortally shall surely be put to death. 18 And he that smiteth a beast mortally shall make it good: life for life. 19 And if a man maim his neighbour; as he hath done, so shall it be done to him: 20 breach for breach, eye for eye, tooth for tooth; as he hath maimed a man, so shall it be rendered unto him. 21 And he that killeth a beast shall make it good; and he that killeth a man shall be put to death. 22 Ye shall have one manner of law, as well for the stranger, as for the home-born; for I am Yehovah your God.'

so, isn't that tantamount to saying that they consider themselves to be **righteous** before אֱלֹהִים [Elohim] (God)?

The Sermon on the Mount

No doubt but the very well known "Sermon on the Mount," the iconic explanation of the meaning of several laws found in the Ten Commandments, and recognized to have been spoken by 'Jesus',[15] has contributed to a **general knowledge of** *law* from the Bible.

Moreover, the **Sermon on the Mount** is a likely source for so many people knowing about some of the codified laws in the **Ten Commandments,** rather than directly reading from the actual source text or translation from the Jewish Scriptures.

Ironically, for such a well known subject, it is surprising that many people do not know where the Ten Commandments are located in the Bible, let alone what they really say!

Oh, sure, most people likely know that they are not supposed to curse the name of God, not steal or murder or commit adultery, not covet anything of their neighbors, etc.

Yet, how can anyone be sure that they can know them without reading the actual Ten Commandments for themselves?

Besides that, translations are actually *interpretations* subject to biases, preconditioned thinking, etc. Sometimes, what is considered as sacred text in a translation, may, instead, be somewhat nuanced and not necessarily a true representation of the original.

---

[15] Matthew 5:17-20, 21-22, 27-28 (ESV); some of the Ten Commandments in Matthew 5:
17 "Do not think that I have come to abolish the Law or the Prophets; I have not come to abolish them but to fulfill them. 18 For truly, I say to you, until heaven and earth pass away, not an iota, not a dot, will pass from the Law until all is accomplished. 19 Therefore whoever relaxes one of the least of these commandments and teaches others to do the same will be called least in the kingdom of heaven, but whoever does them and teaches them will be called great in the kingdom of heaven. 20 For I tell you, unless your righteousness exceeds that of the scribes and Pharisees, you will never enter the kingdom of heaven."
21 "You have heard that it was said to those of old, 'You shall not murder; and whoever murders will be liable to judgment.' 22 But I say to you that everyone who is angry with his brother[c] will be liable to judgment; whoever insults[d] his brother will be liable to the council; and whoever says, 'You fool!' will be liable to the hell[e] of fire."
27 "You have heard that it was said, 'You shall not commit adultery.' 28 But I say to you that everyone who looks at a woman with lustful intent has already committed adultery with her in his heart."

Unless someone can actually read and understand the ancient Hebrew text (where the Ten Commandments originate), how can they be certain of what is written? Can you fully trust a translation?

What If The Christian Source *Is Not* The *de facto* Jewish–Hebrew Source?

How should we react if we discover that the *Christian* source for the Ten Commandments is **NOT** from the definitive Jewish, Hebrew–language based source, but rather from ***their own Greek-language-based* "Scriptures"** (aka **The Septuagint**[16])?

---

[16] "When we trace back through the Alexandrian (southern) stream of Bible manuscripts, we find the legend of a Greek Old Testament called the "Septuagint." Scholars like to say it was made about 285 BC. But, like most of the other documents in this polluted stream, once you ask some basic questions, you start to doubt the official story of its age —and of its being "oldest and best.""

"But what if I could show you where the Greek Old Testament, that they call the "Septuagint," supposedly written in **285 BC,** copied 48 words in a row from the Apostle Paul's letter to the Romans (57-58 AD), into the Psalms, which David originally wrote 1,000 years earlier?"

"I know that was a complex sentence. But please realize this. Trying to explain the creation of the Septuagint Greek Old Testament is like trying to eat an elephant. So let me take this just one tiny bite at a time."

"Why is this important? Because remember, this supposedly "285 BC" Greek Old Testament, called the Septuagint, has been said by Roman Catholics and other professors to have **more authority than the Hebrew,** because they say it was the Bible used by Jesus and the apostles!"

"Because of that, Roman Catholics said it was inspired. Then they took that "Septuagint" Greek Old Testament and had it translated into Latin. That Latin became the Old Testament of the Roman Catholic Latin Vulgate. And that Roman Catholic Latin Vulgate was later translated by Jesuits into an English Bible in 1582-1610 and called the Douay-Rheims Bible. ..."

"The Catholic Bible **didn't** go back to the Hebrew. It only went back to the "Septuagint" **Greek Old Testament."**

David W. Daniels, "Did Jesus Use The Septuagint" (Ontario, CA, Chick Publications), pp 12, 15, 16. Reproduced by permission.

See link to David Daniels' video series, "Was There A B.C. Septuagint?," https://youtube.com/playlist?list=PLhmAbEGx-AnRh2YgrQvayYlEltaAolSWA (playlist); a link can also be found at https://www.the-iconoclast.org/resources/

The Christian Doctrine of "*The Curse Of The Law?*"

Moreover, in the Christian Scriptures, the term **"*the Law*"** appears to have become synonymous with the Hebrew scriptural term **"the Torah."**

Ironically, doesn't **"the Law"** have a **negative connotation** within Christian thinking, theology, practice and expression?

The "Biblical" source for this idea appears to be found in the iconic statement of *"the Apostle Paul"* from the Christian book of Galatians.

Galatians 3:13-14 (ESV):

13 Christ redeemed us from the curse of the law by becoming a curse for us—for it is written, "Cursed is everyone who is hanged on a tree"—14 so that in Christ Jesus the blessing of Abraham might come to the Gentiles, so that we might receive the promised Spirit through faith.

I highly recommend that you reread those two verses again, or do so enough times to fully grasp the real implications and even the intent of its author. I want you to especially understand the portion *"Cursed is everyone who is hanged on a tree"* since its interpretation carries **the weight of the whole of Christian doctrine 'on its back!'**

A Word Of Warning

I want to give a **word of warning** to those of you who believe that the **writings** of "Saul of Tarsus" (in Christianity, known as *the Apostle Paul*) are inherently **"the Word of God."**

Although I want you to continue reading this book, I do not have confidence that many of you will have a **healthy enough belief system** that will allow you to try to understand, let alone appreciate, my exegesis of the Galatians 3 passage.

An Idolatry of the Heart

That is, unless those of you who consider *Paul* a true Apostle of Jesus ("Yeshua," in Hebrew), can remove yourself from what I consider to be an **"idolatry of the heart,"**[17] sincere though it may be; essentially

---

[17] Ezekiel 14:4-8

because anyone who believes that the writings of Saul of Tarsus are the *de facto* **"Word of God" (aka "Holy Scripture")** can but only refuse to question them (a circular reasoning: ***Paul wrote it, therefore it is God breathed, Holy, i.e. the word of God, etc.***).

But, Isn't "The Word of God" Supposed To Be "Without Error?"

Yet, if those statements in the book of Galatians actually ***misquote*** the original Hebrew–language based Jewish Scriptures, take them ***out of context,*** or otherwise are ***incorrect*** in any way, wouldn't it be logical to think it would have been **dishonest** to have included them for consideration as being **"The Words of God?"**

Isn't "the word of God" supposed to be <u>*without error*</u>?

To me, this Galatians passage is not merely in error but also deceptive on many levels! Allow me to explain!

"... for it is written, *"Cursed is everyone who is hanged on a tree"*

For instance, where, at the end of verse 13, it says, ***"for it is written, "Cursed is everyone who is hanged on a tree,"*** it is noteworthy that that phrase, within its New Testament context, has absolutely no correlating passage, in context, in the entire Hebrew–language based Jewish Scriptures (aka, what most Christians refer to as the *Old Testament*)!

Again, the statement *"cursed is everyone who is hanged on a tree"* is *only in the Christian book of Galatians,* but not ***in context*** in its presumptive source, the Hebrew–language based Jewish Scriptures!

---

4 "Therefore speak unto them, and say unto them: Thus saith the Lord GOD [Adonai Yehovi]: Every man of the house of Israel that setteth up his idols in his mind, and putteth the stumblingblock of his iniquity before his face, and cometh to the prophet--I Yehovah will answer him that cometh according to the multitude of his idols; 5 that I may take the house of Israel in their own heart, because they are all turned away from Me through their idols. 6 Therefore say unto the house of Israel: Thus saith the Lord GOD [Adonai Yehovi]: Return ye, and turn yourselves from your idols; and turn away your faces from all your abominations. 7 For every one of the house of Israel, or of the strangers that sojourn in Israel, that separateth himself from Me, and taketh his idols into his heart, and putteth the stumblingblock of his iniquity before his face, and cometh to the prophet, that he inquire for him of Me--I Yehovah will answer him by Myself, 8 and I will set My face against that man, and will make him a sign and a proverb, and I will cut him off from the midst of My people; and ye shall know that I am Yehovah."

Nonetheless, it is quite obvious that most people who believe the writings of *Paul* are definitively **"the Word of God"** cannot even allow those writings to be questioned or examined in any meaningful way. To them, the third chapter of Galatians is unquestioningly true and accurate, and any attempt to influence the change of that view is necessarily *"of the devil!"*

A "Hebrew Of The Hebrews," Or <u>An</u> <u>Abject</u> <u>Liar,</u> <u>A</u> <u>Purposeful</u> <u>Deceiver</u>?

To those who *are able* to question this phrase in Galatians, if the self-proclaimed *Apostle Paul,* who claimed to have been a **Hebrew of the Hebrews**[18] – who was even from that statement, presumably, fully informed of the Hebrew-language based Jewish Scriptures, actually wrote or dictated this passage in Galatians, he could not have been quite so familiar with those Hebrew-language based Jewish Scriptures as the term **Hebrew of the Hebrews** would suggest; and he was, therefore, <u>**an abject liar**</u>.

Otherwise, he was aware that he was taking **Holy Scripture** out of its natural context, and was therefore, <u>**a purposeful deceiver**</u>!

Either of those cases should trouble those who hold *Paul* in such high esteem as to believe his writings are actually **"The Word of God!"**

Just as troubling is that this would necessarily mean that Paul's "God" should **not** also be identified as the אֱלֹהִים [Elohim] (God) recorded in the Hebrew-language based Jewish Scriptures, the Elohim of Abraham, Isaac and Jacob (aka יְהֹוָה [Yehovah]).

There should be no middle ground for anyone to take here.

It is quite noteworthy that these writings relating to the *curse of the law* are absolutely without any basis from a reliable source of truth whatsoever! Yet, they are the **foundation** for much of Christian doctrine, dogma, belief and theology!

---

[18] Philippians 3:3-5 (ESV)
3 "For we are the circumcision, who worship by the Spirit of God and glory in Christ Jesus and put no confidence in the flesh— 4 though I myself have reason for confidence in the flesh also. If anyone else thinks he has reason for confidence in the flesh, I have more: 5 circumcised on the eighth day, of the people of Israel, of the tribe of Benjamin, **a Hebrew of Hebrews**; as to the law, a Pharisee;" [emphasis mine]

Thus, Paul's "God" Should NOT Be Confused with יְהֹוָה [Yehovah] –The אֱלֹהִים [Elohim] of Abraham, Isaac and Jacob!

Anyone familiar with the Hebrew–language based Jewish Scriptures can readily discern that Paul's "God" **should not** be confused with יְהֹוָה [Yehovah], the אֱלֹהִים [Elohim] of Abraham, Isaac and Jacob.

Moreover, anyone truly speaking in the name of יְהֹוָה [Yehovah] ("God"), **by definition cannot be a liar, deceiver, false prophet, or in any other manner, a defiled person**!

The *Curse: Only When A Body Remains Hung After The Sun Sets!*

As a matter of fact, the Hebrew–language based Jewish Scriptures only speak of a *curse* regarding someone hung on a tree **when that person's body remains hung after the setting of the sun!**

The curse has no correlation with the act of hanging itself as the Galatians passage expresses, but only to the corpse remaining hung **after the setting of the sun.**

This is quite evident by looking at two of the three Hebrew–language based Jewish Scripture references that correspond to this idea (Deuteronomy 21:22-23; Joshua 10:26-27):

Deuteronomy 21:22-23

כב וְכִי־יִהְיֶה בְאִישׁ חֵטְא מִשְׁפַּט־מָוֶת וְהוּמָת וְתָלִיתָ אֹתוֹ עַל־עֵץ:

22 And if a man have committed a sin worthy of death, and he be put to death, and thou hang him on a tree,

כג לֹא־תָלִין נִבְלָתוֹ עַל־הָעֵץ כִּי־קָבוֹר תִּקְבְּרֶנּוּ בַּיּוֹם הַהוּא כִּי־קִלְלַת אֱלֹהִים תָּלוּי וְלֹא תְטַמֵּא אֶת־אַדְמָתְךָ אֲשֶׁר יְהֹוָה אֱלֹהֶיךָ נֹתֵן לְךָ נַחֲלָה:

23 his body shall not remain all night upon the tree, but thou shalt surely bury him the same day; for he that is hanged is a reproach unto God; that thou defile not thy land which Yehovah thy God giveth thee for an inheritance.

Joshua 10:26-27

כו וַיַּכֵּם יְהוֹשֻׁעַ אַחֲרֵי־כֵן וַיְמִיתֵם וַיִּתְלֵם עַל חֲמִשָּׁה עֵצִים וַיִּהְיוּ תְּלוּיִם עַל־הָעֵצִים עַד־הָעָרֶב׃

26 And afterward Joshua smote them, and put them to death, and hanged them on five trees; and they were hanging upon the trees until the evening.

כז וַיְהִי לְעֵת ׀ בּוֹא הַשֶּׁמֶשׁ צִוָּה יְהוֹשֻׁעַ וַיֹּרִידוּם מֵעַל הָעֵצִים וַיַּשְׁלִכֻם אֶל־הַמְּעָרָה אֲשֶׁר נֶחְבְּאוּ־שָׁם וַיָּשִׂמוּ אֲבָנִים גְּדֹלוֹת עַל־פִּי הַמְּעָרָה עַד־עֶצֶם הַיּוֹם הַזֶּה׃

27 And it came to pass at the time of the going down of the sun, that Joshua commanded, and they took them down off the trees, and cast them into the cave wherein they had hidden themselves, and laid great stones on the mouth of the cave, unto this very day.

Only by taking Deuteronomy 21:23 **out of the plain meaning in its natural context** can it be interpreted to mean that the act of hanging itself is a *"curse."* **By just quoting *part of the verse*** from the source in the Hebrew–language Jewish Scriptures, the Galatians passage clearly takes the original *out of context* and obfuscates its meaning.

Again, in its natural context, Deuteronomy 21:23 clearly states that a corpse remaining <u>**hung after sunset**</u> is that which **causes "<u>the curse</u>."**

Moreover, the above referenced passage in Joshua 10 shows the carrying out of the scriptural command in taking hung bodies down before sunset. **By knowing that there is a curse for leaving bodies hung on a tree after the setting of the sun,** Joshua fully understood the scriptural command, and was obedient in carrying it out.

Jesus's Body *DID NOT REMAIN* "Hung On The Cross" — After Sunset!

Quite telling is that, even according to the Christian Bible, there is absolutely no indication that the body of Jesus remained hung on the cross (tree) after the setting of the sun.[19]

---

[19] Jesus Is Buried (Passages From ESV, English Standard Version)
Matthew 27:57-61
57 When it was evening, there came a rich man from Arimathea, named Joseph, who also was a disciple of Jesus. 58 He went to Pilate and asked for the body of Jesus. Then Pilate ordered it to be given to him. 59 And Joseph took the body and wrapped it in a clean linen shroud 60 and laid it in his own new tomb, which he had cut in the rock. And he rolled a great stone to the entrance of the tomb and went away. 61 Mary Magdalene and the other Mary were there, sitting opposite the tomb.

Mark 15:42-47.
42 And when evening had come, since it was the day of Preparation, that is, the day before the Sabbath, 43 Joseph of Arimathea, a respected member of the council, who was also himself looking for the kingdom of God, took courage and went to Pilate and asked for the body of Jesus. 44 Pilate was surprised to hear that he should have already died. And summoning the centurion, he asked him whether he was already dead. 45 And when he learned from the centurion that he was dead, he granted the corpse to Joseph. 46 And Joseph bought a linen shroud, and taking him down, wrapped him in the linen shroud and laid him in a tomb that had been cut out of the rock. And he rolled a stone against the entrance of the tomb. 47 Mary Magdalene and Mary the mother of Joses saw where he was laid.

Luke 23:50-56
50 Now there was a man named Joseph, from the Jewish town of Arimathea. He was a member of the council, a good and righteous man, 51 who had not consented to their decision and action; and he was looking for the kingdom of God. 52 This man went to Pilate and asked for the body of Jesus. 53 Then he took it down and wrapped it in a linen shroud and laid him in a tomb cut in stone, where no one had ever yet been laid. 54 It was the day of Preparation, and the Sabbath was beginning. 55 The women who had come with him from Galilee followed and saw the tomb and how his body was laid. 56 Then they returned and prepared spices and ointments. On the Sabbath they rested according to the commandment.

John 19:31-42
31 Since it was the day of Preparation, and so that the bodies would not remain on the cross on the Sabbath (for that Sabbath was a high day), the Jews asked Pilate that their legs might be broken and that they might be taken away. 32 So the soldiers came and broke the legs of the first, and of the other who had been crucified with him. 33 But when they came to Jesus and saw that he was already dead, they did not break his legs. 34 But one of the soldiers pierced his side with a spear, and at once there came out blood and water. 35 He who saw it has borne witness—his testimony is true, and he knows that he is telling the truth—that you also may believe. 36 For these things took place that the Scripture might be fulfilled: "Not one of his bones will be broken." 37 And again another Scripture says, "They will look on him whom they have pierced." 38 After these things Joseph of Arimathea, who was a disciple of Jesus, but secretly for fear of the Jews, asked Pilate that he might take away the body of Jesus, and Pilate gave him permission. So he came and took away his body. 39 Nicodemus also, who earlier had come to Jesus by night, came bringing a mixture of myrrh and aloes, about seventy-five pounds in weight. 40 So they took the body of Jesus and bound it in linen cloths with the spices, as is the burial custom of the Jews. 41 Now in the place where he was crucified there was a garden, and

Therefore, it should easily be seen that **any idea of Jesus being a curse** is not related to the source scriptural context merely regarding a body being hung upon a tree *and remaining there after sunset.*

The *curse* spoken of by Paul, about Jesus, has no basis in the Jewish Scriptures, <u>**since his body was taken down before sunset**</u>!

Therefore, the Christian doctrine relating to *'Christ redeemed us from the curse of the law by becoming a curse for us'* is without merit, having no credible foundation according to **the actual Word of God, the Torah written by Moses!**

Thus, **Paul's rendering** is absolutely not just an incorrect interpretation *but a **great deception** as well.*

Paul is exceptionally subtle. He has arrogantly taken Jewish Scripture out of its natural context to construe an unnatural idea, <u>especially to an audience that is not in the habit of testing his claims</u>!

Yet, it is Paul's declaration which provides the doctrinal foundation for this concept of a de facto *curse of the Law* in Christianity!

It is truly unfortunate for those people who absolutely believe that the "Christian Scriptures" are entirely *God–Breathed*, and, more importantly, that since *Paul* said it, that obviously means it is unquestionably true, since, to them, his words contain no errors whatsoever.

The New Testament Supersedes The Tanakh?

Certainly, there are Christians who espouse the idea that the Christian New Testament *supersedes* all of the Hebrew–language based Jewish Scriptures, and, in fact, interprets "the Old Testament" by providing its "correct meaning!"

Unfortunately, the phrase **"Christ hath redeemed us from the curse of the law,"** (Galatians 3:13a) has so often been shown to be interpreted to mean that the **Torah of Moses** as found in the Hebrew–language based Jewish Scriptures (known in Christendom as **"The Law"**) has, in reality, become ***obsolete*** in the practice of the various versions of the Christian religion.

---

in the garden a new tomb in which no one had yet been laid. 42 So because of the Jewish day of Preparation, since the tomb was close at hand, they laid Jesus there.

The obvious question must be asked, "In Christianity, why else are the Hebrew–language based Jewish Scriptures so readily referred to as *"The Old Testament" or "The Old Covenant"?"*

A well known New Testament passage from the book of Hebrews reinforces this idea. Interestingly, the book of Hebrews was quite likely written by Paul![20]

"He makes the first one obsolete"

Hebrews 8:13 (ESV)

In speaking of a new covenant, he makes the first one obsolete. And what is becoming obsolete and growing old is ready to vanish away. [Emphasis mine]

In my opinion, Jesus is merely the proxy to Paul!

For his unwavering followers, a simple formula might be promulgated: *Paul said it; his words are entirely true; his words are the words of God, and therefore God–breathed; he tells us how to interpret Jesus with the caveat that all opposing views are and should be considered to be **preaching another Gospel**.*[21]

---

[20] Doing a quick "google" search about "who wrote the book of Hebrews?" will find many supporting the idea that it was "the Apostle Paul" who penned it. In one source, https://earlychurchhistory.org/communication/paul-the-apostle-wrote-hebrews/, at the end the author states: "This writer believes, according to the most ancient Clement of Alexandria AND internal evidence, that Paul wrote Hebrews in Hebrew and Luke, the author of the book of Acts, translated Paul's Hebrew/Aramaic into Greek so the Gentile Christians could benefit from it, too."—Sandra Sweeny Silver

Another reference: https://doctrine.org/who-wrote-hebrews (conclusion): "This is where I need write: Game Over. Arguments against Pauline authorship of Hebrews are sickly and feeble. Arguments for alternative authors have all the weaknesses and none of the strengths of Pauline authorship and only highly speculative arguments can be made for non-Paul authors. That modern scholarship has hungrily seized such arguments demonstrates infirmity, not health."

"Evidence for Pauline authorship of Hebrews is more than substantial: it is overwhelming. The most reasonable explanation, recognized early in Church history, is Paul wrote Hebrews. When the internal evidence is examined, it overcomes easily issues of style. It is possible Luke worked with Paul and penned it but that is the only thing in doubt. Paul wrote Hebrews."

Several other references are:
https://purelypresbyterian.com/2018/03/08/proof-that-the-apostle-paul-wrote-hebrews/
https://www.ttb.org/docs/default-source/extra-materials/the-authorship-of-hebrews.pdf?sfvrsn=ff4c1c16_0 (Dr. J. Vernon McGee)

[21] Galatians 1:6-9 ESV "6 I am astonished that you are so quickly deserting him who called you in the grace of Christ and are turning to a different gospel— 7 not that there is another one, but there are some who trouble you and want to distort the gospel of Christ. 8 But even if we or an angel from heaven should preach to you a gospel contrary to the one we preached to you, let

To me, that kind of **fanaticism** ensures **Paul's** popularity in Christianity, **by proxy making him *the de facto son of God*, aka the Messiah**!

Essentially, Paul defined most of Christian doctrine, *doing so 'in the name of Jesus'. Thus, isn't Jesus merely a proxy for Paul*?

Is Paul the de facto Christian Messiah?

Deuteronomy 27:26

כו אָרוּר אֲשֶׁר לֹא־יָקִים אֶת־דִּבְרֵי הַתּוֹרָה־הַזֹּאת לַעֲשׂוֹת אוֹתָם וְאָמַר כָּל־הָעָם אָמֵן׃

26 Cursed be he that confirmeth not the words of this Torah to do them. And all the people shall say: Amen.'

The verse of Deuteronomy 27:26 is the last statement of a list of *curses* expressed to be the result of *sinful behavior*. However, the whole of these "curses" **cannot** readily be interpreted directly in the manner intimated by who I consider to be the **de facto Christian Messiah, Saul of Tarsus** (aka Paul), that the Galatians passage easily infers to as true and accurate.

But, again, if someone holds that the words of the self-proclaimed Christian Apostle Paul are automatically also "the words of God," no other proof is really required for them!

But Are There "Non-Redeemable" Sins?

If the statement that the messiah has redeemed someone from "the curse of the law" bears a presumption that *any* sin may be redeemed or the consequences from it can be removed altogether, might it be that even if any one of the identified sins in Deuteronomy Chapters

---

him be accursed. 9 As we have said before, so now I say again: If anyone is preaching to you a gospel contrary to the one you received, let him be accursed.

6 I am astonished that you are so quickly deserting him who called you in the grace of Christ and are turning to a different gospel— 7 not that there is another one, but there are some who trouble you and want to distort the gospel of Christ. 8 But even if we or an angel from heaven should preach to you a gospel contrary to the one we preached to you, let him be accursed. 9 As we have said before, so now I say again: If anyone is preaching to you a gospel contrary to the one you received, let him be accursed. 10 For am I now seeking the approval of man, or of God? Or am I trying to please man? If I were still trying to please man, I would not be a servant of Christ."

27 and 28 is found to **be non–redeemable**, that no one, including **The Messiah**, could effectively provide redemption for it?

"Sex" With A Beast (Animal); Taking A Bribe To Murder An Innocent Person

In the list from Deuteronomy there are easily two "sins" that **may NOT be redeemable**: laying with a beast (having sexual relations, Deuteronomy 27:21; penalty, Leviticus 20:15 –Death), or taking a bribe and slaying an innocent person (i.e. murder; the death penalty as expressed in Leviticus 24:17; the curse in Deuteronomy 27:25)!

Get-Out-Of-Hell-Free — "Merely by How One Thinks/Believes"

Based upon the specific teachings of Paul (Saul of Tarsus), *"Pauline Christianity"* presumes to have a *get–out–of–HELL–free–"card,"* simply by "stating a belief that *'Jesus' died and was subsequently raised from the dead (by God)."*[22]

That *doctrine* appears even to be able to "save," or "redeem" people who have **forsaken the Torah** of יְהֹוָה [Yehovah]; or for that matter, who have not even known it at all, but that have, nonetheless, transgressed the Laws of יְהֹוָה [Yehovah] (God)!

Do The Ten Commandments Apply To Everyone?

In an ironic twist, many "*Pauline* Christians" seem to believe that the *Ten Commandments* are "mostly" applicable to all peoples!

---

[22] Romans 10:8-13 (ESV)
8 "But what does it say? "The word is near you, in your mouth and in your heart" (that is, the word of faith that we proclaim); 9 because, if you confess with your mouth that Jesus is Lord and believe in your heart that God raised him from the dead, you will be saved. 10 For with the heart one believes and is justified, and with the mouth one confesses and is saved. 11 For the Scripture says, "Everyone who believes in him will not be put to shame." 12 For there is no distinction between Jew and Greek; for the same Lord is Lord of all, bestowing his riches on all who call on him. 13 For "everyone who calls on the name of the Lord will be saved."

Except For The Seventh Day Sabbath (the Fourth Commandment)!

That is, The Ten Commandments (laws) are applicable, except, *of course* **to them** for the **commandment** concerning the **Sabbath rest on <u>Saturday, the Seventh Day of the week</u>**!

This belief can often be attributed to the *"profound Christian argument"* based upon the presumptive claim that, *"<u>because Jesus rose from the dead on the first day of the week</u>,"* that, therefore, the **Seventh Day Sabbath** is definitively **proved** to have been approved to be changed, by "God," to **<u>Sunday, the first day of the week</u>**![23]

Summing this up, that statement of logic is like this: "Christ rose on Sunday, **therefore** "God" has declared that the Sabbath has been changed from the seventh day, Saturday, to the first day, Sunday."

I don't know about you, but if that idea is intended to be a "strong and profound *exegetical* argument," it certainly makes me wonder how to take **Pauline Christians** seriously about so many of their other "inerrant" arguments and revelations, no matter how many of their New Testament Scriptures they can quote from memory!

Hence, as stated earlier, that *by their attitude,* just about everyone acts as if they innately keep the Ten Commandments; again, as if they consider themselves righteous before God!

The Ten Commandments: <u>The *Real* God Code</u>!

It is **not** my intention to make it appear that I want to use this book as a forum to bash Christians or Christianity (OK, except, perhaps, for

---

[23] Some examples using an internet search regarding the Christian Sabbath:
"Who changed the Sabbath to Sunday?," https://www.bibleinfo.com/en/questions/who-changed-the-sabbath
"Sabbath: The First Day of the Week," https://reformedreader.wordpress.com/2015/08/14/sabbath-the-first-day-of-the-week/
"Sabbath Keeping Is Not Required For New Testatment Christians: Seventh-Day Adventists," https://media-cloud.sermonaudio.com/text/3161721584.pdf
"Does the Bible Say Jesus Rose From the Dead on a Sunday," https://www.vision.org/does-bible-say-jesus-rose-dead-sunday-2990
"Was Christ Raised from the Dead on Sunday or Saturday?," https://www.christiancourier.com/articles/195-was-christ-raised-from-the-dead-on-sunday-or-saturday

those *Pauline* Christians, followers of the *false, self*–proclaimed, *apostle* "Paul," Saul of Tarsus — since I do that elsewhere![24]).

In fact, I believe that Christianity has had a very positive influence upon Western Civilization.

However, it is my intention that this book is to focus on the Ten Commandments — those words which יְהֹוָה [Yehovah] wrote with His finger on two stone tablets and which He commanded to be placed within the Ark of the Testimony, also known as Ark of the Covenant!

I have only spoken about the above in order to establish the context by which The Ten Commandments are known about within Western Civilization, which I believe is mostly **through Christian influence.**

Further, I am intending that you will discover the richness of the Ten Commandments by reading this book. After having done so, I am hopeful that you will find yourself in the *minority*, that the Ten Commandments will not be a "passing fancy" to you, but rather a full part of your everyday life and a prominent influence by which you live your life from now on.

May it be a positive influence on your life and may you come to a real relationship with the *Creator of the Universe*, יְהֹוָה [Yehovah], the אֱלֹהִים [Elohim] of Abraham, Isaac and Jacob!

Biblical Hebrew — An Ancient Language

It should be understood that Biblical Hebrew is an ancient language, one used in liturgy throughout past ages, but not regularly spoken as a language for around 2,000 years.

Notwithstanding, some people might presume that modern Israeli Hebrew is so close to the ancient, Biblical Hebrew, that anyone fluent in such is automatically able to interpret the ancient text easily!

---

[24] Robert Pill, 'Paul the False Apostle', last modified 23 Jan 2021, https://www.the-iconoclast.org/reference2/saul-of-tarsus.php;
Robert Pill, 'Obsolete: Calling The Hebrew Scriptures "Old!"', last modified 12 Feb 2021, https://www.the-iconoclast.org/reference2/Obsolete-calling-Hebrew-Scriptures-Old.php;
Robert Pill, 'הַגּוֹיִם Were The 'Christian Scriptures' Written For And By Goyim (Gentiles)?', last modified 2 Feb 2021, https://www.the-iconoclast.org/reference2/scribalstandards.php;
Robert Pill, '', last modified 23 Jan 2021, https://www.the-iconoclast.org/reference2/can-gentiles-join-israel.php

What Is Modern Hebrew?

The modern nation of Israel was established in 1947. British authorities declared the "modern" Hebrew language to be the official language of the nation around that time.

> When Eliezer Ben-Yehuda arrived in Palestine in 1881, Hebrew had not been the spoken language of the Jewish people since the time of the Bible. Yet, thanks to Ben-Yehuda, by 1922 enough Jewish pioneers were speaking Hebrew that the British Mandate authorities recognized it as the official language of Jews in Palestine.[25]

Moment magazine had an article in it's review of the book "Modern Hebrew: The Past and Future of a Revitalized Language" by Norman Berdichevsky:

> While teaching modern Hebrew in England and the United States, Norman Berdichevsky got a shock. Many of his students, he found, "were unable to utter a sentence in the modern language"—despite having attended Hebrew school at their synagogues for four or five years. "In modern Israel, they would be functionally illiterate," Berdichevsky says. The experience led him to write a book on the topic, which came out last month: Modern Hebrew: The Past and Future of a Revitalized Language.

> Stateside, many still equate Hebrew with its rabbinical counterpart, the purview of bar mitzvahs and synagogue prayer. In Israel, the story is different. In the 1880s, early Zionists sought to adopt a modernized version of the ancient biblical language. Most believed it couldn't be done. Today, Israeli Hebrew has become the most successful language revitalization project in history. It is the language de facto, used in every realm of Israeli life, from education to business to picking up groceries. ...

> What major updates did Zionists have to make to biblical Hebrew?

> The language had to change radically. Biblical Hebrew has a vocabulary of about 7,000 words, of which maybe 1,000 or more are totally obscure. It was totally unfit even for the end of the 18th century, let alone the 20th century. An educated Israeli today has

---

[25] David Saiger, 'Eliezer Ben-Yehuda and the Making of Modern Hebrew', My Jewish Learning, accessed 24 Nov 2020, https://www.myjewishlearning.com/article/eliezer-ben-yehuda/.

a vocabulary of at least ten times that. There are also significant differences in the structure and grammar of the language. For instance, if you look at biblical Hebrew the tenses are completely out of joint; the past and the future mix in the same sentence, for stylistic purposes. Modern Hebrew also established a standard pronunciation that didn't exist before. Today there's no more confusion over the tenses: There is a past tense, a present tense and a future tense just like in English. Hebrew has been molded into the format of an Indo-European language, even though it was originally a Semitic language.[26]

The Israel Ministry of Foreign Affairs provides additional information:

Layers of Hebrew: Historical review of the Hebrew language

The Hebrew language and its distinctive history is an indispensable key to understanding Israel's historical and cultural heritage. Just like the Jewish people, the Hebrew language experienced many vicissitudes from the destruction of the Jerusalem Temple by the Romans through to the establishment of the State of Israel in 1948.

This vibrant history can be divided into five main periods:

1. Biblical Hebrew – *Over 3,000 years ago, when the people of Israel first arrived in the Holy Land, Hebrew was established as the national language. Hebrew remained in common usage, even during the Babylonian exile (686-534 BCE), for over 1,500 years, till around 400 CE when, under the weight of the dispersion of the Jews after the destruction of the Second Temple, it fell out of common usage. Biblical Hebrew survived through this time (and indeed through to today) through its role as the language of liturgy and of religious texts.*

2. Mishnaic Hebrew – *The Mishnah, the corpus of Jewish law that was written in Hebrew, was edited during the 2nd century CE. Here we find new words and idioms that were added to the language.*

3. Medieval Hebrew - *At the turn of the first millennium, there was a revival of Hebrew in Jewish communities across the globe, with grammar study that was accompanied by the appearance of*

---

[26] Rachel Gross, 'Modern Hebrew: The Epic Transformation of a Language', Moment Magazine, accessed 24 Nov 2020, https://momentmag.com/hebrew-an-epic-transformation/.

the first Hebrew dictionary. During the golden age of Jewish culture in Spain, Hebrew poetry written by gifted Jewish poets enriched the Hebrew language even further. It was at this time that Hebrew began again to spread outside the traditional fields of liturgy and religious learning.

4. Renaissance Hebrew – In the 15th and 16th centuries, the technological development of printing made its contribution to Hebrew; the first Hebrew printing press in the Holy Land established in Safed in 1577. During this period and later, many European scholars tried to establish Hebrew as "the mother of all languages." They believed that Hebrew was the original source from which all other languages developed.

5. Modern Hebrew – In the 19th century, Hebrew underwent an unprecedented revival. This is the time of Eliezer Ben Yehuda's efforts and accomplishments. Many authors and poets joined his campaign and their efforts helped unleash an era of immense linguistic vitality and creativity. Hebrew became an official language of the State of Israel in 1948.

Since then, as Israel absorbed millions of immigrants and grappled with the myriad challenges of building a modern state, and more recently, with the impact of globalization and immense technological changes, modern Hebrew has grown into a dynamic language with a lexicon of more than 75,000 words. These include over 2,400 deliberately designed Hebrew alternatives for foreign words and recent terms which the ancient language never contained.[27]

Even though it is an ancient language, that does not mean that the ancient Hebrew–language based Jewish Scriptures cannot be understood.

I actually believe that being fluent in modern Hebrew, as those who live in Israel, is not necessarily an advantage in learning Biblical Hebrew. I think they are different enough to consider them distinct languages.

---

[27] MFA, 'Hebrew Language Day: The revival of the language of the Bible', Israel Ministry of Foreign Affairs, last modified 19 Jan 2017,
https://mfa.gov.il/mfa/israelexperience/history/pages/hebrew-language-day-the-revival-of-the-language-of-the-bible.aspx

However, native and fluent speakers of modern Hebrew can typically read and pronounce the Hebrew–language based Jewish Scriptures easier than the rest of us 'mere mortals'!

No doubt everyone brings their own set of "baggage" to learning, but by studying the Hebrew–language based Jewish Scriptures as a course of trying to understand what is intended can truly be achieved. It is my own belief that having access to several Hebrew language aids can greatly facilitate that understanding.[28] A teacher can be of great help as well.

It is my intention to shed light on the ancient Hebrew text of the Ten Commandments. In the course of reading this manuscript, I am hopeful that you will join me in sharing the love of יְהֹוָה [Yehovah] from His written words in that ancient language within which He has chosen to reveal Himself.

---

[28] Ernest Klein, "An Etymological Dictionary of the Hebrew Language For Readers of English," (CARTA, Jerusalem)
Avraham Even-Shoshan, קוֹנְקוֹרְדַּנְצְיָה חֲדָשָׁה New Concordance, (Jerusalem, Kiryat-Sefer)
Reuben Alcalay, "The Complete English Hebrew Dictionary," (Tel Aviv-Jerusalem, Massadah Publishing).

Exodus 20:1–12

א Verse 1

א וַיְדַבֵּר אֱלֹהִים אֵת כָּל־הַדְּבָרִים הָאֵלֶּה לֵאמֹר:

1 And God spoke all these words, saying:

ב Verse 2

ב אָנֹכִי יְהוָה אֱלֹהֶיךָ אֲשֶׁר הוֹצֵאתִיךָ מֵאֶרֶץ מִצְרַיִם מִבֵּית עֲבָדִים:

2 I am Yehovah thy God, who brought thee out of the land of Egypt, out of the house of bondage.

ג Verse 3

ג לֹא יִהְיֶה־לְךָ אֱלֹהִים
אֲחֵרִים עַל־פָּנָי ׃ לֹא תַעֲשֶׂה־
לְךָ פֶסֶל ׀ וְכָל־תְּמוּנָה אֲשֶׁר
בַּשָּׁמַיִם ׀ מִמַּעַל וַאֲשֶׁר בָּאָרֶץ
מִתַּחַת וַאֲשֶׁר בַּמַּיִם ׀ מִתַּחַת
לָאָרֶץ לֹא־תִשְׁתַּחֲוֶה לָהֶם
וְלֹא תָעָבְדֵם כִּי אָנֹכִי יְהוָה
אֱלֹהֶיךָ אֵל קַנָּא פֹּקֵד עֲוֹן
אָבֹת עַל־בָּנִים עַל־שִׁלֵּשִׁים
וְעַל־רִבֵּעִים לְשֹׂנְאָי ׃

3 Thou shalt have no other gods before Me. Thou shalt not make unto thee a graven image, nor any manner of likeness, of any thing that is in heaven above, or that is in the earth beneath, or that is in the water under the earth; thou shalt not bow down unto them, nor serve them; for I Yehovah thy God am a jealous God, visiting the iniquity of the fathers upon the children unto the third and fourth generation of them that hate Me;

ד Verse 4

ד וְעֹשֶׂה חֶסֶד לַאֲלָפִים
לְאֹהֲבַי וּלְשֹׁמְרֵי מִצְוֹתָי ׃

4 and showing mercy unto the thousandth generation of them that love Me and keep My commandments.

ה Verse 5

ה לֹא תִשָּׂא אֶת־שֵׁם־יְהוָה
אֱלֹהֶיךָ לַשָּׁוְא כִּי לֹא יְנַקֶּה
יְהוָה אֵת אֲשֶׁר־יִשָּׂא אֶת־שְׁמוֹ
לַשָּׁוְא׃

5 Thou shalt not lift up the Name of Yehovah thy God as to declare Him worthless; for Yehovah will not hold him guiltless who takes His Name falsely.

ו Verse 6

ו זָכוֹר אֶת־יוֹם הַשַּׁבָּת
לְקַדְּשׁוֹ שֵׁשֶׁת יָמִים תַּעֲבֹד
וְעָשִׂיתָ כָּל־מְלַאכְתֶּךָ וְיוֹם
הַשְּׁבִיעִי שַׁבָּת ׀ לַיהוָה
אֱלֹהֶיךָ לֹא־תַעֲשֶׂה כָל־
מְלָאכָה אַתָּה ׀ וּבִנְךָ־וּבִתֶּךָ
עַבְדְּךָ וַאֲמָתְךָ וּבְהֶמְתֶּךָ
וְגֵרְךָ אֲשֶׁר בִּשְׁעָרֶיךָ כִּי
שֵׁשֶׁת־יָמִים עָשָׂה יְהוָה אֶת־
הַשָּׁמַיִם וְאֶת־הָאָרֶץ אֶת־
הַיָּם וְאֶת־כָּל־אֲשֶׁר־בָּם
וַיָּנַח בַּיּוֹם הַשְּׁבִיעִי עַל־כֵּן
בֵּרַךְ יְהוָה אֶת־יוֹם הַשַּׁבָּת
וַיְקַדְּשֵׁהוּ׃

6 Remember the sabbath day, to keep it holy. Six days shalt thou labour, and do all thy work; but the seventh day is a sabbath unto Yehovah thy God, in it shalt not do any manner of work, thou, nor thy son, nor thy daughter, nor thy man-servant, nor thy maid-servant, nor thy cattle, nor thy stranger that is within thy gates; for in six days Yehovah made heaven and earth, the sea, and all that in them is, and rested on the seventh day; wherefore Yehovah blessed the sabbath day, and hallowed it.

ז Verse 7

ז כַּבֵּד אֶת־אָבִיךָ וְאֶת־אִמֶּךָ לְמַעַן יַאֲרִכוּן יָמֶיךָ עַל הָאֲדָמָה אֲשֶׁר־יְהֹוָה אֱלֹהֶיךָ נֹתֵן לָךְ׃

7 Honour thy father and thy mother, that thy days may be long upon the land which Yehovah thy God giveth thee.

ח Verse 8

ח לֹא תִּרְצָח׃

8 Thou shalt not murder.

ט Verse 9

ט לֹא תִּנְאָף׃

9 Thou shalt not commit adultery.

י Verse 10

י לֹא תִּגְנֹב׃

10 Thou shalt not steal.

יא Verse 11

יא לֹא־תַעֲנֶה בְרֵעֲךָ עֵד שָׁקֶר׃

11 Thou shalt not bear false witness against thy neighbour.

יב Verse 12

יב לֹא תַחְמֹד בֵּית רֵעֶךָ לֹא־תַחְמֹד אֵשֶׁת רֵעֶךָ וְעַבְדּוֹ וַאֲמָתוֹ וְשׁוֹרוֹ וַחֲמֹרוֹ וְכֹל אֲשֶׁר לְרֵעֶךָ׃

12 Thou shalt not covet thy neighbour's house; thou shalt not covet thy neighbour's wife, nor his man-servant, nor his maid-servant, nor his ox, nor his ass, nor any thing that is thy neighbour's.

Getting The Third Commandment Right

I believe that the third commandment is the most mistranslated of all those found in Exodus 20. I also consider that the traditional translation has resulted in great error and misunderstanding. A real word–study showing the author context should demonstrate this.

I will begin this examination with the companion passages for the *ninth* commandment in Exodus 20 and Deuteronomy 5.

By visually comparing these companion verses of the Hebrew texts, I believe that one can readily determine the essence of meanings rarely captured correctly, if ever, in English translations for the third commandment.

Am I saying that, of these original Hebrew passages, the English translations (interpretations) are incorrect, in addition to *NOT* conforming to the Masoretic verse ordering?

YES, ABSOLUTELY!

For instance, the same Hebrew word, לַשָּׁוְא (root: Shin-Vav-Alef), most often translated as "in vain" in the Ten Commandments companion passages of Exodus 20:5 and Deuteronomy 5:11: *"Thou shalt not take the name of Yehovah thy God in vain..."* is NEVER translated "in vain" in Deuteronomy 5:18, where the common translation of that same Hebrew word (לַשָּׁוְא) takes the meaning "false" in the passage *"Thou shalt not bear **false** witness against thy neighbor!"* The word שָׁוְא is most often defined in this order: **lie, falsehood, nothingness, worthlessness, vanity.**

It should prove of interest to learn that the word translated "false," as used in Exodus 20:11 (שָׁקֶר) for that which is translated as *"Thou shalt not bear **false** witness against thy neighbor"* is NOT the same Hebrew word as in its companion passage of Deuteronomy 5:18 (לַשָּׁוְא) mentioned above!

The Hebrew word שָׁקַר (root: Shin-Quf-Resh; defined as **to lie, deal falsely**) has an obvious meaning of falsehood, lying, deception and cannot remotely be considered to be interpreted/translated as *vain, or in vain!*

Thus, it should reasonably be understood that the passages interpreted/translated *"Thou shalt not take the name of Yehovah thy God in vain..."* **are not correct!**

Perhaps a closer interpretation is **"Thou shalt not take the name of Yehovah thy God as nothing, for Yehovah will not hold him guiltless that taketh His name falsely."**

I think it is very unfortunate that so many people believe they have a grasp on the meaning of the Ten Commandments, and particularly on how they rely upon what I call misinterpreted translations for the third commandment. This is because the passage is so often *reinterpreted*, in reality, to say **"Do not take the Name of God as a swear word."**

Obviously, it is a very different thing to consider, rather, that the third commandment would say anything like this **amplified interpretation: "Do not take the Name of the Lord thy God with such contempt as to treat Him so lightly, as if he doesn't exist, as if His Name symbolizes worthlessness!"**

How Could You Otherwise Come To Understand This?

Actually, I don't think that it is likely that you would!

The following two companion verses from Exodus 20:11 and Deuteronomy 5:18 should help to illustrate my "theory":

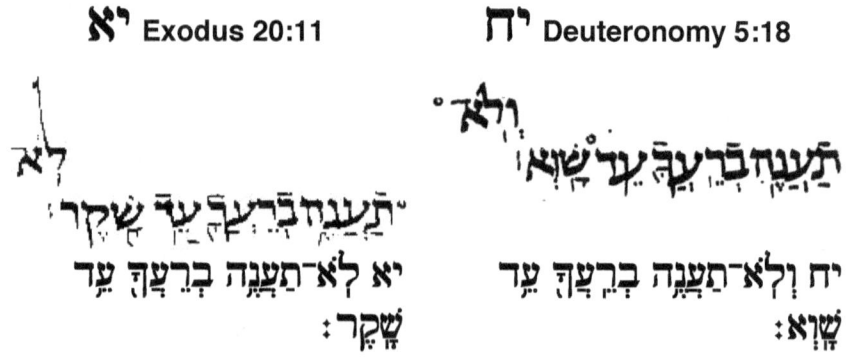

11 Thou shalt not bear false witness against thy neighbour.

18 Neither shalt thou bear false witness against thy neighbour.

Again, these two verses are essentially translated the same, but the Hebrew words expressing "false" are from completely different roots (שֶׁקֶר and שָׁוְא respectively).

I would be remiss if I did not mention a couple of interesting tidbits regarding the Hebrew word שָׁוְא (root: Shin-Vav-Alef).

The Real God Code 37

For instance, Moshe (Moses), who is well known to have written the first five books of the Hebrew–language based Jewish Scriptures, otherwise known as the "Torah," only used the word שָׁוְא one other time outside of the Ten Commandments; in Exodus 23:1, where the interpretation also takes on the natural meaning "false":

Exodus 23:1

א לֹא תִשָּׂא שֵׁמַע שָׁוְא אַל־תָּשֶׁת יָדְךָ עִם־רָשָׁע לִהְיֹת עֵד חָמָס׃

1 Thou shalt not utter a false report; put not thy hand with the wicked to be an unrighteous witness.

Moreover, the word שָׁוְא occurs 53 times in the entire Hebrew–language based Jewish Scriptures.[29]

---

[29] Avraham Even-Shoshan, קוֹנְקוֹרְדַּנְצִיָּה חֲדָשָׁה "*New Concordance*" (Jerusalem, Kiryat-Sefer) page 1117.

ה Verse 5

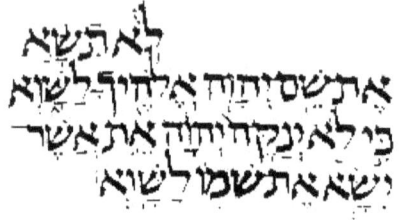

ה לֹא תִשָּׂא אֶת־שֵׁם־יְהוָה
אֱלֹהֶיךָ לַשָּׁוְא כִּי לֹא יְנַקֶּה
יְהוָה אֵת אֲשֶׁר־יִשָּׂא אֶת־שְׁמוֹ
לַשָּׁוְא׃

5 Thou shalt not lift up the Name of Yehovah thy God as to declare Him worthless; for Yehovah will not hold him guiltless who takes His Name falsely.

There is a very nice discussion on this topic which I think is a fitting summation for this chapter. It's from a book by Nehemia Gordon and Keith Johnson, "A Prayer To Our Father," in the section called "PROCLAIMING THE NAME":[30]

> Today, speaking God's name may seem counter-intuitive to many people. Over the centuries we have been taught that the way to sanctify the Almighty's name is by *not* speaking it. As proof of this assertion, people often invoke the Third Commandment, which is translated in the King James Version:
>
>> Thou shalt not take the name of the LORD thy God in vain; for the LORD will not hold him guiltless that taketh his name in vain.[15]
>
> Some interpret this to mean that it is totally forbidden to utter the holy name of God. However, in ancient Hebrew the phrase to "take the name in vain" is a figure of speech that means to make a false vow in that name.[16] Ancient vows were made by invoking the name of God with the statement "As Yehovah lives."[17] To take the name of Yehovah in vain meant to swear falsely while invoking his name in this manner. This might sound radical to some people but it is actually the oldest known interpretation of the verse. *Targum Onkelos*, an ancient Jewish translation of the Torah into Aramaic, translates this verse:

---

[30] Nehemia Gordon and Keith Johnson, "A Prayer To Our Father" (Atascosa, TX, Hilkiah Press), Chapter "May Your Name Be Sanctified," pp104-106. Reproduced by permission.

> You shall not *swear* by the name of the Lord your God in vain because the Lord will not make innocent he who *swears falsely* by his name.[18]

More recently the Jewish Publication Society translated the verse:

> You shall not *swear falsely* by the name of the LORD your God; for the LORD will not clear one who *swears falsely* by His name.[19]

This is not just a Jewish interpretation. The Peshitta, an ancient Aramaic version of the Bible used by the Church of the East, translates the verse:

> You shall not *swear* by the name of the Lord your God *falsely* because the Lord does not make innocent he who *swears falsely* by his name.[20]

Furthermore, the official catechism of the Catholic Church teaches that this commandment "forbids false oaths," and two of the key figures in the Protestant Reformation, Martin Luther and John Calvin, taught this same exact interpretation.[21] This commandment is simply forbidding us to swear falsely in the name of Yehovah. There is no biblical prohibition to utter the divine name as long as one is speaking the truth. On the contrary, in some instances one is required to speak God's holy name. For example, Deuteronomy says:

> You shall fear Yehovah your God, and you shall worship him, and *in his name shall you swear.*[22]

There is an important end-times prophecy in the Book of Jeremiah that involves swearing in God's name. In this prophecy, God speaks to the nations of the world and makes them a promise:

> And it shall comes to pass if they nevertheless learn the way of my people *to swear in my name "As Yehovah lives,"* in the way that they taught my people to swear by Baal, then they shall be built in the midst of my people.[23]

Jeremiah is saying that if the nations learn to swear in the name of Yehovah the way that they taught Israel to swear in the name of Baal, then they shall be grafted into his people.

Before the ban on the name, Jews used to revere the name of God not by suppressing it but by speaking it in prayers, praises, and blessings. In fact, the early Rabbis taught that "a man is required to greet his fellow using the name."[24] They based this teaching on the Book of Ruth, which tells of Boaz, who was walking on the road from Bethlehem when he saw a group of men harvesting grain in the fields. Boaz shouted to the harvesters, "May Yehovah be with you!" to which they responded, "May Yehovah bless you!"[25] To many Jews today it must seem inconceivable that those simple harvesters, covered with dirt and grime of the fields, would shout out the name of the Almighty. But the example of Boaz proves not only that it was permissible to use the divine name in ancient Israel but that it was used in everyday speech.

Notes from "A Prayer To Our Father"

[15] Exodus 20:7 [KJV]. Some Christians count this as the Second Commandment.

[16] A clear example of this is the Ninth Commandment, which speaks about testifying as a "vain witness" in Deuteronomy 5:20. When the commandment first appears in Exodus 20:16, it uses the synonymous phrase "false witness."

[17] Judges 8:19; 1 Samuel 14:39; etc.

[18] *Targum Onkelos* on exodus 20:7 [Aramaic]. Another ancient Aramaic Targum paraphrases the verse: "O my people, Children of Israel, none of you shall swear in the name of the word of the Lord your God in vain because the Lord will not acquit on the great Day of Judgment anyone who swears in his name in vain." (*Pseudo-Jonathan* on Exodus 20:7 [Aramaic]). See also *Babylonian Talmud,* Sabbath 120a.

[19] Exodus 20:7 (*Tanakh: A New Translation of the Holy Scriptures According to the Traditional Hebrew Text*, New York 1985, page 115).

[20] *Peshitta* on Exodus 20:7 (United Bible Societies edition, page 57 [Aramaic]).

[21] *Catechism of the Catholic Church*, Part 3, Section 2, Chapter 1, Article 2.2 section 2150; M. Luther, *The Large Catechism*, translated by R.H. Fischer, Philadelphia 1959, page 15; J. Calvin, *Commentaries on the Last Four Books of Moses*, translated by C. W. Bingham, Grand Rapids 1996, volume 2, pages 408-410.

[22] Deuteronomy 6:13.

[23] Jeremiah 12:16.

[24] *Mishnah*, Berakhot 9:5. According to E. E. Urbach, this ruling predates the ban on the name, see *The Sages: Their Concepts and Beliefs,* translated by I. Abrahams, London 1987, page 128.

[25] Ruth 2:4.

How Many Commandments?

עֲשֶׂרֶת הַדְּבָרִים

It should be known that there are three passages which use the feminine plural of the word for the number ten in Hebrew, עֲשֶׂרֶת (Ah-ser-et), which represents the number *ten* in the often translated phrase **the Ten Commandments,** עֲשֶׂרֶת הַדְּבָרִים (Ah-ser-et ha-Dev-ar-im).

However, the Hebrew word often translated for *commandments in* **The Ten Commandments**, at least in non-Jewish Bibles, הַדְּבָרִים (ha-Dev-ar-im), can also be literally translated "words" or "things."

In my opinion, in this context it should rather be rendered "sayings," "statements," or even "declarations" as representing **The Ten Commandments**.

For the most part, עֲשֶׂרֶת הַדְּבָרִים (Ah-ser-et ha-Dev-ar-im), is the phrase that has been interpreted to give us the phrase *The Ten Commandments!*

The following Hebrew verses with English translations from various Bibles shows the diversity of which this phrase, עֲשֶׂרֶת הַדְּבָרִים (Ah-ser-et ha-Dev-ar-im), is interpreted [emphasis mine].

Exodus 34:28

כח וַיְהִי־שָׁם עִם־יְהֹוָה אַרְבָּעִים יוֹם וְאַרְבָּעִים לַיְלָה לֶחֶם לֹא אָכַל וּמַיִם לֹא שָׁתָה וַיִּכְתֹּב עַל־הַלֻּחֹת אֵת דִּבְרֵי הַבְּרִית עֲשֶׂרֶת הַדְּבָרִים׃

> Exodus 34:28 And he was there with Yehovah forty days and forty nights; he did neither eat bread, nor drink water. And he wrote upon the tables the words of the covenant, **the ten words.** [modified JPS 1917]

> He remained there with HASHEM for forty days and forty nights — he did not eat bread and he did not drink water — and He wrote on the Tablets the words of the covenant, **the Ten Commandments.** [Exodus 34:28 Stone Edition Tanakh]

*So he was there with the LORD forty days and forty nights. He neither ate bread nor drank water. And he wrote on the tablets the words of the covenant, **the Ten Commandments.** [Exodus 34:28 ESV]*

*And he was there with the LORD forty days and forty nights; he did neither eat bread, nor drink water. And he wrote upon the tables the words of the covenant, **the ten commandments.** [Exodus 34:28 KJV]*

Deuteronomy 4:13

יג וַיַּגֵּד לָכֶם אֶת־בְּרִיתוֹ אֲשֶׁר צִוָּה אֶתְכֶם לַעֲשׂוֹת עֲשֶׂרֶת הַדְּבָרִים וַיִּכְתְּבֵם עַל־שְׁנֵי לֻחוֹת אֲבָנִים׃

*Deuteronomy 4:13 And He declared unto you His covenant, which He commanded you to perform, even **the ten words;** and He wrote them upon two tables of stone. [modified JPS 1917]*

*He told you of His covenant that He commanded you to observe, **the Ten Declarations,** and He inscribed them on two stone Tablets. [Deuteronomy 4:13 Stone Edition Tanakh]*

*And he declared to you his covenant, which he commanded you to perform, that is, **the Ten Commandments,** and he wrote them on two tablets of stone. [Deut. 4:13 ESV]*

*And he declared unto you his covenant, which he commanded you to perform, even **ten commandments;** and he wrote them upon two tables of stone. [Deut. 4:13 KJV]*

Deuteronomy 10:4

ד וַיִּכְתֹּב עַל־הַלֻּחֹת כַּמִּכְתָּב הָרִאשׁוֹן אֵת עֲשֶׂרֶת הַדְּבָרִים אֲשֶׁר דִּבֶּר יְהוָה אֲלֵיכֶם בָּהָר מִתּוֹךְ הָאֵשׁ בְּיוֹם הַקָּהָל וַיִּתְּנֵם יְהוָה אֵלָי׃

*Deuteronomy 10:4 And He wrote on the tables according to the first writing, **the ten words,** which Yehovah spoke unto you in the mount out of the midst of the fire in the day of the assembly; and Yehovah gave them unto me. [modified JPS 1917]*

*He inscribed on the Tablets according to the first script, **the Ten Statements** that HASHEM spoke to you on the mountain from the midst of the fire, on the day of the congregation, and HASHEM gave them to me. [Deuteronomy 10:4 Stone Edition Tanakh]*

And he wrote on the tablets, in the same writing as before, **the Ten Commandments** *that the LORD had spoken to you on the mountain out of the midst of the fire on the day of the assembly. And the LORD gave them to me. [Deut. 10:4 ESV]*

And he wrote on the tablets, in the same writing as before, **the Ten Commandments** *that the LORD had spoken to you on the mountain out of the midst of the fire on the day of the assembly. And the LORD gave them to me.[Deut. 10:4 KJV]*

Why I Promote Exodus 20 Over Deuteronomy 5

The Ten Commandments are in Exodus 20 and Deuteronomy 5.

I want to inform you as to why I focus upon Exodus 20 for its verse delineation, and use Deuteronomy 5 as a means to help bring understanding (as with the chapter of the third commandment).

Besides for the natural flow of the Masoretic text of Exodus 20, I consider internal evidence in the timeline of when each record occurred in its scriptural context! Exodus 19:1-3 and Deuteronomy 1:3 show the place in time each was given. [emphasis mine].

Exodus 19:1-3

א בַּחֹדֶשׁ הַשְּׁלִישִׁי לְצֵאת בְּנֵי־יִשְׂרָאֵל מֵאֶרֶץ מִצְרָיִם בַּיּוֹם הַזֶּה בָּאוּ מִדְבַּר סִינָי:

1 In the **third month** *after the children of Israel were gone forth out of the land of Egypt, the same day came they into the wilderness of Sinai.*

ב וַיִּסְעוּ מֵרְפִידִים וַיָּבֹאוּ מִדְבַּר סִינַי וַיַּחֲנוּ בַּמִּדְבָּר וַיִּחַן־שָׁם יִשְׂרָאֵל נֶגֶד הָהָר:

2 And when they were departed from Rephidim, and were come to the wilderness of Sinai, they encamped in the wilderness; and there Israel encamped before the mount.

ג וּמֹשֶׁה עָלָה אֶל־הָאֱלֹהִים וַיִּקְרָא אֵלָיו יְהוָה מִן־הָהָר לֵאמֹר כֹּה תֹאמַר לְבֵית יַעֲקֹב וְתַגֵּיד לִבְנֵי יִשְׂרָאֵל:

3 And Moses went up unto God, and Yehovah called unto him out of the mountain, saying: 'Thus shalt thou say to the house of Jacob, and tell the children of Israel:

Deuteronomy 1:3

ג וַיְהִי֙ בְּאַרְבָּעִ֣ים שָׁנָ֔ה בְּעַשְׁתֵּֽי־עָשָׂ֥ר חֹ֖דֶשׁ בְּאֶחָ֣ד לַחֹ֑דֶשׁ דִּבֶּ֤ר מֹשֶׁה֙ אֶל־בְּנֵ֣י יִשְׂרָאֵ֔ל כְּ֠כֹל אֲשֶׁ֨ר צִוָּ֧ה יְהֹוָ֛ה אֹת֖וֹ אֲלֵהֶֽם׃

3 And it came to pass **in the fortieth year, in the eleventh month, on the first day of the month,** *that Moses spoke unto the children of Israel, according unto all that Yehovah had given him in commandment unto them;*

Thus, it is quite clear that **the Ten Commandments,** as recorded in Exodus 20, were spoken to the Children of Israel near the beginning of their forty year journey in the wilderness within about a year of the tabernacle being constructed and set up.

It is for that reason I use Exodus 20 as the predominant reference for what is written on the two tablets of stone and placed into the Ark of the Covenant! Moreover, I use Exodus 20:1–12 to count the number of **"the Ten Commandments"** herein.

The *Commandments* With Comments

For each "Commandment" (or, statement, declaration) below, I have provided verse images from the Leningrad Codex to the left side of the Hebrew Font based verse, followed by the JPS 1917 English. Although I feel that most verses are self-explanatory, I have provided comments and/or supporting passages from the Tanakh where I feel it is appropriate to do so. Emphasis mine in English Translations where font is **bold**.

Statement/Declaration #1

א Verse 1

א וַיְדַבֵּר אֱלֹהִים אֵת כָּל־הַדְּבָרִים הָאֵלֶּה לֵאמֹר׃

1 And God spoke all these words, saying:

ב Verse 2

ב אָנֹכִי יְהוָה אֱלֹהֶיךָ אֲשֶׁר הוֹצֵאתִיךָ מֵאֶרֶץ מִצְרַיִם מִבֵּית עֲבָדִים׃

2 I am Yehovah thy God, who brought thee out of the land of Egypt, out of the house of bondage.

Without a doubt, these two verses establish who it is that is giving the instructions which follow. אֱלֹהִים [Elohim] spoke these words and He declared His name, יְהוָה [Yehovah], establishing that it was He who brought Israel out of Egyptian bondage with signs and wonders!

I realize that most people think they know who "God" is when "He" is being referred to by a commonly used name. However, just the mentioning of the appellation "God" alone is not enough to ensure that the one spoken of is really the singular Creator of the Universe, the אֱלֹהִים [Elohim] of Abraham, Isaac and Jacob!

This is a very important concept to understand and to get right!

The very best explanation I know for this subject comes from a "podcast" (a digital audio file made available on the internet); the conversation is between Nehemia Gordon, Keith Johnson and Jono Vandor.[31] The following is from the transcript:

> **Nehemia:** That's one other point in this passage, one of my favorite points, is that Melchizedek, it says, is a priest of El elyon, Most High God. Now, one of the things we know from archaeological excavations is they found these Canaanite documents, the biggest cache of them was at a place called Ras Shamra in Syria.
>
> In the Ras Shamra documents, you see that there's a Canaanite deity called "El elyon," the Most High God. Canaanites believed that he created the universe and then he retired. He went off to what they call the mountain of the north, which in Canaanite lore is Lebanon - the mountains of Lebanon. He went to his palace there, and that's the Canaanite equivalent of Mount Olympus in Greece. Then, he left the universe to his son to rule. Actually, he left it to his children who fought it out amongst themselves, and his son Baal, the Lord, he won the battle. You have to imagine, if you're Abraham and this guy Melchizedek, priest of the Most High God, Creator of heaven and earth, comes to you and blesses you by Most High God Creator of heaven and earth, you have to be thinking, "He's a righteous guy." But what does everybody else understand when they're hearing the phrase "Most High God, El elyon, Creator of heaven and earth?" They're thinking of the Canaanite, the father of Baal. That's why when Abraham responds to him, especially when he's speaking to the king of Sodom, who is a complete idolater, he said, "I lift my hand to Yehovah, the Most High God, Creator of heaven and earth." He has

---

[31] Torah Pearls #3 - Lech Lecha (Genesis 12:1-17:27)
https://www.nehemiaswall.com/torah-pearls-lech-lecha, text from "Transcript" link. Conversation between Nehemia Gordon, Keith Johnson, and Jono Vandor.

no problem with that phrase, "the Most High God, creator of heaven and earth," that legitimately describes our God. Let's just say His name because the king of Sodom, he might understand something else if we don't specify who we're talking about. I think that's a very important lesson.

Did you get that?

For this very reason I believe that the first two verses of Exodus 20 *must* be included as part of The Ten Commandments. I also believe that they were most likely to have been included on the two tablets of stone written by the finger of אֱלֹהִים [Elohim] and placed in the ark of the covenant!

Statement/Declaration #2

ב Verse 3

ג לֹא יִהְיֶה־לְךָ אֱלֹהִים
אֲחֵרִים עַל־פָּנָי לֹא תַעֲשֶׂה־
לְךָ פֶסֶל ׀ וְכָל־תְּמוּנָה אֲשֶׁר
בַּשָּׁמַיִם ׀ מִמַּעַל וַאֲשֶׁר בָּאָרֶץ
מִתַּחַת וַאֲשֶׁר בַּמַּיִם ׀ מִתַּחַת
לָאָרֶץ לֹא־תִשְׁתַּחֲוֶה לָהֶם
וְלֹא תָעָבְדֵם כִּי אָנֹכִי יְהוָה
אֱלֹהֶיךָ אֵל קַנָּא פֹּקֵד עֲוֺן
אָבֹת עַל־בָּנִים עַל־שִׁלֵּשִׁים
וְעַל־רִבֵּעִים לְשֹׂנְאָי׃

3 Thou shalt have no other gods before Me. Thou shalt not make unto thee a graven image, nor any manner of likeness, of any thing that is in heaven above, or that is in the earth beneath, or that is in the water under the earth; thou shalt not bow down unto them, nor serve them; for I Yehovah thy God am a jealous God, visiting the iniquity of the fathers upon the children unto the third and fourth generation of them that hate Me;

ד Verse 4

ד וְעֹשֶׂה חֶסֶד לַאֲלָפִים לְאֹהֲבַי וּלְשֹׁמְרֵי מִצְוֺתָי׃

4 and showing mercy unto the thousandth generation of them that love Me and keep My commandments.

Breaking the commandment, "Thou shalt have no other gods before Me..." has consequences! The following passage describes the context and *punishment!*

Deuteronomy 17:2-7

ב כִּי־יִמָּצֵא בְקִרְבְּךָ בְּאַחַד שְׁעָרֶיךָ אֲשֶׁר־יְהוָה אֱלֹהֶיךָ נֹתֵן לָךְ אִישׁ אוֹ־אִשָּׁה אֲשֶׁר יַעֲשֶׂה אֶת־הָרַע בְּעֵינֵי יְהוָה־אֱלֹהֶיךָ לַעֲבֹר בְּרִיתוֹ׃

2 If there be found in the midst of thee, within any of thy gates which Yehovah thy God giveth thee, man or woman, that doeth that which is evil in the sight of Yehovah thy God, in transgressing His covenant,

ג וַיֵּלֶךְ וַיַּעֲבֹד אֱלֹהִים אֲחֵרִים וַיִּשְׁתַּחוּ לָהֶם וְלַשֶּׁמֶשׁ ׀ אוֹ לַיָּרֵחַ אוֹ לְכָל־צְבָא הַשָּׁמַיִם אֲשֶׁר לֹא־צִוִּיתִי׃

3 and hath gone and served other gods, and worshipped them, or the sun, or the moon, or any of the host of heaven, which I have commanded not;

ד וְהֻגַּד־לְךָ וְשָׁמָעְתָּ וְדָרַשְׁתָּ הֵיטֵב וְהִנֵּה אֱמֶת נָכוֹן הַדָּבָר נֶעֶשְׂתָה הַתּוֹעֵבָה הַזֹּאת בְּיִשְׂרָאֵל׃

4 and it be told thee, and thou hear it, then shalt thou inquire diligently, and, behold, if it be true, and the thing certain, that such abomination is wrought in Israel;

ה וְהוֹצֵאתָ אֶת־הָאִישׁ הַהוּא אוֹ אֶת־הָאִשָּׁה הַהִוא אֲשֶׁר עָשׂוּ אֶת־הַדָּבָר הָרָע הַזֶּה אֶל־שְׁעָרֶיךָ אֶת־הָאִישׁ אוֹ אֶת־הָאִשָּׁה וּסְקַלְתָּם בָּאֲבָנִים וָמֵתוּ׃

5 then shalt thou bring forth that man or that woman, who have done this evil thing, unto thy gates, even the man or the woman; **and thou shalt stone them with stones, that they die.**

Notably, verse four (4) ("and showing mercy unto the thousandth generation of them that love Me and keep My commandments.") is especially poignant in that **the promise of mercy** to the thousandth generation **is only given to those who love Yehovah and also keep His commandments**.

Statement/Declaration #3

ו Verse 5

ה לֹא תִשָּׂא אֶת־שֵׁם־יְהוָה אֱלֹהֶיךָ לַשָּׁוְא כִּי לֹא יְנַקֶּה יְהוָה אֵת אֲשֶׁר־יִשָּׂא אֶת־שְׁמוֹ לַשָּׁוְא׃

5 Thou shalt not lift up the Name of Yehovah thy God as to declare Him worthless; for Yehovah will not hold him guiltless who takes His Name falsely.

I have devoted a complete chapter (*Getting the Third Commandment Right*) to help show why I translate the verse as shown, so I'll not belabor the point here except for the following verses that I hope will help drive home its significance by showing the *penalty* for its violation.

Leviticus 19:11-12

יא לֹא תִּגְנֹבוּ וְלֹא־תְכַחֲשׁוּ וְלֹא־תְשַׁקְּרוּ אִישׁ בַּעֲמִיתוֹ׃

*11 Ye shall **not steal; neither shall ye deal falsely, nor lie** one to another.*

יב וְלֹא־תִשָּׁבְע֥וּ בִשְׁמִ֖י לַשָּׁ֑קֶר וְחִלַּלְתָּ֛ אֶת־שֵׁ֥ם אֱלֹהֶ֖יךָ אֲנִ֥י יְהוָֽה׃

*12 And **ye shall not swear by My name falsely**, so that thou profane the name of thy God: I am Yehovah.*

Leviticus 24:16

יו וְנֹקֵ֤ב שֵׁם־יְהוָה֙ מ֣וֹת יוּמָ֔ת רָג֥וֹם יִרְגְּמוּ־ב֖וֹ כָּל־הָעֵדָ֑ה כַּגֵּר֙ כָּאֶזְרָ֔ח בְּנָקְבוֹ־שֵׁ֖ם יוּמָֽת׃

*16 And **he that blasphemeth the name of Yehovah, he shall surely be put to death;** all the congregation shall certainly stone him; as well the stranger, as the home-born, when he blasphemeth the Name, **shall be put to death.***

Statement/Declaration #4

ו Verse 6

ו זָכוֹר אֶת־יוֹם הַשַּׁבָּת
לְקַדְּשׁוֹ שֵׁשֶׁת יָמִים תַּעֲבֹד
וְעָשִׂיתָ כָּל־מְלַאכְתֶּךָ וְיוֹם
הַשְּׁבִיעִי שַׁבָּת ׀ לַיהוָה
אֱלֹהֶיךָ לֹא־תַעֲשֶׂה כָל־
מְלָאכָה אַתָּה ׀ וּבִנְךָ־וּבִתֶּךָ
עַבְדְּךָ וַאֲמָתְךָ וּבְהֶמְתֶּךָ
וְגֵרְךָ אֲשֶׁר בִּשְׁעָרֶיךָ כִּי
שֵׁשֶׁת־יָמִים עָשָׂה יְהוָה אֶת־
הַשָּׁמַיִם וְאֶת־הָאָרֶץ אֶת־
הַיָּם וְאֶת־כָּל־אֲשֶׁר־בָּם
וַיָּנַח בַּיּוֹם הַשְּׁבִיעִי עַל־כֵּן
בֵּרַךְ יְהוָה אֶת־יוֹם הַשַּׁבָּת
וַיְקַדְּשֵׁהוּ׃

6 Remember the sabbath day, to keep it holy. Six days shalt thou labour, and do all thy work; but the seventh day is a sabbath unto Yehovah thy God, in it thou shalt not do any manner of work, thou, nor thy son, nor thy daughter, nor thy man-servant, nor thy maid-servant, nor thy cattle, nor thy stranger that is within thy gates; for in six days Yehovah made heaven and earth, the sea, and all that in them is, and rested on the seventh day; wherefore Yehovah blessed the sabbath day, and hallowed it.

Quite obviously, the Sabbath stands out prominently and the commandment is straightforward. Nonetheless, the passage does not infer "any day in the week, of one's own choosing," but specifically the seventh day.

The following passages indicate the **penalty** for violating the Sabbath. If יְהוָה [Yehovah] gave such importance to the Sabbath, in addition to the following verses where the penalty is given, how seriously should we consider for observing it ourselves?

Exodus 31:13-15

יג וְאַתָּה דַּבֵּר אֶל־בְּנֵי יִשְׂרָאֵל לֵאמֹר אַךְ אֶת־שַׁבְּתֹתַי תִּשְׁמֹרוּ כִּי אוֹת הִוא בֵּינִי וּבֵינֵיכֶם לְדֹרֹתֵיכֶם לָדַעַת כִּי אֲנִי יְהוָה מְקַדִּשְׁכֶם׃

13 'Speak thou also unto the children of Israel, saying: **Verily ye shall keep My sabbaths,** *for it is a sign between Me and you throughout your generations, that ye may know that I am Yehovah who sanctify you.*

יד וּשְׁמַרְתֶּם אֶת־הַשַּׁבָּת כִּי קֹדֶשׁ הִוא לָכֶם מְחַלְלֶיהָ מוֹת יוּמָת כִּי כָּל־הָעֹשֶׂה בָהּ מְלָאכָה וְנִכְרְתָה הַנֶּפֶשׁ הַהִוא מִקֶּרֶב עַמֶּיהָ׃

14 Ye shall keep the sabbath therefore, for it is holy unto you; **every one that profaneth it shall surely be put to death;** *for whosoever doeth any work therein, that soul shall be cut off from among his people.*

יה שֵׁשֶׁת יָמִים יֵעָשֶׂה מְלָאכָה וּבַיּוֹם הַשְּׁבִיעִי שַׁבַּת שַׁבָּתוֹן קֹדֶשׁ לַיהוָה כָּל־הָעֹשֶׂה מְלָאכָה בְּיוֹם הַשַּׁבָּת מוֹת יוּמָת׃

15 Six days shall work be done; but on the seventh day is a sabbath of solemn rest, holy to Yehovah; **whosoever doeth any work in the sabbath day, he shall surely be put to death.**

Exodus 35:2-3

ב שֵׁשֶׁת יָמִים תֵּעָשֶׂה מְלָאכָה וּבַיּוֹם הַשְּׁבִיעִי יִהְיֶה לָכֶם קֹדֶשׁ שַׁבַּת שַׁבָּתוֹן לַיהוָה כָּל־הָעֹשֶׂה בוֹ מְלָאכָה יוּמָת׃

2 Six days shall work be done, but on the seventh day there shall be to you a holy day, a sabbath of solemn rest to Yehovah; **whosoever doeth any work therein shall be put to death.**

ג לֹא־תְבַעֲרוּ אֵשׁ בְּכֹל מֹשְׁבֹתֵיכֶם בְּיוֹם הַשַּׁבָּת׃

3 **Ye shall kindle no fire throughout your habitations upon the sabbath day.**'

Statement/Declaration #5

ז Verse 7

ז כַּבֵּד אֶת־אָבִיךָ וְאֶת־אִמֶּךָ
לְמַעַן יַאֲרִכוּן יָמֶיךָ עַל
הָאֲדָמָה אֲשֶׁר־יְהוָה אֱלֹהֶיךָ
נֹתֵן לָךְ׃

7 Honour thy father and thy mother, that thy days may be long upon the land which Yehovah thy God giveth thee.

Exodus 21:15, 17

יה וּמַכֵּה אָבִיו וְאִמּוֹ מוֹת יוּמָת׃

15 And he that smiteth his father, or his mother, **shall be surely put to death.**

יז וּמְקַלֵּל אָבִיו וְאִמּוֹ מוֹת יוּמָת׃

17 And he that curseth his father or his mother, **shall surely be put to death.**

Leviticus 20:9

ט כִּי־אִישׁ אִישׁ אֲשֶׁר יְקַלֵּל אֶת־אָבִיו וְאֶת־אִמּוֹ מוֹת יוּמָת אָבִיו
וְאִמּוֹ קִלֵּל דָּמָיו בּוֹ׃

9 **For whatsoever man there be that curseth his father or his mother shall surely be put to death;** he hath cursed his father or his mother; his blood shall be upon him.

Statement/Declaration #6

ח Verse 8

ח לֹא תִּרְצָח׃

תִּרְצָח

לֹא

8 Thou shalt not murder.

Exodus 21:12

יב מַכֵּה אִישׁ וָמֵת מוֹת יוּמָת:

12 He that smiteth a man, so that he dieth, **shall surely be put to death**.

Numbers 35:16-21, 30

טז וְאִם־בִּכְלִי בַרְזֶל ׀ הִכָּהוּ וַיָּמֹת רֹצֵחַ הוּא מוֹת יוּמַת הָרֹצֵחַ:

16 But if he smote him with an instrument of iron, so that he died, he is a murderer; **the murderer shall surely be put to death.**

יז וְאִם בְּאֶבֶן יָד אֲשֶׁר־יָמוּת בָּהּ הִכָּהוּ וַיָּמֹת רֹצֵחַ הוּא מוֹת יוּמַת הָרֹצֵחַ:

17 And if he smote him with a stone in the hand, whereby a man may die, and he died, he is a murderer; **the murderer shall surely be put to death.**

יח אוֹ בִּכְלִי עֵץ־יָד אֲשֶׁר־יָמוּת בּוֹ הִכָּהוּ וַיָּמֹת רֹצֵחַ הוּא מוֹת יוּמַת הָרֹצֵחַ:

18 Or if he smote him with a weapon of wood in the hand, whereby a man may die, and he died, he is a murderer; **the murderer shall surely be put to death.**

יט גֹּאֵל הַדָּם הוּא יָמִית אֶת־הָרֹצֵחַ בְּפִגְעוֹ־בוֹ הוּא יְמִיתֶנּוּ:

19 **The avenger of blood shall himself put the murderer to death**; when he meeteth him, he shall put him to death.

כ וְאִם־בְּשִׂנְאָה יֶהְדָּפֶנּוּ אוֹ־הִשְׁלִיךְ עָלָיו בִּצְדִיָּה וַיָּמֹת:

20 And if he thrust him of hatred, or hurled at him any thing, lying in wait, so that he died;

כא אוֹ בְאֵיבָה הִכָּהוּ בְיָדוֹ וַיָּמֹת מוֹת־יוּמַת הַמַּכֶּה רֹצֵחַ הוּא גֹּאֵל הַדָּם יָמִית אֶת־הָרֹצֵחַ בְּפִגְעוֹ־בוֹ:

21 or in enmity smote him with his hand, that he died; **he that smote him shall surely be put to death: he is a murderer;** the

avenger of blood shall put the murderer to death when he meeteth him.

לְ כָּל־מַכֵּה־נֶפֶשׁ לְפִי עֵדִים יִרְצַח אֶת־הָרֹצֵחַ וְעֵד אֶחָד לֹא־יַעֲנֶה בְנֶפֶשׁ לָמוּת׃

30 **Whoso killeth any person, the murderer shall be slain at the mouth of witnesses;** but one witness shall not testify against any person that he die.

Statement/Declaration #7

ט Verse 9

לֹא

תִּנְאָף׃

ט לֹא תִּנְאָף׃

9 Thou shalt not commit adultery.

What is the penalty for committing adultery? –**Death!**

Leviticus 20:10

י וְאִישׁ אֲשֶׁר יִנְאַף אֶת־אֵשֶׁת אִישׁ אֲשֶׁר יִנְאַף אֶת־אֵשֶׁת רֵעֵהוּ מוֹת־יוּמַת הַנֹּאֵף וְהַנֹּאָפֶת׃

10 And the man that committeth adultery with another man's wife, even he that committeth adultery with his neighbour's wife, **both the adulterer and the adulteress shall surely be put to death.**

Statement/Declaration #8

י Verse 10

לֹא

תִּגְנֹב

י לֹא תִּגְנֹב׃

10 Thou shalt not steal.

Exodus 21:37; 22:1-3

לז כִּי יִגְנֹב־אִישׁ שׁוֹר אוֹ־שֶׂה וּטְבָחוֹ אוֹ מְכָרוֹ חֲמִשָּׁה בָקָר יְשַׁלֵּם תַּחַת הַשּׁוֹר וְאַרְבַּע־צֹאן תַּחַת הַשֶּׂה:

37 If a man steal an ox, or a sheep, and kill it, or sell it, **he shall pay five oxen for an ox, and four sheep for a sheep.**

א אִם־בַּמַּחְתֶּרֶת יִמָּצֵא הַגַּנָּב וְהֻכָּה וָמֵת אֵין לוֹ דָּמִים:

1 If a thief be found breaking in, and be smitten so that he dieth, there shall be no bloodguiltiness for him.

ב אִם־זָרְחָה הַשֶּׁמֶשׁ עָלָיו דָּמִים לוֹ שַׁלֵּם יְשַׁלֵּם אִם־אֵין לוֹ וְנִמְכַּר בִּגְנֵבָתוֹ:

2 If the sun be risen upon him, there shall be bloodguiltiness for him--**he shall make restitution; if he have nothing, then he shall be sold for his theft.**

ג אִם־הִמָּצֵא תִמָּצֵא בְיָדוֹ הַגְּנֵבָה מִשּׁוֹר עַד־חֲמוֹר עַד־שֶׂה חַיִּים שְׁנַיִם יְשַׁלֵּם:

3 If the theft be found in his hand alive, whether it be ox, or ass, or sheep, **he shall pay double.**

Statement/Declaration #9

יא Verse 11

יא לֹא־תַעֲנֶה בְרֵעֲךָ עֵד שָׁקֶר:

לֹא־תַעֲנֶה בְרֵעֲךָ עֵד שָׁקֶר

11 Thou shalt not bear false witness against thy neighbour.

Bearing **false witness** and **lying** is a serious matter before Elohim. Here are some passages which speak to it.

Deuteronomy 19:15-21

יה לֹא־יָקוּם עֵד אֶחָד בְּאִישׁ לְכָל־עָוֺן וּלְכָל־חַטָּאת בְּכָל־חֵטְא אֲשֶׁר יֶחֱטָא עַל־פִּי ׀ שְׁנֵי עֵדִים אוֹ עַל־פִּי שְׁלֹשָׁה־עֵדִים יָקוּם דָּבָר׃

15 One witness shall not rise up against a man for any iniquity, or for any sin, in any sin that he sinneth; at the mouth of two witnesses, or at the mouth of three witnesses, shall a matter be established

יו כִּי־יָקוּם עֵד־חָמָס בְּאִישׁ לַעֲנוֹת בּוֹ סָרָה׃

16 If an **unrighteous witness** rise up against any man to bear perverted witness against him;

יז וְעָמְדוּ שְׁנֵי־הָאֲנָשִׁים אֲשֶׁר־לָהֶם הָרִיב לִפְנֵי יְהוָה לִפְנֵי הַכֹּהֲנִים וְהַשֹּׁפְטִים אֲשֶׁר יִהְיוּ בַּיָּמִים הָהֵם׃

17 then both the men, between whom the controversy is, shall stand before Yehovah, before the priests and the judges that shall be in those days.

יח וְדָרְשׁוּ הַשֹּׁפְטִים הֵיטֵב וְהִנֵּה עֵד־שֶׁקֶר הָעֵד שֶׁקֶר עָנָה בְאָחִיו׃

18 And the judges shall inquire diligently; and, behold, **if the witness be a false witness, and hath testified falsely against his brother;**

יט וַעֲשִׂיתֶם לוֹ כַּאֲשֶׁר זָמַם לַעֲשׂוֹת לְאָחִיו וּבִעַרְתָּ הָרָע מִקִּרְבֶּךָ׃

19 **then shall ye do unto him, as he had purposed to do unto his brother; so shalt thou put away the evil from the midst of thee.**

כ וְהַנִּשְׁאָרִים יִשְׁמְעוּ וְיִרָאוּ וְלֹא־יֹסִפוּ לַעֲשׂוֹת עוֹד כַּדָּבָר הָרָע הַזֶּה בְּקִרְבֶּךָ׃

20 And those that remain shall hear, and fear, and shall henceforth commit no more any such evil in the midst of thee.

כא וְלֹא תָחוֹס עֵינֶךָ נֶפֶשׁ בְּנֶפֶשׁ עַיִן בְּעַיִן שֵׁן בְּשֵׁן יָד בְּיָד רֶגֶל בְּרָגֶל׃

21 And thine eye shall not pity: **life for life, eye for eye, tooth for tooth, hand for hand, foot for foot.**

Statement/Declaration #10

ב׳ Verse 12

לֹא תַחְמֹד בֵּית רֵעֶךָ לֹא־
יב לֹא תַחְמֹד בֵּית רֵעֶךָ לֹא־
תַחְמֹד אֵשֶׁת רֵעֶךָ וְעַבְדּוֹ
וַאֲמָתוֹ וְשׁוֹרוֹ וַחֲמֹרוֹ וְכֹל אֲשֶׁר
לְרֵעֶךָ׃

12 Thou shalt not covet thy neighbour's house; thou shalt not covet thy neighbour's wife, nor his man-servant, nor his maid-servant, nor his ox, nor his ass, nor any thing that is thy neighbour's.

This last commandment appears to be about actions that can be brought about by having an unnatural desire (coveting) for that which belongs to your neighbor.

I had a Hebrew teacher that would often speak about "*a fence around the Torah*" (v'asu s'yag laTorah - from Pirke Avot 1:1),[32] which is similar to what this last "declaration" expresses. Quite simply, the "fence" idea is about insulating oneself from exposure to any potential temptation that can result in a transgression.

The delineation of Exodus 20:1-12, above, follows the original verse breaks given to us by the Masoretes themselves.

---

[32] Josh Franklin, "Building a Fence Around Torah," Sefaria, accessed 18 May 2021, https://www.sefaria.org/sheets/112806.1?lang=bi&with=all&lang2=en

To me, this presents **the Ten Commandments** with a very natural flow. It keeps each group of ideas as individual units.

The first "statement" declares who the author is to provide a point of reference. From the very outset, אָנֹכִי יְהוָה אֱלֹהֶיךָ [I am Yehovah your Elohim] was intended to be recognized as the source, The *Law Giver!*

Again, it is my opinion that all of the above statements/declarations in Exodus 20:1–12 were what was written on the two tablets of stone inscribed by the finger of Elohim [בְּאֶצְבַּע אֱלֹהִים] and placed within the Ark of the Testimony, also known as the Ark of the Covenant!

Moreover, Exodus 40:17 shows at what time the tabernacle (where the Ark of the Covenant was to reside) was erected during the 40 year wandering of the Children of Israel in the wilderness. From this timing, it is clear to me that the Exodus 20 version of the Ten Commandments was that which were written on the stone tablets and placed within the Ark of the Covenant.

Exodus 40:17

יז וַיְהִי בַּחֹדֶשׁ הָרִאשׁוֹן בַּשָּׁנָה הַשֵּׁנִית בְּאֶחָד לַחֹדֶשׁ הוּקַם הַמִּשְׁכָּן:

17 And it came to pass **in the first month in the second year, on the first day of the month,** *that the tabernacle was reared up.*

The Idea of Ten In Idiomatic Phrasing

If you were to strictly count the number of definitive *commands* in Exodus 20 as codified in **the Leningrad Codex,** they would just add up to ***nine***!

Since so many English translations refer to עֲשֶׂרֶת הַדְּבָרִים as the Ten Commandments I believe it necessary to set the record straight that **the number *ten* used in this way really should not be taken literally!**

I am hoping that I made it clear earlier that the translation of עֲשֶׂרֶת הַדְּבָרִים as "The Ten Commandments" is also not quite right.

Nevertheless, because the term has become so iconic, I think we are just stuck with using it!

To illustrate the idea that the number ten should not necessarily be taken literally, I am providing additional passages and comments.

Numbers 14:22

כִּי כָל־הָאֲנָשִׁים הָרֹאִים אֶת־כְּבֹדִי וְאֶת־אֹתֹתַי אֲשֶׁר־עָשִׂיתִי בְמִצְרַיִם וּבַמִּדְבָּר וַיְנַסּוּ אֹתִי זֶה עֶשֶׂר פְּעָמִים וְלֹא שָׁמְעוּ בְּקוֹלִי׃

*22 surely all those men that have seen My glory, and My signs, which I wrought in Egypt and in the wilderness, yet have **put Me to proof these ten times,** and have not hearkened to My voice;*

There are several places in the Hebrew–language based Jewish Scriptures which present the idea of completion using the number ten, as in the Numbers passage above. I am of the opinion that this phrasing, and others like it, often deploys language as a rhetorical device,[33] an idiom,[34] not intended to be taken literally but rather, as here, just to express a large quantity.

A similar use of "ten" is where Jacob tells his father-in-law, Laban, that he has changed his wages ten times:

Genesis 31:7, 41

ז וַאֲבִיכֶן הֵתֶל בִּי וְהֶחֱלִף אֶת־מַשְׂכֻּרְתִּי עֲשֶׂרֶת מֹנִים וְלֹא־נְתָנוֹ אֱלֹהִים לְהָרַע עִמָּדִי׃

---

[33] I. What is a Rhetorical Device? A rhetorical device is any language that helps an author or speaker achieve a particular purpose (usually persuasion, since rhetoric is typically defined as the art of persuasion). But "rhetorical device" is an extremely broad term, and can include techniques for generating emotion, beauty, and spiritual significance as well as persuasion. 'Rhetorical Device', Proofed, accessed 12 May 2021, https://literaryterms.net/rhetorical-device/
[34] Definition of idiom
1 : an expression in the usage of a language that is peculiar to itself either in having a meaning that cannot be derived from the conjoined meanings of its elements (such as up in the air for "undecided") or in its grammatically atypical use of words (such as give way)
2a : the language peculiar to a people or to a district, community, or class : dialect
b : the syntactical, grammatical, or structural form peculiar to a language
3 : a style or form of artistic expression that is characteristic of an individual, a period or movement, or a medium or instrument the modern jazz idiom broadly : manner, style a new culinary idiom
'idiom', Merriam-Webster, accessed 12 May 2021, https://www.merriam-webster.com/dictionary/idiom

*7 And your father hath mocked me, **and changed my wages ten times**; but God suffered him not to hurt me.*

מָא זֶה־לִּי עֶשְׂרִים שָׁנָה בְּבֵיתֶךָ עֲבַדְתִּיךָ אַרְבַּע־עֶשְׂרֵה שָׁנָה בִּשְׁתֵּי בְנֹתֶיךָ וְשֵׁשׁ שָׁנִים בְּצֹאנֶךָ וַתַּחֲלֵף אֶת־מַשְׂכֻּרְתִּי עֲשֶׂרֶת מֹנִים׃

*41 These twenty years have I been in thy house: I served thee fourteen years for thy two daughters, and six years for thy flock; **and thou hast changed my wages ten times.***

There is little doubt that this phrase, *"changed my wages ten times"* is an idiomatic expression and it is used similarly elsewhere.[35] To presume that "ten" means exactly ten, to me, is a bit naive!

Another type of rhetorical phrasing is as when Ahasuerus tells his wife, Esther, he will grant her up to *half of his kingdom*.[36] Again, I do not believe the "grant" is to be considered literally, but rather a common expression from the time of the "ancients."

When King David went to fulfill a command to "rear up an altar unto Yehovah," Araunah the Jebusite said **'Let my Lord take and offer what seemeth good unto him; behold the oxen...'.** David's response was 'Nay; but I will verily buy it at a price;.'[37]

Abraham, when he was burying his wife, Sarah, came to the children of Heth, after asking to buy the field of the cave of Machpelah.

Ephron the Hittite answered, 'Nay, my lord, hear me: **the field give I thee, and the cave that is therein, I give thee;**..." And when Abraham asked for the price, Ephron responded, 'My lord, hearken unto me: a piece of land worth four hundred shekels of silver, what is that betwixt me and thee? ...."[38]

---

[35] Genesis 31:7, 41; Numbers 14:22, Nehemia 4:6; Job 19:3; Daniel 1:20, 7:10.
[36] Esther 5:3 Then said the king unto her: 'What wilt thou, queen Esther? for whatever thy request, even to the half of the kingdom, it shall be given thee.'
[37] 2 Samuel 24:22-24 22 And Araunah said unto David: 'Let my lord the king take and offer up what seemeth good unto him; behold the oxen for the burnt-offering, and the threshing-instruments and the furniture of the oxen for the wood.' 23 All this did Araunah the king give unto the king. {S} And Araunah said unto the king: 'Yehovah thy God accept thee.' 24 And the king said unto Araunah: 'Nay; but I will verily buy it of thee at a price; neither will I offer burnt-offerings unto Yehovah my God which cost me nothing.' So David bought the threshing-floor and the oxen for fifty shekels of silver.
[38] Genesis 23:1-20.

These are just some examples of the use of colorful, exaggerated phrasing of ancient language often expressed in Scripture. Simply stated, the number "Ten" in **The Ten Commandments** can be interpreted correctly as to be *"around ten!"*

Root Definitions[39] For Exodus 20:1-12

Common Hebrew Prefixes and Suffixes

Table Source: https://www.jewfaq.org/root.htm

Prefix	Meaning	Comments and Examples
ו	And, but	Vav used as a prefix can make the "v" sound or the "u" sound. When used with other prefixes, this is always the first prefix. *V*ahavta (*and* you shall love); *U*vayom (*and* on the day).
ב	In, on, with, by, etc.	Beit as a prefix sometimes makes the soft sound (v). *B*ereishit (*in* the beginning); u'*v*ayom (and *on* the day).
ה	The	When Hei used with other prefixes, this is always the last prefix before the root. It is often absorbed into the Beit or Lamed prefix. *Ha*olam (*the* universe); u'vayom (and on the day; note that the v' (on) combines with the ha (the) to become va (on the)).
כ	Like, as	Mi *k*amokha (who is *like* you?).
ל	To, for	*L*'chayim (*to* life).
מ	From; also turns a verb into a noun	*Mi*mitzrayim (*from* Egypt); *mi*tzvah (commandment, a noun derived from the root verb tzavah meaning command)
ש	Turns a verb into the person who does it	*She*hecheyanu (*who* has kept us alive); *she*asah (*who* performed)

Suffix	Meaning	Comments and Examples
ים	Masculine plural	Yam*im* (days).
ות	Feminine plural	Mitzv*ot* (commandments).
ךָ	You, your	B'khol l'vavi*kha* uv'khol naf'shikha uv'khol m'odekha (with all *your* heart and with all *your* soul and with all *your* means).

---

[39] Ernest Klein, "An Etymological Dictionary of the Hebrew Language For Readers of English" (CARTA, Jerusalem);
Ernest Klein, 'A Comprehensive Etymological Dictionary of the Hebrew Language for Readers of English', Sefaria, accessed 9 Mar 2021, https://www.sefaria.org/Klein_Dictionary

נוּ֫ We, us, our Avi*nu* malkey*nu* (*our* Father, *our* King); asher kidisha*nu* (who has sanctified *us*); ashamnu (*we* have been guilty).

Common Prepositions / Prefixes / Suffixes (Klein Dictionary[40])

אַ pref. PBH on, upon. [Aram., equivalent of Heb. עַל.]

בְּ prep. (also בַּ. בָּ. בֵּ. בִּ. בְּ, according to its position) 1 in, within (as in בְּעֵינֵי, 'in the eyes of'). 2 on (as in בַּמִּזְבֵּחַ, 'on the altar'). 3 with (as in בַּשֵּׁבֶט. בַּמַּטֶּה, 'with the rod'). 4 for, for the price of (as in בְּרָחֵל, 'for רָחֵל'; בְּכֶסֶף מָלֵא, 'for the full price'). 5 as, in the condition of (as in בְּעֶזְרִי, 'as my help'). [cp. Ugar., Phoen. ב (= in, with), Aram.-Syr. בּ (= in, with), Arab. bi- (= in, by), Ethiop. ba (= in).]

הָ. הַ. הֶ. הֵ def. art. the (usually הַ, with the doubling of the next letter, as in הַבַּיִת; הָ before the letters א, ה, ח, ע, ר, as in הָאָדָם, הֶ before an accented הָ. תָ. עָ, as in הֶחָכָם). [Related to Moabite and Phoen. ה. According to Brockelmann, the doubling of the next letter is due to the compensation of the shortened vowel; he compares מַה, shortened form of מָה (= what). This shows the Ungnad was wrong in assuming that the Heb. art. derives from the form han. The supposition that the Heb. art. developed from hal had been given up by most Sem. scholars long ago.]

וְ I conj. (waw copulative) and, but, therefore. 2 as, since, seeing, while, whereas, although; usually in circumstantial clauses as in וְהוּא יֹשֵׁב (= as he sat ... Gen. 18:1) and in וְהוּא הַצָּעִיר (= although he was the younger ... Gen. 48:14). Before a labial (i.e. any of the sounds ב. ו. מ. פ) and before a sound with a shwa, it becomes וּ, e.g. וּמִי (= and who), וּדְבַר (= and the word of). With following יְ it coalesces into וִי, e.g. וִיהִי (= and let him be). Before an accented syllable it often becomes וָ, e.g. וָחֹרֶף (= and winter). Before a letter with ḥataph it takes the vowel of the ḥataph, e.g. וַאֲנָשִׁים (= and men), וֶאֱמֶת (= and

---

[40] ibid.

truth), וָאֳנִיָה (= and a ship). Before אֱלֹהִים it becomes וַ.
[Related to Aram., Syr. and Phoen, Arab. wa, Ethiop. w–,
Akka. u–.]

ו II conj. (waw consecutive, also waw conversive) 1 turns the
future tense into past tense. With verbs in the second person
and third person sing., and in all the three persons plu., it
always has the form וַ, as in וַתֹּאמַר (= and you said). With a
verb standing in the first person sing. it has the form וָ‎־, as in
וָאֹמַר (= and I said). 2 turns the past tense into future tense. It
may have the form וְ, וִ, וּ, וָ, e.g. וְאָמַרְתִּי (= and I will say),
וּבֵרַכְתָּ (= and you will bless), וִהְיִיתֶם (= and you will be),
וַאֲכַלְתֶּם (= and you will eat).

כְּ pref. (prob. orig. a noun) meaning 'the likeness of, the like of'.
Used qualitatively, i.e. in the senses 'like, as' e.g. כְּאִישׁ (= like
a man); 'according to', as in כִּדְבַר (= according to the word of)
and corresponding to Arab. mithl (= likeness, model), and to L.
instar (= resemblance, image). Also used quantitatively, i.e. in
the sense 'about', 'approximately', as in כְּעֶשֶׂר שָׁנִים (= about
ten years), and corresponding to Arab. qadr (= quantity,
amount, number). כְּ becomes כִּ before a consonant with
'schwa', as in כִּשְׁלֹמֹה (= like Solomon). With following יְ it
coalesces into כִּי, as in כִּירוּשָׁלַיִם (= like Jerusalem). Before a
'hataph' (see חֲטָף) it takes the vowel of the hataph, as in
כֶּאֱדוֹם (= like Edom). Before the art. the ה is usually dropped
and its vowel is taken over by the pref., as in כַּמֶּלֶךְ for כְּהַמֶּלֶךְ
(= like the king), כָּאוֹר for כְּהָאוֹר (= like the light). Before the
Tetragrammaton it becomes כַּ, before אֱלֹקִים it becomes כֵּ.
(cp. the prefixes בְּ and לְ, which undergo changes similar to
those of כְּ.) [Related to Phoen. כ, BAram. and Aram. כְּ, Arab.
ka; Akka. ki, aki (= like as), from Sem. ka. See כֹּה and cp.
words there referred to. cp. also כְּלָא, כְּמוֹ, כַּמָּה, and כַּאֲשֶׁר.]

לְ pref. 1 to, unto. 2 toward. 3 at, by. 4 into. 5 belonging to. 6
written by (the so-called 'Lamed auctoris', as in מִזְמוֹר לְדָוִד (=
psalm written by David). 7 לְ serves to introduce the inf.
construction, as in לְדַבֵּר (= to speak), לְבָרֵךְ (= to bless). לְ
becomes לִ before a consonant with 'schwa', as in לִשְׁלֹמֹה (=

to Solomon); with following יְ it coalesces into יִ, as in לִירוּשָׁלַיִם (= to Jerusalem); before a 'hateph' (see חָטָף) it takes the vowel of the hateph, as in לֶאֱדוֹם (= to Edom); before the art. the ה is usually dropped and its vowel taken over by the prep. ל as in לַבֶּגֶד, for לְהַבֶּגֶד (= to the garment), לָאָב for לְהָאָב (= to the father); before אֱלֹקִים, לְ becomes לֵ; cp. also לְאֱמֹר (= to say), which becomes לֵאמֹר (q.v.). [Related to Aram.-Syr. לְ, Ugar. l-, Arab. li-, Ethiop. l- (= to), Akka. la- (= Heb. לִפְנֵי).]

מִ prep. from, of (form of מִן before gutturals).

מ (also מִ, מָ, מָ, מוֹ, מָ, מֶ, מֵ, מִי) subst. pref. which serves 1 to form abstract nouns, as מַדָּע (= knowledge), 2 to denote places, as מָאֲבוּס (= granary, storehouse), and 3 to form names of instruments, as מָגֵן (= shield). On some occasions it becomes מֵ (as in מֵיטָב), מָ (as in מוֹדַע), מִי (as in מִדְבָּר), מוֹ (as in מָעֹז), מְ (as in מְבוּכָה), and מָ is sometimes lengthened into מָ (as in מֶרְחָק). Prefixes מ and ת are sometimes interchangeable. cp. e.g. מוֹצָא and תּוֹצָא (= outgoing). Pref. ma is common to all Sem. languages.

תְּ, תּוֹ, תִּ, תַּ subst. pref. Nouns with prefixed ת generally serve: **1** as verbal nouns of the Qal, usually strengthening the basic meaning of the verb; **2** in most cases, esp. in the form 'taqtīl', as verbal nouns of the Pi'ēl, corresponding to Arab. 'taqtīl', verbal n. of the second (intensive) conjugation; see **3**; תַּשְׁמִישׁ However, since in Hebrew the intensive conjugation (Pi'ēl) and the causative conjugation (Hiph'īl) are closely related in sense (e.g. the Pi'ēl often has a causative meaning, which is the primary sense of the Hiph'īl), and because the form 'taqtīl' is very similar to the Hiph'īl (perf. הִפְעִיל, imperf. יַפְעִיל), therefore it often occurs that 'taqtīl' is the verbal noun form for verbs in the Hiph'īl; **4** Quite rarely verbal nouns with pref. ת are related to the Niph'āl or the Hithpa'ēl. ת is the mostly used prefix forming verbal nouns in Hebrew. It is related to Aram-Syr. תְּ, תַּ, Arab. ta-, ti-, Ethiop. ta-, ti-, Akka. ta. In all Sem. languages the prefixes מ and ת are often interchangeable. cp. e.g. תַּרְבִּית and מַרְבִּית (= interest, profit), תּוֹצָא and מוֹצָא (= outgoing), תְּשׁוּבָה (= return), and מְשׁוּבָה (= backsliding), תַּאֲוָה

and מַאֲוַיִּים (= desire), תַּחֲלוּאִים and מַחֲלוּיִים (= sickness), תִּירוֹשׁ and Aram. מֵירְתָא, Syr. מְאִרִיתָא (= must, new wine), Syr. תַּרְנִיתָא and מַרְנִיתָא (= meditation), Arab. *tiqwāl* and *miqwāl* (= chatterer, babbler), *tīfāq* and *mīfāq* (= first appearance). cp. pref. מ.

Common Suffixes

א II the most common subst. and adj. suff. in Aram. (corresponding to Heb. first suff. ה.]

אי PBH suff. forming nomina opificum from ל״ה verbal stems, as בַּנַּאי (= builder), from בנה (= to build); גַּבַּאי (= collector), from גבה (= to collect).

ה I the most common f. subst. and adj. suff. cp. e.g. סוּסָה (= mare) from סוּס (= horse); גְּדוֹלָה, f. of גָּדוֹל (= great). This suff. developed from ת, which had perhaps orig. a demonstrative force, and it became ה orig. only in pause. Later, however, the form ה penetrated also into context in the form of the absolute state. The form ת remained in the construction state (which can never appear in pausal position) and before pron. suffixes. All this applies also to Aramaic and Arabic. cp. suff. תִי. See suffixes ת, ת — collateral forms of ה.

ה II suff. serving to form nomina unitatis (nouns of individuality). cp. e.g. אֶבְרָה (= pinion), from אֵבֶר (= pinions); אֳנִיָּה (= ship), from אֳנִי (= fleet); נִצָּה (= blossom, flower), from נֵץ (= collectively); שִׁירָה (= song, ode), from שִׁיר (collectively); שִׁמְשָׁה (= sun disk), prob. from שֶׁמֶשׁ (= sun); שַׂעֲרָה (= a single hair), from שֵׂעָר (= hair). [Orig. and formally identical with ה I. cp. Arab. ḥamāma (= one dove), from ḥamām (= doves); dhahaba (= a piece of gold), from dhahab (= gold).]

ה III f. collective suff. [In most cases suff. of the f. part., used substantively in a collective sense (see אוֹרְחָה and גּוֹלָה). In some other cases as in דָּגָה (= fish, coll.) and in אַרְזָה (= cedar panel), formed from a noun. In both cases, orig. and formally identical with ה I.]

ן ֿ¹ suff. forming abstract nouns, as in בִּנְיָן (= construction, building), מִנְיָן (= number), עִנְיָן (= occupation, affair, business). [This suff. occurs in all Sem. languages. It forms before all verbal nouns, but also agential nouns, diminutives and adjectives; see ן ᴵᴵ. In Heb. it mostly appears in the form וֹן (q.v.). The few Heb. words ending in ן belong to a later period or are borrowed from Aramaic.]

ן ᴵᴵ PBH suff. forming agential nouns and adjectives, as in קַפְּדָן (= an irascible person), לַמְדָן (= a learned man), mostly from Aram. [The form פַּעֲלָן differs from the form פָּעָל inasmuch as פַּעֲלָן denotes someone who performs an action incidentally, whereas the form פָּעָל denotes someone's permanent occupation or profession. cp. e.g. בַּלְעָן, דַּגָּל and בַּלְעָן and קַסְמָן, שַׁתָּל and תַּבְלָן, קַסָּם and הַלְכָן, הַלָּךְ and דַּגְלָן, הַלְכָן and שַׁתְלָן, שַׁקְּרָן. cp. also ן ᴵ, תָן, נִי, נוּת, and the second element in יִסְטָן.]

ן ᴵᴵᴵ NH suff. forming names of chemical elements, as in חַמְצָן (= oxygen), מֵימָן (= hydrogen), חַנְקָן (= nitrogen), פֶּחְמָן (= carbon). [Coined on the basis of ן ᴵᴵ, suff. forming agential nouns: the word חַמְצָן (= oxygen) lit. means 'he who makes sour, acidifier', etc.]

לְךָ (in pause לָךְ) inflected m. pers. pron. meaning 'to thee', 'to you'. [Formed from לְ with suff. ךָ. cp. לְכָה ᴵᴵ and the second element in מַלְךָ.]

ם ᴵᴵ adv. suff., added to nouns, as in חִנָּם (= gratis), from חֵן (= grace), יוֹמָם (= by day), from יוֹם (= day), and to adjectives, as רֵיקָם (= empty-handed), from רֵיק (= empty). This suff. prob. served orig. as the indef. art. (= mimmation).

ת (after gutturals ת) f. subst. & adj. suff. cp. e.g. דֶּלֶת (= door), קֶשֶׁת (= bow), שֶׁבֶת (= to sit), לֶדֶת (= to bear), דַּעַת (= to know), גְּבֶרֶת (= mistress, lady), נְחֹשֶׁת (= copper), שׁוֹמֶרֶת (= watching). It is esp. common in participles and infinitives: שׁוֹמֶרֶת is more frequent than שׁוֹמְרָה, לֶדֶת than לֵדָה. [This suff. developed from t which had perhaps orig. demonstrative force. It appears in the Sem. languages in two forms: 1 as t, whence: Heb. ת, as in בַּת (= daughter), שְׁתַּיִ (= two), ת in אוֹהֶבֶת (= loving), יוֹשֶׁבֶת (= sitting), etc.; t appears also in Arabic in a few nouns, as in bint (= daughter), 'uḫt (= sister), and in thintai (= two) (f.); in Ethiop. bent (= pupil of the eye), 'eḫt (= sister), walat (= daughter), tamart (= palm tree), negesht (= queen; f. of negūsh, 'king'); in Akka. bintu (= daughter), shattu (= year), talīmtu (= sister), batūltu (= virgin), ti'āmtu (= sea); and prob. in the Aram. nouns בָּת (= daughter), שְׁתָּא (= year). 2 as -at, which became ה (orig. only in pause), whence Heb. ה, as in סוּסָה (= mare; from סוּס, 'horse'); see first suff. ה.]

Verses 1-12 And Root Definitions Of Each Word[41]

א Verse 1

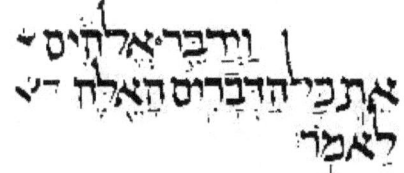

א וַיְדַבֵּר אֱלֹהִים אֵת כָּל־הַדְּבָרִים הָאֵלֶּה לֵאמֹר:

1 And God spoke all these words, saying:

וַיְדַבֵּר (word 1, verse 1)

דבר [I] to speak.

— Qal - דָּבַר (used only in the act. part. דֹּבֵר, 'saying, speaking', and in the pass. part. דָּבוּר, 'said, spoken').

— Niph. - 1 נִדְבַּר (pl.) they spoke to one another, talked; MH 2 was said, was spoken.

— Pi. - 1 דִּבֶּר he spoke of; 2 he spoke to or with.

— Pu. - 1 דֻּבַּר was spoken; NH 2 was stipulated, was agreed.

---

[41] Definitions From: Ernest Klein, 'A Comprehensive Etymological Dictionary of the Hebrew Language for Readers of English', Sefaria, accessed 9 Mar 2021, https://www.sefaria.org/Klein_Dictionary.
Formatting changed to conform to book format; Ezra SIL SR for Hebrew; Helvetica for English.

— Hith. - **1** הִתְדַּבֵּר he spoke, talked; NH 2 he came to an agreement. [Prob. an imitative base with the orig. meaning 'to buzz, hum' and base of דְּבוֹרָה (= bee).] Derivatives: דָּבָר, דָּבוּר, דִּבּוּר, דִּבְרַת, דַּבְרָן, דַּבֶּרֶת, הִתְדַּבְּרוּת, מְדַבֵּר, מִדְבָּר, (n.), מְדֻבָּר II.

אֱלֹהִים (word 2, verse 1)

אֱלֹהִים, אֱלוֹהִים m.n. pl. 1 gods. 2 God (pl. of majesty). 3 supernatural beings. 4 judges. [According to some scholars אֱלֹהִים is the pl. of אֱלוֹהַּ, according to others it is the pl. of אֵל I.]

אֵת (word 3, verse 1)

אֵת I, אֶת prep. the mark of the accusative. Usually prefixed only to a definite noun, as in אֶת־הָאִישׁ (= the man). [Related to Moabite את, Phoen. אית (to be read אַיַּת), Aram. (also BAram.) and Syr. יָת (this latter mostly used as a noun), Egypt.-Aram. ות, Arab. 'iyyā (only used with a suff. to emphasize the pron.) and possibly also to Ethiop. kīyā (also used only with a suff. for the sake of emphasis). Orig. — as Syr. יָת, יָתָא — a noun in the sense of 'being, essence, existence'. The orig. form prob. was 'iwyath (cp. the Phoen. form), which ultimately derives from base אוה (= to sign, mark), whence also אוֹת (= sign).]

כָּל (word 4, verse 1)

כֹּל m.n. all, whole, the whole of. [From כלל I (= to comprehend, include). cp. Aram. (also BAram.) כֹּל, כָּל, Ugar. kl, Arab. kull, Ethiop. kellā, OSArab. כל, Akka. kullatu (= the whole of). See כְּלִי.]

הַדְּבָרִים (word 5, verse 1)

דבר I to speak.

— Qal - דָּבַר (used only in the act. part. דּוֹבֵר, 'saying, speaking', and in the pass. part. דָּבוּר, 'said, spoken').

— Niph. - **1** נִדְבַּר (pl.) they spoke to one another, talked; MH 2 was said, was spoken.

— Pi. - **1** דִּבֶּר he spoke of; 2 he spoke to or with.

— Pu. - **1** דֻּבַּר was spoken; NH 2 was stipulated, was agreed.

— Hith. - **1** הִתְדַּבֵּר he spoke, talked; NH 2 he came to an agreement. [Prob. an imitative base with the orig. meaning 'to buzz, hum' and base of דְּבוֹרָה (= bee).] Derivatives: דָּבָר, דָּבוּר, דִּבּוּר, דִּבְרָה, דִּבְרָן, דַּבֶּרֶת, הִדָּבְרוּת, מְדַבֵּר, מִדְבָּר (n.), דִּבֵּר, מְדֻבָּר‍ᴵᴵ.

הָאֵלֶּה (word 6, verse 1)

אֵלֶּה pron. m. & f. pl. these. [Related to MH אֵלוּ, Phoen. אל, האל, Punic ily, BAram. אֵלֶּה, also אִלֵּין, אֵל, Aram. אִלֵּין, Arab. 'ulā, Ethiop. 'elū, SArab. אלת, אלן, אלי, אלו. cp. אֵל ᴵᴵᴵ, אֵלּוּ.]

לֵאמֹר (word 7, verse 1)

אמר ᴵ to say.
  — Qal - 1 אָמַר he said, told, uttered; 2 he commanded, ordered; 3 he said in his heart, thought.
  — Niph. - נֶאֱמַר it was said.
  — Hiph. - הֶאֱמִיר he caused to say, induced to say; he avouched. [Moabite and Phoen. אמר, Aram. אֲמַר, Syr. אֱמַר (= he said, spoke), Arab. 'amara (= he commanded).] Derivatives: אָמוֹרָא, אֲמִירָה, אֹמֶר, אִמְרָה, הַאֲמָרָה, כְּלוֹמַר, לֵאמֹר, מֵימְרָה. cp. ימר and אָמִיר.

ב Verse 2

ב אָנֹכִי יְהוָה אֱלֹהֶיךָ אֲשֶׁר
הוֹצֵאתִיךָ מֵאֶרֶץ מִצְרַיִם
מִבֵּית עֲבָדִים׃

2 I am Yehovah thy God, who brought thee out of the land of Egypt, out of the house of bondage.

אָנֹכִי (word 1, verse 2)

אָנֹכִי pers. pron. I. [Related to Phoen. אנך and אנכי, Moabite אנך, Punic anec, OAram. אנך, אנכי, Ugar. ạnk, Akka. anāku, and cogn. with Egypt. ynk, Coptic anok, nok. It has no correspondences in Aram., Arab. and Ethiop. (in this latter, kū appears as the suff. of the first pers. in the conjugation of the verb, as in waladkū, Heb. יָלַדְתִּי, 'I bore'). The endings כִי, resp. - ku, etc. in אָנֹכִי, anāku, etc., are prob. related to Heb. כֹה, Aram.-Syr. כָּא (= here).] Derivatives: אָנֹכִיּי, אָנֹכִיּוּת.

יְהוָה (word 2, verse 2)

יְהוָה, יְהֹוָת m.n. the proper name of God in the Bible, Tetragrammaton. [It prob. derives from הוה (= to be). The usual transliteration 'Jehovah' is based on the supposition that the Tetragrammaton is the imperfect Qal or Hiph'il of הוה and lit. means 'the one who is', 'the existing', resp. 'who calls into existence'. In reality, however, the pronunciation and literal meaning of the Tetragrammaton is unknown. cp. יָהּ ¹.]

אֱלֹהֶיךָ (word 3, verse 2)

אֱלֹהַּ, אֱלֹהַּ m.n. 1 god. 2 God. [According to some scholars אֱלוֹהַּ is a back formation from the pl. אֱלוֹהִים, this latter being the plural of אֵל ¹ with the infix ה, which has an analogy in Heb. אִמָּהוֹת, pl. of אֵם (= mother), in Aram. אבהת, pl. of אַב (= father), שְׁמָהָת, pl. of שְׁמָא (= name), to which may be added Ugar. 'mht, pl. of 'mt (= Heb. אָמָה, 'bondwoman'), bhtm, pl. of bt (= Heb. בַּיִת, 'house'), and 'lht, pl. of 'lt (= goddess), f. of 'l (= Heb. אֵל ¹, 'god'). Others see in אֱלוֹהַּ the orig. form from which the pl. אֱלוֹהִים was formed. The consideration of the fact that אֵל has the pl. אֵלִים, shows that the second view is surely preferable to the first. Fleischer sees in אֱלוֹהַּ the derivative of base אלה, which he connects with Arab. aliha (= he sought refuge in anxiety), whence אֱלוֹהַּ would have meant orig. 'fear', hence 'object of fear or reverence', 'the revered one'. However, Nöldeke and others are prob. right when they maintain that the verb aliha in the above sense is prob. denominated from 'ilāh (= god).]

אֲשֶׁר (word 4, verse 2)

1 אֲשֶׁר who, which, that, that which. 2 in order that. [Related to Ugar. aṯr (= that which). cp. Moabite אשר. According to most scholars these words were originally nouns meaning 'trace, place', and are related to Arab. 'athira (= to leave traces), 'lthr (= trace, place), and to Aram. אֲתַר, אַתְרָא, Syr. אַתְרָא (= place). See אָתַר.]

הוֹצֵאתִיךָ (word 5, verse 2)

הוֹצָאָה f.n. PBH 1 carrying out, taking out, bringing forth. PBH 2 expenditure, expenses. NH 3 edition. NH 4 publication. [Verbal

n. of הוֹצִיא (= he brought out, brought forth), Hiph. of יצא. For the ending see first suff. ה.]

יצא to go or come out.

— Qal - יָצָא he went out, came out, went forth, came forth.

— Hiph. - 1 הוֹצִיא he brought out, brought forth, carried out; PBH 2 he released, discharged; PBH 3 he excluded; PBH 4 he spent; NH 5 he published (short for הוֹצִיא לָאוֹר).

— Hoph. - 1 הוּצָא was brought forth, was taken out; PBH 2 was spent.

— Pi. - יִצֵּא he exported.

— Pu. - יֻצָּא was exported. [Aram. יְעָא (= went forth; burst forth, bloomed), Ugar. yṣ' (= to go out), Ethiop. waḍa'a (= went out), Arab. waḍu'a (= was or became beautiful, neat or clean), Akka. aṣū, earlier waṣū (= to go out; to rise — said of the sun). cp. אָסְיָה.] Derivatives: יָצִיא I, יוֹצְאָנִית, יָצוּא, יְצוּא, יָצִיא II, יְצִיאָה, יַצְאָן, יַצְאָנוּת, הוֹצָאָה, הַמּוֹצִיא, מוֹצָא, מוֹצָא, מִיצָא, תּוֹצָאָה, צֶאֱצָא.

מֵאֶרֶץ (word 6, verse 2)

אֶרֶץ f.n. (pl. 1 אֲרָצוֹת) earth. 2 land, country. 3 ground. [Related to BAram. אַרְקָא (for the change of צ to ק cp. Heb. קָטַר, 'he caused to smoke', with Aram. עֲטַר), Aram. אַרְעָא, אֲרַע, Ugar. arṣ, Arab. arḍ, Akka. erṣetu (= earth), Tigre 'ard. cp. Arakiel — name of the earth in the Book of Enoch 8:3. cp. אַרְעָה, אַרְק. אַרְקָה.] Derivatives: אַרְצִי, אַרְצָן.

מִצְרַיִם (word 7, verse 2)

מִצְרִי adj. Egyptian. [Gentilic name formed from מִצְרַיִם (= Egypt). For the ending see suff. י.]

מִבֵּית (word 8, verse 2)

מִבֵּית adv. from within, inside, internally. [Formed from pref. מִ (= from), and the noun בַּיִת (= house).]

בֵּי m.n. house, home (occurring in numerous phrases quoted from Talmud or Midrash, as in בֵּי־כְנִשְׁתָּא, 'synagogue'; בֵּי־מַסּוּתָא, 'bath'; בֵּי־רַב, 'school'; בֵּי־שֻׁתָּפֵי, 'partnership). Aram., c. st. of בֵּיתָא (= house). See בַּיִת.]

בַּיִת m.n. (pl. 1 בָּתִּים) house, home, family. 2 school. MH 3 stanza (of a poem). [Related to Akka. bītu, Ugar. bt, Phoen. בת,

Aram. בֵּיתָא, Aram.–Syr. בָּת, Arab. bayt.] Derivatives: בֵּית
בִּית, בַּיָת, בֵּיתִי, בֵּיתָנִי.

עֲבָדִים (word 9, verse 2)

עבד to work; to serve.

— **Qal.** - עָבַד v. **1** he worked, labored, tilled, cultivated (the soil); **2** he served. **3** he worshiped.

— **Niph.** - נֶעֱבַד. **1** was tilled, was cultivated; PBH **2** was worshiped; PBH **3** was dressed, was tanned (said of hides).

— **Pi.** - עִבֵּד **1** he cultivated; **2** he dressed, tanned (said of hides); he elaborated, adapted.

— **Pu.** - עֻבַּד **1** was worked; PBH **2** was dressed, was tanned (said of hides); NH **3** was elaborated, adapted.

— **Nith.** - הִתְעַבֵּד, נִתְעַבֵּד **1** was worked; **2** was dressed, was tanned (said of hides); NH **3** was adapted.

— **Shiph. (see . -** שִׁעְבֵּד).

— **Hiph.** - הֶעֱבִיד **1** he caused to work, made to serve; **2** he enslaved.

— **Hoph.** - הָעֳבַד was made to serve. [Aram. (also BAram.) and Syr. עֲבַד (= he worked, did, performed, made), whence BAram. עֲבַד, Aram. and Syr. עַבְדָּא (= slave, servant), Ugar. bd (= to work, serve, worship), Arab. 'abada (= he served, worshiped, obeyed), whence 'abd (= slave, worshiper), OSArab. עבד (= servant), Ethiop. 'abbaṭa (= he imposed forced labor), Akka. abdu (= slave). Derivatives: עֶבֶד, עָבָד, עֲבֻדָּה, עִבְדָּן, עַבְדוּת, עָבוּד, עִבּוּד, עֲבוּדָה, עוֹבֵד, הַעֲבָדָה, עָבַד, עַבְדָּא, עָבְדָּא cp. מִעְבָּד, מַעְבָּדָה, מַעֲבִיד, תַּעֲבוּד.

עֶבֶד m.n. **1** servant; **2** slave, bondman; **3** worshipper. [From עבד.]

עַבְדָּא m.n. PBH servant; slave. [Aram. and Syr., denominated from עֲבַד (q.v.). cp. עֶבֶד.]

עָבְדָּא PBH, עֶבְדָּה NH **1** deed, act. **2** occurrence. **3** fact. [From Aram. עוֹבָדָא, Syr. עָבְדָּא (= work, fact, deed), from עֲבַד (= he did).] Derivative: עָבְדָּתִי.

עֲבֻדָּה f.n. household servants (occurring in the Bible only Gen. 26:14 and Job 1:3). [From עבד.]

עַבְדוּת f.n. slavery, servitude, bondage (in the Bible occurring only Ez. 9:8 following and Neh. 9:17). [Formed from עבד with suff. וּת. cp. Syr. עַבְדּוּתָא (of s.m.).] Derivative: עַבְדוּתִי.

עַבְדוּתִי adj. NH slavish, servile. [Formed from עַבְדוּת with suff. ִי.]

עֲבוֹדָה f.n. 1 work, labor. 2 deed, action. 3 service. 4 divine service, worship. PBH 5 'abodah', the first of the last three benedictions of the 'Amidah'. MH 6 liturgy for the 'Musaph' service on the Day of Atonement. [From עבד.]

ג Verse 3

ג לֹא יִהְיֶה־לְךָ אֱלֹהִים אֲחֵרִים עַל־פָּנָי ׃ לֹא תַעֲשֶׂה־לְךָ פֶסֶל ׀ וְכָל־תְּמוּנָה אֲשֶׁר בַּשָּׁמַיִם ׀ מִמַּעַל וַאֲשֶׁר בָּאָרֶץ מִתַּחַת וַאֲשֶׁר בַּמַּיִם ׀ מִתַּחַת לָאָרֶץ לֹא־תִשְׁתַּחֲוֶה לָהֶם וְלֹא תָעָבְדֵם כִּי אָנֹכִי יְהוָה אֱלֹהֶיךָ אֵל קַנָּא פֹּקֵד עֲוֹן אָבֹת עַל־בָּנִים עַל־שִׁלֵּשִׁים וְעַל־רִבֵּעִים לְשֹׂנְאָי ׃

3 Thou shalt have no other gods before Me. Thou shalt not make unto thee a graven image, nor any manner of likeness, of any thing that is in heaven above, or that is in the earth beneath, or that is in the water under the earth; thou shalt not bow down unto them, nor serve them; for I Yehovah thy God am a jealous God, visiting the iniquity of the fathers upon the children unto the third and fourth generation of them that hate Me;

לֹא (word 1, verse 3)

לֹא adv. no, not. [Related to Aram. (also BAram) and Syr. לָא, Ugar. *l*, Arab. *lā*, Akka. *lā* (= not, no). cp. לָאו, and the second element in אֶלָּא. אוּלַי. אֲלוּלֵא. לוּלֵא.]

לֹא־ combining form meaning 'non-'. [From לֹא (= no, not).]

לֹא adv. PBH no, not. [Aram., related to Heb. לֹא (q.v.).]

יִהְיֶה (word 2, verse 3)

היה to be, exist, happen, become.

— Qal - הָיָה **1** was, existed; **2** came into being, became; **3** he remained; **4** it came to pass, happened.

— Niph. - נִהְיָה **1** he became; **2** it was done, was brought about.

— Pi. - הִיָּה he caused (something) to become, he made. [A parallel form of הוה ᴵᴵ.] Derivative: הָיוֹת.

הָיוֹת **1** inf. to be. MH **2** existence. [Inf. construction of הָיָה (= he was). See היה.]

לְךָ (word 3, verse 3)

לְךָ (in pause לָךְ) inflected m. pers. pron. meaning 'to thee', 'to you'. [Formed from לְ with suff. ךָ. cp. לְכָה ᴵᴵ and the second element in מֶלֶךְ.]

לָךְ inflected f. pers. pron. meaning 'to thee', 'to you'. [Formed from לְ with suff. ךְ.]

אֱלֹהִים (word 4, verse 3)

אֱלֹהִים, אֱלוֹהִים m.n. pl. 1 gods. 2 God (pl. of majesty). 3 supernatural beings. 4 judges. [According to some scholars אֱלֹהִים is the pl. of אֱלוֹהַּ, according to others it is the pl. of אֵל ᴵ.]

אֲחֵרִים (word 5, verse 3)

אחר to be or remain behind.

— Qal - אָחַר he was late, tarried (a hapax legomenon in the Bible, occurring Gen. 32:5 in the form וָאֵחַר).

— Pi. - **1** אִחַר he delayed, tarried; **2** he caused one to delay, kopt back

— Pu. - אֻחַר he was late.

— Hith. - הִתְאַחֵר he came late.

— Hiph. - הֶאֱחִיר he delayed, postponed.

— Hoph. - הָאֳחַר was delayed, postponed. [Aram. אֲחַר, Syr. אוֹחַר, Arab. 'aḥḥara (= he put off), 'ta'áḥḥara (= he was behind, was late, tarried), Akka. uḫḫuru (= he remained behind), Ugar. aḥr (= later, afterward).] Derivatives: מְאַחֵר

אַחֲרוֹן, אַחֲרָיוּת, הָאֶחָרַת, הִתְאַחֲרוּת, מְאַחֵר, אָחוֹר, אָחוּר, אַחַר, אַחַר, אַחֲרָאִי,, prob. also מָחָר.

1 אַחַר after, behind, afterward. 2 behind, after. [Orig. a noun meaning 'the hinder part' and a derivative of אחר, whence also Moabite אחר, Ugar. 'hr (= after), Aram. אָחֳרָא (= behind). cp. אַחֲרֵי.] Derivatives: אַחַר, אַחֲרֵי.

עַל (word 6, verse 3)

עַל I **1** height, upper part. **2** , above. [From עלה. See עַל II.]

עַל II prep. **1** on, upon, above. **2** at, beside. **3** toward(s). **4** against. **5** concerning, about. **6** because of, on account of. **7** together with. [Shortened from עֲלֵי, which is preserved in poetry (see עֲדֵי and אֱלֵי), from עלה. Related to Phoen. and Moabite על, עלת, Aram., BAram.) and Syr. עַל, Ugar. 'l, Arab. 'alā, OSArab. עלי, Ethiop. lā'la, Akka. eli (= on, upon). cp. עַל I. cp. also עֲלִיָּה II.] Derivative: עַל.

פְּנֵי (word 7, verse 3)

פנה to turn.

— **Qal** - **1** פָּנָה he turned, turned toward (אֶל), turned away; **2** he turned and looked, looked, looked at (אֶל), considered, regarded; PBH **3** he freed himself, was free.

— **Niph.** - **1** נִפְנָה he turned away; **2** was free, was at leisure; **3** was removed; **4** he eased nature, eased himself.

— **Pi.** - פִּנָּה MH **1** he removed, cleaned, emptied; NH **2** he vacated, evacuated.

— **Pu.** - פֻּנָּה MH **1** was removed, was emptied; NH **2** was vacated, was evacuated.

— **Hith.** - **1** הִתְפַּנָּה was removed, was emptied; **2** he became free, had leisure.

— **Hiph.** - **1**. הִפְנָה v. he turned, caused to turn; **2** intr. v., he turned, made a turn.

— **Hoph.** - **1** הָפְנָה was turned, was directed; PBH **2** was disengaged, was free. [JAram.–Syr. פְּנָא (= he turned), Arab. faniya (= he passed away, vanished), fanā (= passing away), Ethiop. fannawa (= he sent away). cp. פָּנִים. cp. also פֶּן, אֹפֶן.] Derivatives: פַּנַאי, פָּנוּי, פְּנוּי, פְּנוּת, פְּנִיָּה, פּוֹנָה, פְּנָאָה, הַפְנָיָה, פֶּנֶת. cp. הַפָּנוּת, הִתְפַּנּוּת, מִפְנֶה, מְפֻנֶּה, תַּפְנִית.

לֹא (word 8, verse 3)

לֹא adv. no, not. [Related to Aram. (also BAram) and Syr. לָא, Ugar. *l*, Arab. *lā*, Akka. *lā* (= not, no). cp. לָאו לֵא, and the second element in אֶלָּא. אוּלַי. אִלּוּלֵא. לוּלֵא.]

לֹא combining form meaning 'non-'. [From לֹא (= no, not).]

לָא adv. PBH no, not. [Aram., related to Heb. לֹא (q.v.).]

תַעֲשֶׂה (word 9, verse 3)

עשׂה to do, make.

— **Qal** - עָשָׂה v. **1** he did, made; **2** he worked, labored; **3** he acted, dealt; **4** he produced, yielded, performed, accomplished; **5** he brought about, caused, effected; **6** he appointed; **7** he acquired, gained; **8** he spent (his time).

— **Niph.** - נַעֲשָׂה **1** was done, was made; **2** was produced, was performed, was accomplished; **3** was offered (as a sacrifice); **4** was observed; **5** was used.

— **Pi.** - עִשָּׂה PBH **1** he caused somebody to do; **2** he pressed, squeezed.

— **Pu.** - עֻשָּׂה **1** was made, was formed; PBH **2** was done by force, was forced.

— **Hiph.** - הֶעֱשָׂה he caused to be done, forced to do. [Moabite עשׁת. ואעשׁ, Ugar. *'shy* (= he made), OSArab. עסו, Arab. *sa'ā (y)* (= he did, made, acted).] Derivatives: עָשָׂה, עָשׂוּי, עָשׂוּי, עֲשִׂיָּה, הֵעָשׂוֹת, מַעֲשֶׂה, מִעֲשֶׂה, תַּעֲשִׂיָּה.

עֲשֵׂה m.n. PBH (pl. עֲשִׂין) positive command. [Shortened from מִצְוַת־עֲשֵׂה (see מִצְוָה). Properly imper. of עָשָׂה (see עשׂה), used as a noun.]

לְךָ (word 10, verse 3)

לְךָ (in pause לָךְ) inflected m. pers. pron. meaning 'to thee', 'to you'. [Formed from לְ with suff. ךָ. cp. לְכָה II and the second element in מֶלֶךְ.]

לָךְ inflected f. pers. pron. meaning 'to thee', 'to you'. [Formed from לְ with suff. ךְ.]

פֶּסֶל (word 11, verse 3)

פסל I to hew, hew out, carve.

— **Qal** - פָּסַל v. he hewed, hewed out, carved.

— **Niph.** - נִפְסַל was hewn, was hewn out, was carved, was sculptured.

— **Pi.** - 1 פִּסֵּל he carved, sculptured; 2 he cut dry twigs.
— **Pu.** - פֻּסַּל was carved, was sculptured. [Aram.–Syr. פְּסַל (= he hewed, hewed out, carved), Ugar. *psl*, Nab. פסלא (= stonecutter), Egypt.–Aram. פסילה, פסלה (= ashlar). cp. פסל ᴵᴵ.] Derivatives: פְּסֹלֶת, מְפֻסָּל, מַפְסֶלֶת ᴵ, פַּסָּל, פֶּסֶל, פְּסִיל, פָּסוּל.

פֶּסֶל m.n. (pl. פְּסָלִים, in the Bible פְּסִילִים) carved image, idol. [From פסל ᴵ.] Derivative: פִּסָלוֹן.

וְכָל (word 12, verse 3)

כֹּל m.n. all, whole, the whole of. [From כלל ᴵ (= to comprehend, include). cp. Aram. (also BAram.) כֹּל, כָּל, Ugar. *kl*, Arab. *kull*, Ethiop. *kellā*, OSArab. כל, Akka. *kullatu* (= the whole of). See כְּלִי.]

תְּמוּנָה (word 13, verse 3)

תְּמוּנָה f.n. 1 likeness, image. 2 form. NH 3 description. NH 4 (fig.) image. MH 5 geometric figure. [According to most scholars formed from base מין, מון (= to furrow, split; to invent, fabricate, lie), with pref. תְּ and first suff. ה. It is more probable, however, that the ת in תְּמוּנָה belongs to the base.] Derivatives: תמן ᴵᴵ, תְּמוּנִי, תְּמוּנוֹן.

אֲשֶׁר (word 14, verse 3)

אֲשֶׁר 1 who, which, that, that which. 2 in order that. [Related to Ugar. aṯr (= that which). cp. Moabite אשר. According to most scholars these words were originally nouns meaning 'trace, place', and are related to Arab. 'athira (= to leave traces), 'ithr (= trace, place), and to Aram. אֲתַר, אַתְרָא, Syr. אַתְרָא (= place). See אָתַר.]

בַּשָּׁמַיִם (word 15, verse 3)

שָׁמַיִם m.n. pl. 1 visible heavens, sky. 2 Heaven, abode of God. 3 (fig.) God. [Related to Phoen. שמם, OAram. שמין, Aram. (also BAram.), Egypt. and Syr. שְׁמַיָּא, Samar. שומיא, Ugar. *shmn* (= heaven, sky), proper name בעלשמם (transliterated by Philo into *Beelsamen*), Arab. *samā*', OSArab. שמו, שמה, Ethiop. *samay*, Akka. *shamū*, pl. *shamē*, also *shamāmu*, *shamai*, TA *shamūma*, *shamēma* (= heaven, sky). The orig. meaning of these words is prob. 'high place', height'. cp. Aram. and Syr. שְׁמַיָּא, which besides 'heaven, sky', also mean 'height, highest part; ceiling, roof'; Arab. *samā* (= was high, was lofty; rose high), *sumūw* (= height, altitude); Akka. *shamai* in the meaning 'roof'; Talmudic Heb. שְׁמֵי קוֹרָה (= ceiling, roof).] Derivative: שְׁמֵימִי.

שְׁמֵימִי adj. MH heavenly, celestial. [Formed from שָׁמַיִם with suff. ִי.]

מִמַּעַל (word 16, verse 3)

מַעַל II m.n. high place, height (used only in the adv. form מִמַּעַל, 'from above, above'). [Formed from עלה (= to go up, ascend), with pref. מ.] Derivative: מַעֲלָה.

מְעַל m.n. raising, lifting. [From עלה (= to go up, ascend).]

מַעֲלָה I m.n. (pl. מַעֲלוֹת) ascent. [From עלה (= to go up, ascend).]

מַעֲלָה II adj. raising, lifting. [Part. of הֶעֱלָה (= he raised, lifted, brought up), Hiph. of עלה.]

מַעֲלָה f.n. 1 step, stair. 2 ascent. MH 3 grade, degree. NH 4 virtue, merit. [From עלה (= to go up, ascend). For the pref. see מ.]

מַעְלָה adv. upwards, up, high up. [From מַעַל II.]

מְעֻלָּה adj. PBH distinguished, prominent, excellent. [Part. of עֻלָּה, Pu. of עלה (= to go up, ascend). cp. מְעַלְיָא.]

מְעַלְיָא adj. PBH excellent. [Aram., corresponding to Heb. מְעֻלָּה. See מְעֻלָּה.]

וַאֲשֶׁר (word 17, verse 3)

אֲשֶׁר 1 who, which, that, that which. 2 in order that. [Related to Ugar. aṯr (= that which). cp. Moabite אשר. According to most scholars these words were originally nouns meaning 'trace, place', and are related to Arab. 'athira (= to leave traces), 'ithr (= trace, place), and to Aram. אֲתַר, אַתְרָא, Syr. אַתְרָא (= place). See אֲתַר.]

בָּאָרֶץ (word 18, verse 3)

אֶרֶץ f.n. (pl. 1 אֲרָצוֹת) earth. 2 land, country. 3 ground. [Related to BAram. אַרְקָא (for the change of צ to ק cp. Heb. קְטַר, 'he caused to smoke', with Aram. עֲטַר), Aram. אַרְעָה. אֲרַע, Ugar. arṣ, Arab. arḍ, Akka. erṣetu (= earth), Tigre 'arḍ. cp. Arakiel — name of the earth in the Book of Enoch 8:3. cp. אַרְעָה, ארק. אַרְקָה.] Derivatives: אַרְצִי, אַרְצָן.

מִתַּחַת (word 19, verse 3)

תַּחַת ¹ **1** the under part. **2** underneath, below. **3** under, below, beneath. **4** in one's place, where one stands. **5** in place of, instead of. **6** because of, on account of. [Related to BAram., Aram., Egypt.–Aram. תְּחוֹת (= under), Syr. תְּחֵית, adv. (= below), תְּחוֹת, prep. (= under), Ugar. tḥt, Arab. and Ethiop. taḥta (= under, below).] Derivatives: תַּחַת ᴵᴵ, תַּחְתִּי, תַּחְתּוֹן. cp. תַּת, תַּתָּא, תַּתָּאָה.

וַאֲשֶׁר (word 20, verse 3)

אֲשֶׁר 1 who, which, that, that which. **2** in order that. [Related to Ugar. aṯr (= that which). cp. Moabite אשר. According to most scholars these words were originally nouns meaning 'trace, place', and are related to Arab. 'athira (= to leave traces), 'ithr (= trace, place), and to Aram. אֲתַר, אַתְרָא, Syr. אַתְרָא (= place). See אֲתַר.]

בַּמָּיִם (word 21, verse 3)

מַיִם m.n. pl. (pl. also מֵימוֹת) water. [Related to Aram. מַיָּא, מַיִּין, Syr. מַיָּא, Ugar. my and mym, Arab. mā', OSArab. מו, מה, Ethiop. māy, Akka. mū (= water).] Derivatives: מֵימִי, מֵימוֹן, מֵימָה, מִים, מֵימֶת, מֵימָן, מֵימִיָה. cp. מְ. cp. also the second element in מַדְמַיִם, חוֹפָמִי, פַּחְמִיָה.

מים to mix with water, to hydrate.
— Pi. - מַיֵּם he mixed with water, watered; he hydrated.
— Pu. - מֻיַּם was watered, was hydrated.
— Hith. - הִתְמַיֵּם was watered, was hydrated. [Denominated from מַיִם.] Derivative: מִיּוּם.

מִתַּחַת (word 22, verse 3)

תַּחַת ¹ **1** the under part. **2** underneath, below. **3** under, below, beneath. **4** in one's place, where one stands. **5** in place of, instead of. **6** because of, on account of. [Related to BAram., Aram., Egypt.–Aram. תְּחוֹת (= under), Syr. תְּחֵית, adv. (= below), תְּחוֹת, prep. (= under), Ugar. tḥt, Arab. and Ethiop. taḥta (= under, below).] Derivatives: תַּחַת ᴵᴵ, תַּחְתִּי, תַּחְתּוֹן. cp. תַּת, תַּתָּא, תַּתָּאָה.

לָאָרֶץ (word 23, verse 3)

אֶרֶץ f.n. (pl. 1 אֲרָצוֹת) earth. 2 land, country. 3 ground. [Related to BAram. אַרְקָא (for the change of צ to ק cp. Heb. קָטַר, 'he caused to smoke', with Aram. עֲטַר), Aram. אַרְעָה, אֲרַע, Ugar. arṣ, Arab. arḍ, Akka. erṣetu (= earth), Tigre 'ard. cp. Arakiel — name of the earth in the Book of Enoch 8:3. cp. ארק, אַרְעָה, אַרְקָה.] Derivatives: אַרְצָן, אַרְצִי.

לֹא (word 24, verse 3)

לֹא adv. no, not. [Related to Aram. (also BAram) and Syr. לָא, Ugar. l, Arab. lā, Akka. lā (= not, no). cp. לָאו, לָא, and the second element in לוּלָא, אִלּוּלָא, אוּלַי, אֶלָּא.]
לֹא combining form meaning 'non-'. [From לֹא (= no, not).]
לָא adv. PBH no, not. [Aram., related to Heb. לֹא (q.v.).]

תִשְׁתַּחֲוֶה (word 25, verse 3)

שחה to bow down, bend low.

— **Qal** - שָׁחָה he bowed down, bent low.
— **Hiph.** - הִשְׁחָה MH **1** he caused to bow down; **2** he depressed.
— **Hith.** - הִשְׁתַּחֲוָה he bowed down, bent low, prostrated himself. [Prob. related to Akka. shiḫū (= to bow down). A secondary form of שוּת, שחח.] Derivatives: שְׁחִי, שְׁחוּת, שְׁחוּי, שְׁחִיָּה, הִשְׁתַּחֲוָיָה, הִשְׁתַּחֲוָאָה.

לָהֶם (word 26, verse 3)

לָהֶם inflected pers. pron. meaning 'to them' (m.). [Formed from לְ with suff. הֶם.]
לָהֶן inflected pers. pron. meaning 'to them' (f.). [Formed from לְ with suff. הֶן.]

וְלֹא (word 27, verse 3)

לֹא adv. no, not. [Related to Aram. (also BAram) and Syr. לָא, Ugar. l, Arab. lā, Akka. lā (= not, no). cp. לָאו, לָא, and the second element in לוּלָא, אִלּוּלָא, אוּלַי, אֶלָּא.]
לֹא combining form meaning 'non-'. [From לֹא (= no, not).]
לָא adv. PBH no, not. [Aram., related to Heb. לֹא (q.v.).]

תַּעֲבְדֵם (word 28, verse 3)

עבד to work; to serve.

— **Qal.** - עָבַד v. **1** he worked, labored, tilled, cultivated (the soil); **2** he served. **3** he worshiped.

— **Niph.** - נֶעֱבַד. **1** was tilled, was cultivated; PBH **2** was worshiped; PBH **3** was dressed, was tanned (said of hides).

— **Pi.** - עִבֵּד **1** he cultivated; **2** he dressed, tanned (said of hides); he elaborated, adapted.

— **Pu.** - עֻבַּד **1** was worked; PBH **2** was dressed, was tanned (said of hides); NH **3** was elaborated, adapted.

— **Nith.** - הִתְעַבֵּד, נִתְעַבֵּד **1** was worked; **2** was dressed, was tanned (said of hides); NH **3** was adapted.

— **Shiph. (see** . - שִׁעְבֵּד).

— **Hiph.** - הֶעֱבִיד **1** he caused to work, made to serve; **2** he enslaved.

— **Hoph.** - הָעֳבַד was made to serve. [Aram. (also BAram.) and Syr. עֲבַד (= he worked, did, performed, made), whence BAram. עֲבַד, Aram. and Syr. עַבְדָּא (= slave, servant), Ugar. bd (= to work, serve, worship), Arab. 'abada (= he served, worshiped, obeyed), whence 'abd (= slave, worshiper), OSArab. עבד (= servant), Ethiop. 'abbaṭa (= he imposed forced labor), Akka. abdu (= slave). Derivatives: עֶבֶד, עָבָד, עֲבָדָה, עִבְדָּן, עַבְדוּת, עָבוּד, עֲבוּד, עֲבוֹדָה, עוֹבֵד, הַעֲבָדָה, עָבַד, עַבְדָּא, עֶבְדָּא. cp. מְעֻבָּד, מַעֲבָדָה, מַעֲבִיד, תַּעֲבוּד.

עֶבֶד m.n. **1** servant; **2** slave, bondman; **3** worshipper. [From עבד.]

עַבְדָּא m.n. PBH servant; slave. [Aram. and Syr., denominated from עֲבַד (q.v.). cp. עֶבֶד.]

עֶבְדָּא PBH, עֲבָדָה NH **1** deed, act. **2** occurrence. **3** fact. [From Aram. עוֹבָדָא, Syr. עֲבָדָא (= work, fact, deed), from עֲבַד (= he did).] Derivative: עֶבְדָּתִי.

עֲבֻדָּה f.n. household servants (occurring in the Bible only Gen. 26:14 and Job 1:3). [From עבד.]

עַבְדוּת f.n. slavery, servitude, bondage (in the Bible occurring only Ez. 9:8 following and Neh. 9:17). [Formed from עבד with suff. וּת. cp. Syr. עַבְדּוּתָא (of s.m.).] Derivative: עַבְדוּתִי.

עַבְדוּתִי adj. NH slavish, servile. [Formed from עַבְדוּת with suff. ִי.]

עֲבוֹדָה f.n. **1** work, labor. **2** deed, action. **3** service. **4** divine service, worship. PBH **5** 'abodah', the first of the last three benedictions of the 'Amidah'. MH **6** liturgy for the 'Musaph' service on the Day of Atonement. [From עבד.]

כִּי (word 29, verse 3)

כִּי ᴵ conj. **1** that. **2** because. **3** when, while, as. **4** if, in case. **5** although, though. [כִּי was orig. a demonstrative pron. meaning 'thus', 'therefore', 'then'. It is related to Phoen. כ, Moabite כי, Punic כא, כה, כע, Aram. כִּי (= as, like), Ugar. k (= as, when, that), Akka. kī (= as, like), prob. also to Arab. kay (= that, in order that), Syr. כָּי (= then). See prefix כְּ and כֹּה.]

אָנֹכִי (word 30, verse 3)

אָנֹכִי pers. pron. I. [Related to Phoen. אנך and אנכי, Moabite אנך, Punic anec, OAram. אנך, אנכי, Ugar. ạnk, Akka. anāku, and cogn. with Egypt. ynk, Coptic anok, nok. It has no correspondences in Aram., Arab. and Ethiop. (in this latter, kū appears as the suff. of the first pers. in the conjugation of the verb, as in waladkū, Heb. יָלַדְתִּי, 'I bore'). The endings כִּי, resp. - ku, etc. in אָנֹכִי, anāku, etc., are prob. related to Heb. כֹּה, Aram.-Syr. כָּא (= here).] Derivatives: אָנֹכִיּוּת, אָנֹכִיִּי.

יְהוָה (word 31, verse 3)

יְהֹוָה, יָהֳוָה m.n. the proper name of God in the Bible, Tetragrammaton. [It prob. derives from הוה (= to be). The usual transliteration 'Jehovah' is based on the supposition that the Tetragrammaton is the imperfect Qal or Hiph'il of הוה and lit. means 'the one who is', 'the existing', resp. 'who calls into existence'. In reality, however, the pronunciation and literal meaning of the Tetragrammaton is unknown. cp. יָהּ ᴵ.]

אֱלֹהֶיךָ (word 32, verse 3)

אֱלֹהַּ, אֱלָהּ m.n. **1** god. **2** God. [According to some scholars אֱלוֹהַּ is a back formation from the pl אֱלֹהִים, this latter being the plural of אֵל ᴵ with the infix ה, which has an analogy in Heb. אִמָּהוֹת, pl. of אֵם (= mother), in Aram. אֲבָהָת, pl. of אַב (= father), שְׁמָהָת, pl. of שְׁמָא (= name), to which may be added Ugar. 'mht, pl. of 'mt (= Heb. אָמָה, 'bondwoman'), bhtm, pl. of bt (= Heb. בַּיִת, 'house'), and 'lht, pl. of 'lt (= goddess), f. of 'l (= Heb. אֵל ᴵ, 'god'). Others see in אֱלוֹהַּ the orig. form from which the pl. אֱלֹהִים was formed. The consideration of the fact that

אֵל has the pl. אֵלִים, shows that the second view is surely preferable to the first. Fleischer sees in אֱלוֹהַּ the derivative of base אלה, which he connects with Arab. aliha (= he sought refuge in anxiety), whence אֱלוֹהַּ would have meant orig. 'fear', hence 'object of fear or reverence', 'the revered one'. However, Nöldeke and others are prob. right when they maintain that the verb aliha in the above sense is prob. denominated from 'ilāh (= god).]

אֵל (word 33, verse 3)

אֵל ¹ m.n. 1 god. 2 God. [Of uncertain etymology. Formerly most scholars derived the word from the base אול (= to be strong). Nöldeke connected it with base אול (= to be in front), which is probably identical orig. with אול (= to be strong); see אול ¹. According to Lagarde it is a derivative of אלה (= to strive or reach after a person), hence lit. means 'He whom everyone strives to reach'. Ewald and König derive it from base אלה (= to be strong). None of these etymologies, nor any others suggested, is convincing. Related to Phoen. אל, אלן, Samaritan אל, Ugar. 'l (= the mightest god. 'El'), 'lt (= name of the wife of 'El'), Akka. ilu (= god). Arab. al-ilāt (= goddess). cp. אֵל ², אֵלָה ². cp. also the second element in יִשְׂרָאֵל.]

אֵל ² m.n. power. [Prob. derived from אול (= to be strong), and possibly to אֵל ¹.]

קָנָא (word 34, verse 3)

קנא to be jealous; to be zealous; to be envious.

 — **Pi.** - 1 קִנֵּא was jealous; 2 was zealous; 3 was envious; 4 he suspected (his wife) of adultery.

 — **Hith.** - 1 הִתְקַנֵּא was jealous; 2 was envious.

 — **Hiph.** - הִקְנִיא he excited one's jealousy. [Related to JAram. and Syr. קְנָא, Ethiop. qan'a (= was jealous, was zealous), Ugar. qn' (= to have zeal), iqnu (= I am zealous), and prob. also with Arab. qana'a (= became or was intensely red).] Derivatives: קָנָא, קִנְאָה, קַנָּא, קַנַּאי, קַנְאָן, קִנּוּי.

קַנָּא adj. jealous (said only of God; with reference to man the adj. קַנַּאי is used). [From קנא. cp. קַנּוֹא.] Derivatives: קַנָּאִי, קַנָּאוּת.

קִנְאָה f.n. 1 jealousy. 2 envy. 3 zeal, zealousness. 4 anger; object of anger. 5 passion. [Formed from קנא with first suff. ה. cp. Syr. קִנְאתָא (= zeal, zealousness).]

קַנְאוּת f.n. MH fanaticism. [Formed from קָנָא with suff. וּת.]

קַנַּאי m.n. PBH 1 zealot, fanatic. 2 a jealous person. [A secondary form of קַנָּא.]

קַנָּאִי adj. NH zealous, jealous. [Formed from קַנָּא with suff. י.]

קַנְאָן adj. filled with envy. [Formed from קנא with agential suff. ן. cp. קַנְאָתָן.] Derivative: קַנְאָנוּת.

קַנְאָנוּת f.n. NH being filled with envy, enviousness. [Formed from קַנְאָן with suff. וּת. cp. קַנְאֲתָנוּת.]

קַנְאָתָן adj. PBH filled with envy. [A secondary form of קַנְאָן.] Derivatives: קַנְאֲתָנוּת, קַנְאֲתָנִי.

קַנְאֲתָנוּת f.n. NH being filled with envy. [Formed from קַנְאָתָן with suff. וּת.]

קַנְאֲתָנִי adj. NH filled with envy, enviousness. [Formed from קַנְאָתָן with suff. י.]

קַנּוֹא adj. jealous (said only of God); occurring only Josh. 24:19 and Nah. 1:2). [A secondary form of קַנָּא.]

פָּקַד (word 35, verse 3)

פְּקֻדָּה f.n. 1 mustering, numbering. 2 visitation, punishment. 3 oversight, charge. 4 officers. NH 5 command, order. [From פקד.]

פקד to attend to; to visit, muster; to appoint.

— Qal - 1 פָּקַד he attended to, observed; 2 he commanded, ordered; 3 he mustered, passed in review, he numbered, counted, enumerated, passed in review; 4 he remembered, recalled; 5 he punished, took revenge; 6 he visited; 7 he missed, was lacking; PBH 8 he had marital relations with.

— Niph. - 1 נִפְקַד was visited; 2 was lacking, was missing; 3 was appointed; 4 was punished; MH 5 was deposited with; NH 6 was commanded, was commissioned.

— Pi. - 1 פִּקֵּד he mustered, numbered, enumerated; PBH 2 he commanded.

— Pu. - 1 פֻּקַּד was mustered, was numbered, was enumerated; MH 2 was commanded.

— Hith. - הִתְפַּקֵּד, הִתְפָּקַד , was mustered, was numbered.

— Hiph. - 1 הִפְקִיד he committed, entrusted; 2 he deposited; 3 he appointed.

— Hoph. - 1 הָפְקַד was committed, was entrusted; 2 was deposited; 3 was appointed. [Phoen. פקד (= to attend to, take care of, provide), Akka. paqādu (= to attend to; to visit, muster; to appoint), Aram. פְּקַד (= he commanded), Syr. פְּקַד (= he visited, inquired, saw to, he commanded), Nab. פקד (= he commanded), Ugar. pqd (= to command to, take care of), Arab. faqada (= he sought, he missed), Ethiop. faqada (= he visited, mustered; he needed, desired). The original meaning of this base prob. was 'to miss'.] Derivatives: פָּקָד I, פָּקָד II, פְּקִידָה I, פֶּקֶד, פְּקָדָה, פִּקָּדוֹן, פְּקִידוּת, פָּקוּד, פָּקִיד, פְּקִידָה II, הַפְקָדָה, הַפְקָדוּת, הִתְפַּקְּדוּת, מִפְקָד, מְפֻקָּד, מְפַקֵּד, מִפְקָדָה, מַפְקִיד, נִפְקָד, תַּפְקִיד.

- **פְּקֻדָּה** f.n. **1** mustering, numbering. **2** visitation, punishment. **3** oversight, charge. **4** officers. NH **5** command, order. [From פקד.]

עָוֹן (word 36, verse 3)

עָוֹן see עָוֹן.

עָוֹן, עָוֹן m.n. (pl. עֲוֹנוֹת, also עֲוֹנִים) **1** iniquity, guilt. **2** punishment. [From עוה.]

אָבֹת (word 37, verse 3)

- **אָב** I m.n. (pl. **1** אָבוֹת) father. 2 forefather, patriarch. 3 ancestor, progenitor. 4 head (of a family), leader, chief. 5 God. 6 master, teacher. 7 important, great. PBH 8 parent (male). PBH 9 basic factor, origin, source. NH 10 Father (of the Christian Church). [cp. Aram. אַבָּא, Ugar. 'b, Akka. abu, Arab. abu.] Derivatives: אֲבָהוּת, אֲבָהִי, אָבוּת.
- **אַבָּא** m.n. PBH 1 father, daddy. PBH 2 'Abba' — title of ancient Rabbis. NH 3 reverend (father). [Aram., properly 'the father' (= הָאָב in Heb.).]
- **אָבוֹת** m.n. pl. 1 pl. of אָב (= father). 2 parents, patriarchs.
- **אָבוּת** f.n. MH fatherhood, paternity. [Formed with suff. וּת from אָב (= father). cp. אֲבָהוּת.]

עַל (word 38, verse 3)

- **עַל** I **1** height, upper part. **2** , above. [From עלה. See עַל II.]
- **עַל** II prep. **1** on, upon, above. **2** at, beside. **3** toward(s). **4** against. **5** concerning, about. **6** because of, on account of. **7** together with. [Shortened from עֲלֵי, which is preserved in poetry (see עֲלֵי and עֲדֵי), from עלה. Related to Phoen. and Moabite עַל, עלת, Aram., BAram.) and Syr. עַל, Ugar. 'l, Arab. 'alā, OSArab.

עֲלִי, Ethiop. lā'la, Akka. eli (= on, upon). cp. עַל ¹. cp. also עֲלִיָה ᴵᴵ.] Derivative: עַל.

בָּנִים (word 39, verse 3)

בֵּן m.n. 1 son; offspring. 2 branch, shoot. 3 inhabitant of. 4 worthy of, deserving. [Related to Moabite, Phoen., OSArab. בן, Ugar. bn, Arab. ibn, Akka. bin(= son), BAram. and Aram.–Syr. בַּר (pl. בְּנִין), Mehri ber (= son). All these words prob. derive from בנה ᴵ (= to build). The change of n to r in Aram., Syr. and Mehri is difficult to explain; it may be due to regressive dissimilation. cp. בנה ᴵᴵ. cp. also בַּר and בַּת.] Derivatives: בְּנָהוּת, בְּנָיוּת.

עַל (word 40, verse 3)

עַל ᴵ 1 height, upper part. 2 , above. [From עלה. See עַל ᴵᴵ.]

עַל ᴵᴵ prep. 1 on, upon, above. 2 at, beside. 3 toward(s). 4 against. 5 concerning, about. 6 because of, on account of. 7 together with. [Shortened from עֲלֵי, which is preserved in poetry (see אֱלֵי and עֲדֵי), from עלה. Related to Phoen. and Moabite על, עלת, Aram., BAram.) and Syr. עַל, Ugar. 'l, Arab. 'alā, OSArab. עלי, Ethiop. lā'la, Akka. eli (= on, upon). cp. עַל ᴵ. cp. also עֲלִיָה ᴵᴵ.] Derivative: עַל.

שְׁלֹשִׁים (word 41, verse 3)

שָׁלֹשׁ, שָׁלוֹשׁ f. adj. three. [From שׁלשׁ ᴵ. Related to Phoen. שלש, OAram. שלשא, BAram.–Aram. and Syr. תְּלָת (f.), תְּלָתָה, תְּלָתָא (m.), Ugar. tlt, Arab. talāth (f.), talātha (m.), OSArab. תלת, older form שלת, Ethiop. shalā (f.), shalāstu (m.), Akka. shalāshi (f.), shalāshti (m.) (= three).] Derivatives: שָׁלֹשׁ, שְׁלֹשִׁים, שָׁלֵשׁ, שִׁלֵּשׁ, שִׁלַּשׁ, שְׁלֹשָׁה, שִׁלְשׁוֹם, שְׁלִישִׁי, שִׁלְשְׁתַּיִם ᴵᴵ, שָׁלִישׁ ᴵ, שָׁלִישׁ ᴵᴵᴵ, שְׁלִישִׁי ᴵⱽ, שְׁלִישׁוֹן, שָׁלִישׁ. cp. תְּלָת.

שׁלשׁ ᴵ base of שָׁלֹשׁ (= three). [See שָׁלֹשׁ and words there referred to.]

שׁלשׁ ᴵᴵ to multiply by three.

— Pi. - 1 שִׁלֵּשׁ he did something three times; 2 he divided into three parts; NH 3 he multiplied by three.

— Pu. - 1 שֻׁלַּשׁ was threefolded, was threefold; 2 was three years old (Gen. 15:9; according to several scholars the meaning is 'was of the third' — i.e. best — litter); PBH 3 was said (or written) three times.

— Hith. - הִשְׁתַּלֵּשׁ PBH 1 he did something a third time; PBH

2 it was divided into three parts; MH **3** he was appointed arbitrator (in this sense denominated from שָׁלִישׁ IV).

— **Hiph.** - **1** הִשְׁלִישׁ he deposited (with a third person; denominated from שָׁלִישׁ IV); **2** he divided into three parts.

— **Hoph.** - הֻשְׁלַשׁ was deposited (with a third person). [Denominated from שָׁלֹשׁ.] Derivatives: שִׁלּוּשׁ, הַשְׁלָשָׁה, הִשְׁתַּלְּשׁוּת, מְשֻׁלָּשׁ, מְשַׁלֵּשׁ.

שִׁלֵּשׁ m.n. one of the third generation; great grandson. [Formed from שָׁלֹשׁ (= three) and lit. meaning 'pertaining to the third'. cp. רִבֵּר.]

שֶׁלֶשׁ m.n. NH drill. [Derived from שָׁלֹשׁ and so called because woven through three threads.]

שִׁלּוּשׁ m.n. NH triplicate. [From שָׁלֹשׁ.] Derivative: שְׁלָשׁוּת.

שָׁלֹשׁ, שְׁלֹשָׁה f. adj. three. [See שָׁלֹשׁ.]

שְׁלָשׁוּת f.n. NH triplicity. [Formed from שָׁלֹשׁ with suff. וּת.]

שְׁלָשִׁי adj. PBH **1** three-year old. NH **2** tripartite. [Lit.: 'third'; a secondary form of שְׁלִישִׁי (q.v.). cp. רְבָעִי, חֲמָשִׁי.]

שְׁלֹשִׁים, שְׁלוֹשִׁים **1** thirty. **2** the thirty days of mourning. [Properly pl. of שָׁלֹשׁ (= three). cp. Aram.–Syr. תְּלָתִין, Arab. *thalāthūna* (= thirty).]

שְׁלִשִׁית f.n. NH trio (music). [Formed from שָׁלֹשׁ (= three), with suff. ית.]

וְעַל (word 42, verse 3)

עַל I **1** height, upper part. **2** , above. [From עלה. See עַל II.]

עַל II prep. **1** on, upon, above. **2** at, beside. **3** toward(s). **4** against. **5** concerning, about. **6** because of, on account of. **7** together with. [Shortened from עֲלֵי, which is preserved in poetry (see אֱלֵי and עֲדֵי), from עלה. Related to Phoen. and Moabite על, עלת, Aram., BAram.) and Syr. עַל, Ugar. *'l*, Arab. *'alā*, OSArab. עלי, Ethiop. *lā'la*, Akka. *eli* (= on, upon). cp. עַל I. cp. also עֲלִיָּה II.] Derivative: עַל.

רִבֵּעִים (word 43, verse 3)

רְבִיעַ I m.n. PBH **1** a quarter. MH **2** a quadrant (geometry). [From רבע I; a secondary form of רֶבַע.]

רְבִיעוֹן m.n. NH Quaternary (geology). [Formed from רְבִיעִי (= fourth), with suff. וֹן.] Derivative: רְבִיעוֹנִי.

רְבִיעוֹנִי adj. NH quaternary (geology). [Formed from רְבִיעוֹן with adj. suff. ִי.]

רְבִיעִי adj. 1 fourth. PBH 2 the fourth person called to the reading of the 'Torah' in the synagogue. [From אַרְבַּע. cp. BAram. רְבִיעִי, Aram. רְבִיעָי, רְבִיעַאי, רְבִיעָאָה, Syr. רְבִיעָיָא, Akka. rebū.] Derivatives: רְבִיעוֹן, רְבִיעִיָּה, רְבִיעִית.

רְבִיעִיָּה f.n. NH 1 a group of four, quartet. 2 quadruplets. [Formed from רְבִיעִי (= fourth), with first suff. יָּה.]

רְבִיעִית ᴵ f.n. 1 one-fourth, a quarter. PBH 2 a liquid measure, the fourth of a 'log'. [Subst. use of the f. of רְבִיעִי (= fourth).]

רבע ᴵ to square, quadruple, quadrate.

— Pi. - רִבַּע PBH 1 he made a quadrilateral; PBH 2 he did something four times; NH 3 he divided into four; NH 4 he squared (a member); NH 5 he multiplied by four.

— Pu. - רֻבַּע was squared (in the Bible occurring only in the form of the part. (see מְרֻבָּע).

— Hith. - הִתְרַבַּע MH 1 was made into a quadrilateral; MH 2 was divided into four; NH 3 was done four times. [Base of אַרְבַּע (= four).] — The Qal occurs only in the act. part. (see רָבוּעַ). Derivatives: רֶבַע ᴵ, רֹבַע ᴵ, רְבִיעִית, רְבוּעַ, רְבָעִי, רִבֵּעַ.

רֶבַע ᴵ m.n. 1 the fourth part, one quarter. 2 side of a square. [From רבע ᴵ. cp. Aram. רִבְעָא, Syr. רֶבְעָא (= the fourth part, one quarter). cp. also רְבָעָה, רִבְעָה, רִבְעוֹן.]

רֹבַע ᴵ m.n. 1 the fourth part (Kin. II 6:25). 2 the fourth part of a 'kab' (short for הַקַּב רֹבַע). NH 3 quarter (of a city). NH 4 quadrant (astronomy). [From רבע ᴵ. cp. רוּבְעָא, JAram. and Syr. רוּבְעָא, Arab. rub' (= the fourth part, a quarter). cp. also רֶבַע ᴵ.]

רִבֵּעַ m.n. one of the fourth generation; great great grandchild (in the Bible, a pl. tantum, occurring Ex. 20:5; 34:7; Num. 14:18; Deut. 5:9). [From רבע ᴵ.]

רִבְעָה f.n. PBH one quarter of a denar. [Formed from רֶבַע ᴵ, with first suff. ה.]

רְבָעָה f.n. NH group of four, quartet. [Formed from רֶבַע ᴵ with first suff. ה.]

רִבְעוֹן m.n. NH quarterly (periodical). [Coined on the analogy of עִתּוֹן (= journal), from רֶבַע (= quarter). For the ending see subst. suff. וֹן.]

רְבָעִי adj. PBH of the fourth year (of planting). [A secondary form of רְבִיעִי (= fourth). cp. שְׁלִשִׁי, חֲמִשִׁי.]

רְבָעִית f.n. NH quartet (music). [Formed from רבע ᴵ with suff. ית.]

לְשֹׂנְאָי (word 44, verse 3)

שׂנא to hate.

— Qal - שָׂנֵא he hated.

— Niph. - נִשְׂנָא was hated.

— Hiph. - הִשְׂנִיא he caused to be hated, made hateful.

— Hoph. - הָשְׂנָא was made hateful.

— Pi. - שִׂנֵּא he hated violently (in the Bible occurring only Ps. 139:21).

— Hith. - הִשְׂתַּנֵּא he became hateful. [BAram. שְׂנָא, JAram. שְׂנָא, סְנָא, Syr. and New Syr. סְנָא (= he hated), Aram. סִנְאָה, Syr. סָנְאָא (= hater), Samaritan part. סנ(א), Mand. part. סאנא (= hating), Arab. shani'a (= he hated), OSArab. שׂנא (= to hate).] Derivatives: שׂוֹנֵא, שָׂנוּא, שַׂנְאוּי, שָׂנוּי, שָׂנִיא, שִׂנְאָה, הַשְׂנָאָה, מְשַׂנֵּא.

שִׂנְאָה f.n. hatred, hate, enmity. [Properly inf. of שָׂנֵא (= he hated). For other infinitives ending in ה and used as nouns see אַהֲבָה and words there referred to.] Derivatives: שִׂנְאָתָנוּת, שִׂנְאָתָנִי.

שַׂנְאוּי adj. PBH hated. [A secondary form of שָׂנוּא. cp. שָׂנוּי.]

ד Verse 4

ד וְעֹשֶׂה חֶסֶד לַאֲלָפִים לְאֹהֲבַי וּלְשֹׁמְרֵי מִצְוֹתָי׃

4 and showing mercy unto the thousandth generation of them that love Me and keep My commandments.

וְעֹשֶׂה (word 1, verse 4)

עשׂה to do, make.

— Qal - עָשָׂה v. 1 he did, made; 2 he worked, labored; 3 he acted, dealt; 4 he produced, yielded, performed, accomplished; 5 he brought about, caused, effected; 6 he appointed; 7 he acquired, gained; 8 he spent (his time).

— Niph. - נַעֲשָׂה 1 was done, was made; 2 was produced,

was performed, was accomplished; **3** was offered (as a sacrifice); **4** was observed; **5** was used.

— **Pi.** - עָשָׂה PBH **1** he caused somebody to do; **2** he pressed, squeezed.

— **Pu.** - עָשָׂה **1** was made, was formed; PBH **2** was done by force, was forced.

— **Hiph.** - הֶעֱשָׂה he caused to be done, forced to do. [Moabite ואעש. עשתי, Ugar. 'shy (= he made), OSArab. עסו, Arab. saʻā(y) (= he did, made, acted).] Derivatives: עָשׂוּי, עָשׂוּי, עֲשִׂיָּה, הֵעָשׂוֹת, מַעֲשָׂה, מְעֻשָּׂה, תַּעֲשִׂיָּה.

עֲשֵׂה m.n. PBH (pl. עֲשִׂין) positive command. [Shortened from מִצְוַת־עֲשֵׂה (see מִצְוָה). Properly imper. of עָשָׂה (see עשה), used as a noun.]

חֶסֶד (word 2, verse 4)

חסד ᴵ to be kind, to be pious.

— **Pi.** - חִסֵּד he dealt kindly.

— **Hith.** - הִתְחַסֵּד **1** he showed himself kind; MH **2** he pretended to be pious. [Prob. denominated from חָסִיד.] Derivatives: הִתְחַסְּדוּת, מִתְחַסֵּד.

חֶסֶד ᴵ m.n. **1** kindness, goodness, mercy. **2** affection. **3** lovely appearance. [Related to חָסִיד. cp. Aram. חִסְדָּא, Syr. חֶסְדָּא (= kindness, mercy). These words are perhaps related to Arab. ḥashada, usually in pl. (= they assembled).] Derivative: חָסוּד.

לַאֲלָפִים (word 3, verse 4)

אלף ᴵᴵ to bring forth thousands.

— **Hiph.** - הֶאֱלִיף brought forth thousands (in the Bible a hapax legomenon occurring Ps. 144:18). [Denominated from אֶלֶף ᴵ (= thousand).]

אֶלֶף ᴵ m.n. thousand. [Related to Moabite אלף, BAram. אֲלַף, אַלְפָא, Aram. אֲלַף, אַלְפָּא, Ugar. 'lp, Arab. alf (= one thousand), Ethiop. Tigre, Amharic 'elf (= ten thousand). All these words prob. derive from אלף ᴵ and orig. denoted 'group, crowd'. cp. אַלְפִּית, אֶלֶף ᴵᴵ, אֶלֶף ᴵᴵᴵ, אלף ᴵᴵ.]

אַלְפִּית f.n. NH one thousandth, a thousandth part. [Formed from אֶלֶף ᴵ (= a thousand) with dimin. suff. ית.]

לְאֹהֲבַי (word 4, verse 4)

אהב to love.

— Qal - אָהַב he loved, liked.
— Niph. - נֶאֱהַב he was loved, was liked.
— Pi. - אִהַב he loved passionately.
— Pu. - **1** אֹהַב he became beloved; **2** he fell in love.
— Hith. - **1** הִתְאָהֵב he was loved by; **2** he fell in love with.
— Hiph. - הֶאֱהִיב he caused to love. [Related to Ugar. ahb (= to love), perhaps also to Arab. hábba (= he got in motion).] Derivatives: אֲהַבְהָבִים אַהֲב, אַהֲבָה, אֲהָבִים, מַאֲהָב, הִתְאַהֲבוּת, אהבהב, אַהֲבָן, אוֹהֵב, אָהוּב, נֶאֱהָב, מְאֹהָב, מְאַהֵב.

אֲהָב see אֲהָבִים.

אֹהַב m.n. MH (in Biblical Heb. only in the pl. אֹהָבִים) love, amour. [Back formation from אַהֲבָה.]

אַהֲבָה f.n. love. [Properly inf. of אָהַב (= he loved). For the ending see subst. suff. ה. For the infinitival origin of the word cp. e.g. Deut. 7:8 and 11:3 לְאַהֲבָה (= to love); cp. also יִרְאָה (= fear), אָכְלָה (= eating food).] Derivative: אַהֲבְתָן.

אֲהָבִים m.n. pl. love (a hapax legomenon in the Bible, occurring Pr. 7:18). Pl. of אֹהַב, from אהב (= to love).]

אַהֲבָן m.n. NH lover. [Formed from אהב with agential suff. ן.]

אַהֲבְתָן adj. NH amorous, flirtatious. [Formed from אַהֲבָה with agential suff. ן.]

וּלְשֹׁמְרֵי (word 5, verse 4)

שמר ¹ to keep, to heed, watch over, guard, to observe.

— Qal - **1** שָׁמַר he kept; **2** he heeded, watched over, guarded; **3** he preserved, protected; **4** he observed, celebrated.

— Niph. - **1** נִשְׁמַר he took heed, was careful; PBH **2** was kept, was guarded.

— Pi. - **1** שִׁמֵּר he paid regard; PBH **2** he watched, guarded; PBH **3** he took care.

— Pu. - שֻׁמַּר (mostly used in the part. מְשֻׁמָּר) was watched, was guarded.

— Hith. - **1** הִשְׁתַּמֵּר he took care, took heed; **2** was kept, was observed. [Phoen. in proper names, Pun. שמר (= watchman), Mand. סמירא (= preserved), Ugar. shmr (= to watch, guard), Arab. *thamala* (= he supported, aided, protected), *thumāla* (= residue, remnant, dregs of a liquid; see שְׁמָרִים), Akka. *shamāru* (= to wait upon, attend).] Derivatives:

שְׁמוּרָה 'I, שְׁמָרָה 'I, שְׁמָרִים, שְׁמָרָן. שָׁמוּר. שָׁמוּר 'II, שֶׁמֶר 'I, שֶׁמֶר
שְׁמִירָה. שׁוֹמֵר. שׁוֹמֵרָה. אַשְׁמוּרָה 'III, שְׁמוּרִים. שָׁמִיר 'II, שְׁמוּרָה,
אַשְׁמֹרֶת. הַשְׁמָרוּת. הִשְׁתַּמְּרוּת. מִשְׁמָר. מִשַּׁמָּר. מִשְׁמָר. מִשְׁמָרָה
מִשְׁמֶרֶת. מִשְׁמֹרֶת. תִּשְׁמֹרֶת. cp. the first element in שְׁמַרְחֹם and
in שְׁמַרְטַף.

שֶׁמֶר 'II m.n. MH watching, guarding. [From שׁמר 'I.]

שָׁמְרָה f.n. watch, guard (a hapax legomenon in the Bible, occurring
Ps. 141:3). [Properly inf. of שָׁמַר (= he watched, guarded; see
שׁמר 'I). For other infinitives ending in ה and used as nouns see
אַהֲבָה and words there referred to.]

מִצְוֺתַי (word 6, verse 4)

צַו m.n. command, order. [From צוה.]

צַוָּאָה f.n. PBH **1** command, order. **2** last will, testament. [From צִוָּה
in the phrase צִוָּה לְבֵיתוֹ, 'he declared his last will'. See צוה.
For the ending see first suff. ה.]

צוה to command, order.

— **Pi.** - **1** צִוָּה he commanded, ordered; **2** he appointed,
charged.

— **Pu.** - צֻוָּה was commanded, was ordered.

— **Nith.** - נִצְטַוָּה was commanded, was ordered. [Arab.
waṣā(y) (= he bound, united), waṣṣā(y) and auṣā(y) (= he
enjoined, bequeathed), waṣiyya (= injunction, testament). For
the differentiation of the Heb.–Aram. and Arab. stem by
metathesis cp. Heb. חִוָּה (= he showed, declared), with Arab.
waḥā(y) (= he inspired, revealed). cp. also לוה 'II.] Derivatives:
צִיּוּן and צִיּוֹן. cp. צַו. צַוָּאָה. צִוּוּי. מִצְוָה. מִצְוָה. מִצַּוֶּה.

צִוּוּי m.n. PBH **1** command, order. MH **2** imper. (grammar). [Verbal
n. of צִוָּה, Pi. of צוה.]

ה Verse 5

ה לֹא תִשָּׂא אֶת־שֵׁם־יְהוָה
אֱלֹהֶיךָ לַשָּׁוְא כִּי לֹא יְנַקֶּה
יְהוָה אֵת אֲשֶׁר־יִשָּׂא אֶת־שְׁמוֹ
לַשָּׁוְא׃

לא תשא
את־שם־יהוה אלהיך לשוא
כי לא ינקה יהוה את אשר
ישא את־שמו לשוא

The Real God Code

> **5 Thou shalt not lift up the Name of Yehovah thy God as to declare Him worthless; for Yehovah will not hold him guiltless who takes His Name falsely.**

לֹא (word 1, verse 5)

לֹא adv. no, not. [Related to Aram. (also BAram) and Syr. לָא, Ugar. *l*, Arab. *lā*, Akka. *lā* (= not, no). cp. לָאו, לֻא, and the second element in אֱלָא, אוּלַי, אִלּוּלָא, לוּלָא.]

לֹא combining form meaning 'non-'. [From לֹא (= no, not).]

לָא adv. PBH no, not. [Aram., related to Heb. לֹא (q.v.).]

תִשָּׂא (word 2, verse 5)

נשׂא PBH to lift, carry, take.

— **Qal** - נָשָׂא **1** he lifted, raised; **2** he bore, carried; **3** he took, took away, carried off; PBH **4** he married; **5** it contained; **6** he swept away, destroyed; **7** he forgave, pardoned; **8** he suffered, endured.

— **Niph.** - נִשָּׂא **1** was lifted up, was raised; **2** was exalted, was respected; **3** was carried from place to place; **4** (in the f.) was married.

— **Pi.** - נִשֵּׂא **1** he lifted up, raised; **2** he carried from place to place, carried away.

— **Pu.** - נֻשָּׂא **1** was carried; **2** was exalted.

— **Hith.** - הִתְנַשֵּׂא **1** he lifted himself up; **2** he exalted himself.

— **Hiph.** - הִשִּׂיא **1** he caused to bear; **2** he caused to bring; PBH **3** he transported, transferred.

— **Hoph.** - הֻשָּׂא **1** was lifted, was raised; **2** was given in marriage. [BAram. נְשָׂא, Aram. נְסָא (= he lifted, carried, took), Ugar. *nshạ* (= to lift, carry), Arab. *nasha'a* (= he rose, was high, grew up), Ethiop. *nas'a, nash'a* (= he took), Akka. *nashū* (= to lift; to carry), Syr. מְסָאתָא (= scales). cp. תְשׁוּאָה. cp. also 'munshi' in my CEDEL.] Derivatives: נְשׂוּא, נָשָׂא, (adj. and n.), הִנָּשְׂאוּת, הַשָּׂאָה, נְשִׂיאָה ^{III}, נְשִׂיאָה ^{II}, נְשִׂיאָה ^I, נָשִׂיא ^{II}, נָשׂוּי, נָשִׂיא ^I, הִתְנַשְּׂאוּת, מַשָּׂא, מִנְשָׂא, מִנְשָׂאָה, מַשָּׂאָה, נוֹשֵׂאת, מַשֵּׂאת, שׂוֹא, שִׂיא, תְּשׂוּאָה ^{II}, שְׂאֵת ^I, מַשּׂוֹאִי, מַשּׂוֹא, מַשּׂוּאָה, שְׂאֵת.

נִשָּׂא adj. high, exalted. [Part. of נִשָּׂא (= was lifted up, was raised), Niph. of נשׂא.]

אֶת (word 3, verse 5)

> אֵת ¹, אֶת prep. the mark of the accusative. Usually prefixed only to a definite noun, as in אֶת־הָאִישׁ (= the man). [Related to Moabite את, Phoen. אית (to be read אֵית), Aram. (also BAram.) and Syr. יָת (this latter mostly used as a noun), Egypt.-Aram. ות, Arab. 'iyyā (only used with a suff. to emphasize the pron.) and possibly also to Ethiop. kīyā (also used only with a suff. for the sake of emphasis). Orig. — as Syr. יָתָא — a noun in the sense of 'being, essence, existence'. The orig. form prob. was 'iwyath (cp. the Phoen. form), which ultimately derives from base אוה (= to sign, mark), whence also אוֹת (= sign).]

שֵׁם (word 4, verse 5)

> שֵׁם ¹ m.n. (pl. שֵׁמוֹת) **1** name, designation. **2** reputation, renown, fame. **3** name, as designation of God. [Related to BAram. שֻׁם, Aram. שֵׁם, שְׁמָא, שׁוּם, Syr. שְׁמָא, OAram., Palm. שׁם, Mand. שומא, Ugar. shm, Arab. ism, usm, sim, Ethiop. sem, Akka. shumu (= name). Some scholars connect the above names with Arab. wasama (= he branded cattle, stamped, marked, branded), wasm (= branding cattle, stamp, mark, brand).] Derivatives: שֵׁמִי, שִׁמּוֹן, לְשֵׁם, כְּשֵׁם, בְּשֵׁם, הַשֵּׁם ¹, שְׁמָנִי. cp. שְׁמָא.

> שְׁמָא m.n. PBH name. [Aram., emphatic state of שֵׁם (= name). See שֵׁם.]

יְהוָה (word 5, verse 5)

> יְהוָֹת, יֶהְוָה m.n. the proper name of God in the Bible, Tetragrammaton. [It prob. derives from הוה (= to be). The usual transliteration 'Jehovah' is based on the supposition that the Tetragrammaton is the imperfect Qal or Hiph'il of הוה and lit. means 'the one who is', 'the existing', resp. 'who calls into existence'. In reallly, however, the pronunciation and literal meaning of the Tetragrammaton is unknown. cp. יָהּ ¹.]

אֱלֹהֶיךָ (word 6, verse 5)

> אֱלֹהַּ, אֱלוֹהַּ m.n. **1** god. **2** God. [According to some scholars אֱלוֹהַּ is a back formation from the pl. אֱלוֹהִים, this latter being the plural of אֵל ¹ with the infix ה, which has an analogy in Heb. אִמָּהוֹת, pl. of אֵם (= mother), in Aram. אבהת, pl. of אַב (= father), שְׁמָהָת, pl. of שְׁמָא (= name), to which may be added

Ugar. 'mht, pl. of 'mt (= Heb. אָמָה, 'bondwoman'), bhtm, pl. of bt (= Heb. בַּיִת, 'house'), and 'lht, pl. of 'lt (= goddess), f. of 'l (= Heb. אֵל ᴵ, 'god'). Others see in אֱלוֹהַּ the orig. form from which the pl. אֱלוֹהִים was formed. The consideration of the fact that אֵל has the pl. אֵלִים, shows that the second view is surely preferable to the first. Fleischer sees in אֱלוֹהַּ the derivative of base אלה, which he connects with Arab. aliha (= he sought refuge in anxiety), whence אֱלוֹהַּ would have meant orig. 'fear', hence 'object of fear or reverence', 'the revered one'. However, Nöldeke and others are prob. right when they maintain that the verb aliha in the above sense is prob. denominated from 'ilāh (= god).]

לַשָּׁוְא (word 7, verse 5)

שָׁוְא m.n. **1** lie, falsehood. **2** nothingness, worthlessness, vanity. [Related to Arab. sa'a (= was or became bad, was or became evil, was foul, was unseemly), sau' (= evil), Ethiop. say' (= wickedness, baseness).]

כִּי (word 8, verse 5)

כִּי ᴵ conj. **1** that. **2** because. **3** when, while, as. **4** if, in case. **5** although, though. [כִּי was orig. a demonstrative pron. meaning 'thus', 'therefore', 'then'. It is related to Phoen. כ, Moabite כי, Punic כא, כה, כע, Aram. כִּי (= as, like), Ugar. k (= as, when, that), Akka. kī (= as, like), prob. also to Arab. kay (= that, in order that), Syr. כִּי (= then). See prefix כְּ and כֹּה.]

לֹא (word 9, verse 5)

לֹא adv. no, not. [Related to Aram. (also BAram) and Syr. לָא, Ugar. l, Arab. lā, Akka. lā (= not, no). cp. לְאוּ לְאָ, and the second element in אֶלָּא, אוּלַי, אֱלוּלָא, לוּלֵא.]
לֹא combining form meaning 'non-'. [From לֹא (= no, not).]
לָא adv. PBH no, not. [Aram., related to Heb. לֹא (q.v.).]

יְנַקֶּה (word 10, verse 5)

נקה to be clean, be pure, be innocent.
— **Pi.** - נִקָּה PBH **1** he cleansed; **2** he pronounced innocent (denominated from נָקִי); **3** he left unpunished.
— **Pu.** - נֻקָּה PBH **1** was acquitted, was absolved; MH **2** was cleansed, was cleared.

— **Niph.** - נִקָּה **1** was clean, was pure; **2** was free from guilt, was free from punishment; MH **3** was cleaned, was cleansed, was purified.

— **Hith.** - הִתְנַקָּה **1** was cleaned, was cleansed, was purified; **2** he tried to exonerate himself. [Phoen. נקי (= pure), Aram. נְקָא (= was clean), נְקִי (= be cleansed), Syr. נְקָא (= was inclined, was apt, was ready, was eager), נָק (= he poured out a libation), BAram. נְקֵא (= pure), Ugar. nqy (= clean), Arab. naqiya (= was clean), Akka. naqu (= to pour out a libation).] Derivatives: נִקּוּי, נָקִי, נִקָּיוֹן, הִתְנַקּוּת, הִנָּקוּת, מְנֻקָּה, מְנַקִּיָּה.

יְהֹוָה (word 11, verse 5)

יְהֹוָה, יֱהֹוִה m.n. the proper name of God in the Bible, Tetragrammaton. [It prob. derives from הוה (= to be). The usual transliteration 'Jehovah' is based on the supposition that the Tetragrammaton is the imperfect Qal or Hiph'il of הוה and lit. means 'the one who is', 'the existing', resp. 'who calls into existence'. In reality, however, the pronunciation and literal meaning of the Tetragrammaton is unknown. cp. יָהּ ᴵ.]

אֵת (word 12, verse 5)

אֵת ᴵᴵ prep. with. [Related to Akka. itti (= with). These words possibly stand for int, resp. inti, and derive from Sem. base אנה (= to bring about), whence also Ethiop. enta (= in the direction of, toward). cp. תִּתִּי (= my giving), from תֵּת (= to give). According to some scholars, Akka. itti and Heb. אֵת ᴵᴵ lit. mean 'to the side of', and derive from Old Sem. יָד (= hand). cp. מֵאֵת (= from).]

אֲשֶׁר (word 13, verse 5)

1 אֲשֶׁר who, which, that, that which. **2** in order that. [Related to Ugar. aṯr (= that which). cp. Moabite אשר. According to most scholars these words were originally nouns meaning 'trace, place', and are related to Arab. 'athira (= to leave traces), 'ithr (= trace, place), and to Aram. אֲתַר, אַתְרָא, Syr. אַתְרָא (= place). See אָתַר.]

יִשָּׂא (word 14, verse 5)

נשא PBH to lift, carry, take.

— **Qal** - נָשָׂא **1** he lifted, raised; **2** he bore, carried; **3** he took, took away, carried off; PBH **4** he married; **5** it contained;

The Real God Code

6 he swept away, destroyed; **7** he forgave, pardoned; **8** he suffered, endured.

— **Niph.** - נִשָּׂא **1** was lifted up, was raised; **2** was exalted, was respected; **3** was carried from place to place; **4** (in the f.) was married.

— **Pi.** - נִשֵּׂא **1** he lifted up, raised; **2** he carried from place to place, carried away.

— **Pu.** - נֻשָּׂא **1** was carried; **2** was exalted.

— **Hith.** - הִתְנַשֵּׂא **1** he lifted himself up; **2** he exalted himself.

— **Hiph.** - הִשִּׂיא **1** he caused to bear; **2** he caused to bring; PBH **3** he transported, transferred.

— **Hoph.** - הֻשָּׂא **1** was lifted, was raised; **2** was given in marriage. [BAram. נְשָׂא, Aram. נְסָא (= he lifted, carried, took), Ugar. nshạ (= to lift, carry), Arab. nasha'a (= he rose, was high, grew up), Ethiop. nas'a, nash'a (= he took), Akka. nashū (= to lift; to carry), Syr. מַסְאָתָא (= scales). cp. תְּשׂוּאָה. cp. also 'munshi' in my CEDEL.] Derivatives: נְשָׂא, נָשׂוּא, (adj. and n.), הַנְּשָׂאוּת, הַשָּׂאָה, נְשִׂיאָה I, נְשִׂיאָה II, נְשִׂיאָה III, נָשׂוּי, נָשִׂיא I, נָשִׂיא II, הִתְנַשְּׂאוּת, מַשָּׂא, מְשָׂא, מִנְשָׂא, מַשָּׂאָה, מְנַשְּׂאָה, נוֹשֵׂאת, מַשֵּׂאת, שׂוֹא, שִׂיא, תְּשׂוּאָה I, שְׂאֵת II, מַשְׂאוֹי, מַשּׂוֹא, מַשּׂוּאָה, שְׂאֵת.

נָשָׂא adj. high, exalted. [Part. of נָשָׂא (= was lifted up, was raised), Niph. of נשׂא.]

אֵת (word 15, verse 5)

אֵת I, אֶת prep. the mark of the accusative. Usually prefixed only to a definite noun, as in אֶת־הָאִישׁ (= the man). [Related to Moabite את, Phoen. אית (to be read אֵיָת), Aram. (also BAram.) and Syr. יָת (this latter mostly used as a noun), Egypt.-Aram. ית, Arab. 'iyyā (only used with a suff. to emphasize the pron.) and possibly also to Ethiop. kīyā (also used only with a suff. for the sake of emphasis). Orig. — as Syr. יָת, יָתָא — a noun in the sense of 'being, essence, existence'. The orig. form prob. was 'iwyath (cp. the Phoen. form), which ultimately derives from base אוה (= to sign, mark), whence also אוֹת (= sign).]

שְׁמוֹ (word 16, verse 5)

שֵׁם I m.n. (pl. שֵׁמוֹת) **1** name, designation. **2** reputation, renown, fame. **3** name, as designation of God. [Related to BAram. שֻׁם, Aram. שׁוּם, שְׁמָא, Syr. שְׁמָא, שֵׁם, OAram., Palm. שׁם,

Mand. שומא, Ugar. *shm*, Arab. *ism, usm, sim*, Ethiop. *sem*, Akka. *shumu* (= name). Some scholars connect the above names with Arab. *wasama* (= he branded cattle, stamped, marked, branded), *wasm* (= branding cattle, stamp, mark, brand).] Derivatives: הַשֵּׁם. בְּשֵׁם. כְּשֵׁם. לְשֵׁם. שֵׁמוֹן. שְׁמִי, ¹, שְׁמָנִי. cp. שְׁמָא.

שְׁמָא m.n. PBH name. [Aram., emphatic state of שֵׁם (= name). See שֵׁם.]

לַשָּׁוְא (word 17, verse 5)

שָׁוְא m.n. **1** lie, falsehood. **2** nothingness, worthlessness, vanity. [Related to Arab. *sa'a* (= was or became bad, was or became evil, was foul, was unseemly), *sau'* (= evil), Ethiop. *say'* (= wickedness, baseness).]

ו Verse 6

ו זָכוֹר אֶת־יוֹם הַשַּׁבָּת
לְקַדְּשׁוֹ שֵׁשֶׁת יָמִים תַּעֲבֹד
וְעָשִׂיתָ כָּל־מְלַאכְתֶּךָ וְיוֹם
הַשְּׁבִיעִי שַׁבָּת ׀ לַיהוָה
אֱלֹהֶיךָ לֹא־תַעֲשֶׂה כָל־
מְלָאכָה אַתָּה ׀ וּבִנְךָ־וּבִתֶּךָ
עַבְדְּךָ וַאֲמָתְךָ וּבְהֶמְתֶּךָ
וְגֵרְךָ אֲשֶׁר בִּשְׁעָרֶיךָ כִּי
שֵׁשֶׁת־יָמִים עָשָׂה יְהוָה אֶת־
הַשָּׁמַיִם וְאֶת־הָאָרֶץ אֶת־
הַיָּם וְאֶת־כָּל־אֲשֶׁר־בָּם
וַיָּנַח בַּיּוֹם הַשְּׁבִיעִי עַל־כֵּן
בֵּרַךְ יְהוָה אֶת־יוֹם הַשַּׁבָּת
וַיְקַדְּשֵׁהוּ׃

> 6 Remember the sabbath day, to keep it holy. Six days shalt thou labour, and do all thy work; but the seventh day is a sabbath unto Yehovah thy God, in it thou shalt not do any manner of work, thou, nor thy son, nor thy daughter, nor thy man-servant, nor thy maid-servant, nor thy cattle, nor thy stranger that is within thy gates; for in six days Yehovah made heaven and earth, the sea, and all that in them is, and rested on the seventh day; wherefore Yehovah blessed the sabbath day, and hallowed it.

זָכוֹר (word 1, verse 6)

זְכִירָה f.n. PBH 1 remembrance, recollection. NH 2 memory. [Verbal n. of זָכַר. See זכר and first suff. ה.]

זכר ᴵ to remember.

— Qal - זָכַר 1 he remembered, called to mind. 2 he mentioned.
— Niph. - נִזְכַּר 1 was remembered. 2 was mentioned.
— Hith. - הִזְדַּכֵּר was remembered, was brought to mind.
— Hiph. - הִזְכִּיר 1 he caused to be remembered. 2 he mentioned. 3 he commemorated. 4 he offered a memorial sacrifice.
— Hoph. - הָזְכַּר was mentioned. [Phoen. זכר, סכר, BAram. דְּכַר, Aram. דְּכַר and זְכַר, Syr. דְּכַר (= he remembered). Arab. *dhakara*, Ethiop. *zakara* (= he remembered), Akka. *zakāru, sakāru, saqāru* (= to say, name, swear), *zikru* (= name). According to some scholars the orig. meaning of this base would have been 'to prick, pierce', whence 'to fix in one's mind' — 'to remember'.] Derivatives: זֵכֶר, זִכָּרוֹן, זְכִירָה, זָכוּר, זִכָּרוֹן, זַכְרָן, זִכְרָה, זִכְרָיָה, זִכְרִינִי, אַזְכָּרָה, הַזְכָּרָה, הִזְדַּכְּרוּת, הִזָּכְרוּת, מַזְכִּיר, מְזֻכָּר, מָזְכָּר, מַזְכֶּרֶת, תַּזְכִּיר, תִּזְכֹּרֶת. cp. זָכָר.

זֵכֶר m.n. (also זֶכֶר) 1 remembrance, memory. 2 name. [From זכר ᴵ. cp. Arab. *dhikr*, Akka. *zikru* and *sikru* (= uttering, commemoration, name). For the variant זֶכֶר cp. חֵשֶׁק and חֶשֶׁק (= desire), יֵשַׁע and יֶשַׁע (= help), נֵצֶר and נֶצֶר (= vow), נֵצַח and נֶצַח (= eternity), שֵׂכֶל and שֶׂכֶל (= understanding).]

זִכָּרוֹן m.n. (pl. זִכְרוֹנוֹת, also זִכְרוֹנִים) (also זִכָּרוֹן) memorial, remembrance, reminder. [Formed from זכר with suff. וֹן. cp. BAram. דִּכְרוֹנָה (= record).]

זַכְרָן m.n. PBH a person endowed with a retentive memory. [Formed from זָכַר (see זכר ᴵ) with agential suff. ן.] Derivative: זַכְרָנוּת.

זַכְרָנוּת f.n. MH power of memory. [Formed from זַכְרָן with suff. וּת.]

אֶת (word 2, verse 6)

אֵת ᴵ, אֶת prep. the mark of the accusative. Usually prefixed only to a definite noun, as in אֶת־הָאִישׁ (= the man). [Related to Moabite את, Phoen. אית (to be read אַיַת), Aram. (also BAram.) and Syr. יָת (this latter mostly used as a noun), Egypt.-Aram. ות, Arab. 'iyyā (only used with a suff. to emphasize the pron.) and possibly also to Ethiop. kīyā (also used only with a suff. for the sake of emphasis). Orig. — as Syr. יָתָא, יָת — a noun in the sense of 'being, essence, existence'. The orig. form prob. was 'iwyath (cp. the Phoen. form), which ultimately derives from base אוה (= to sign, mark), whence also אוֹת (= sign).]

יוֹם (word 3, verse 6)

יוֹם m.n. (pl. יָמִים 1) day. 2 time. 3 year. [Related to BAram., Aram., and Syr. יוֹם. יוֹמָא, Ugar. ym, Arab. yaum, Akka. ūmu (= day), Ethiop. yōm (= today), Aram. יָמָא, Syr. אִימָמָא (= day; in contradistinction to 'night'). cp. יָמָמָה. יוֹמָא.] Derivatives: יוֹמוֹן, יוֹמִי. יוֹמָם. יוֹמָן. יוֹמְיוֹמִי. cp. the second element in בָּרְיוֹם.

יוֹמָא m.n. PBH 1 day, the day. 2 name of a Mishnah, Tosephta and Talmud tractate in the order מוֹעֵד dealing with the laws referring to the Day of Atonement, hence lit. meaning 'the tractate dealing with the Day' by pre-eminence. [Aram., 'the day', i.e. 'the day by pre-eminence'. See יוֹם.]

יוֹמִי adj. MH daily. [Formed from יוֹם (= day), with suff. י.]

יוֹמַיִם adv. everyday, daily. [For [[illegible]] יוֹם־יוֹם (= day by day, every day, daily), repetition of יוֹם (= day).] Derivative: יוֹמְיוֹמִי.

יוֹמִית adv. daily. [Formed from יוֹם (= day), with adv. suff. ית.]

יוֹמָם adv. daily. [Formed from יוֹם (= day), with the adv. suff. ם. The same suff. appears in אָמְנָם. See אָמְנָם and words there referred to.]

הַשַׁבָּת (word 4, verse 6)

שׁבת to cease, desist; to rest.

— **Qal** - **1** שָׁבַת he ceased, desisted; **2** he desisted from labor, rested; PBH **3** he observed the Sabbath, he spent the Sabbath; NH **4** he struck, was on strike (properly 'he stopped working').

— **Niph.** - נִשְׁבַּת ceased.

— **Hiph.** - **1** הִשְׁבִּית he caused to cease, put an end to; **2** he removed, exterminated, destroyed; NH **3** he locked out (workers).

— **Hoph.** - הָשְׁבַּת PBH **1** was made to cease, was stopped; PBH **2** he ceased, perished; NH **3** was locked out (from his work). [JAram. שְׁבַת (= he rested; he observed the Sabbath), Arab. sabata (= he cut off, interrupted, ceased, rested). Akka. shabātu, which prob. means 'to complete, cease, desist'. cp. שֶׁבֶת I.] Derivatives: שְׁבִיתָה, שׁוֹבֵת, שַׁבָּת, מִשְׁבָּת II, מִשְׁבָּת, שְׁבוּת, שֶׁבֶת.

שַׁבָּת m.n. (pl. שַׁבָּתוֹת) **1** day of rest, Sabbath. **2** week, i.e. the seven days from Sunday to Sabbath (the JAram. and Syr. loan words also have both meanings: 'Sabbath', and 'week'; cp. also Gk. sabbaton and sabbata, which also have both these meanings). **3** feast, festival. **4** of years, i.e. a period of seven years. **5** the Sabbathical year, 'shemittah'. PBH **6** 'Sabbath', name of the first Mishnah and Talmud tractate of the order מוֹעֵד. [Derived from שׁבת and lit. meaning 'day of rest'. Aram.–Syr. שַׁבְּתָא, Arab. sabt, Ethiop. sanbat, are Heb. loan words. So are Gk. sabbaton (whence L. sabbatum, It. sabato, Old Provençal–Catalan dissapte, Spanish–Portuguese sábado, Serbo-Croatian subota, Czech and Slovak sobota, Russ. subbóta, etc.), and its Gk. vulgar var. sambaton, whence VL sambatum, Rumanian sîmbătă, Old Slavic sǫbota, Hungarian szombat (= Saturday), and sambatīdiēs (= the day of Sabbath), whence Old Fren. sambe-di, whence Fren. samedi (= Saturday), and prob. through the medium of the Gothic — the first element in Old High Ger. sambaz-tac, middle High Ger. samez-tac, Ger. Samstag (= Saturday). However, also Akka. shabbatu, shappatu, and Egypt. smdt, in the sense '15th day of the month' (but not in the meaning '7th day of the week', nor in that of '7th or 14th day of the month', as supposed by many scholars), are borrowed from ancient Hebrew. As shown by the above facts, the name שַׁבָּת and the idea it conveys are of Hebrew origin.] Derivatives: שַׁבְּתַאי, שַׁבָּתוֹן, שַׁבַּתִּי, שַׁבָּתִין. cp. סַמְבַּטְיוֹן.

לְקַדְּשׁוֹ (word 5, verse 6)

קדש to be holy, be sacred.

— Qal - 1 קָדַשׁ was set apart, was consecrated; 2 was forbidden.

— Niph. - 1 נִקְדַּשׁ was hallowed, was sanctified, 2 was consecrated, was dedicated.

— Pi. - 1 קִדֵּשׁ he hallowed, sanctified; 2 he dedicated; consecrated; 3 he declared holy; 4 he cleansed, purified; 5 he devoted, assigned; PBH 6 he sanctified the Sabbath or the festivals; PBH 7 he pronounced the benediction of Kiddush; PBH 8 he made something prohibited; PBH 9 he betrothed, wedded.

— Pu. - 1 קֻדַּשׁ was hallowed, was sanctified; 2 was dedicated was consecrated; PBH 3 was betrothed, was wedded.

— Hith. - 1 הִתְקַדֵּשׁ he kept himself separated, purified himself; 2 he became sanctified; 3 he prepared himself; PBH 4 it was forbidden (as food).

— Hiph. - 1 הִקְדִּישׁ he set apart as holy, devoted as holy; 2 he regarded as holy; 3 he designated, appointed; NH 4 he dedicated.

— Hoph. - 1 הֻקְדַּשׁ was set apart as holy, was devoted as holy; MH 2 was regarded as holy; NH 3 was designated, was appointed; NH 4 was dedicated. [Related to Ugar. *qdsh* (= sanctuary), Phoen. קדש (= holy), מקדש (= sanctuary, holy place), Aram.-Syr. קְדַשׁ (= he hallowed, sanctified, consecrated), Palm. קדש (= to sanctify, consecrate), Arab. *qadusa* (= was holy, was pure), *quaddasa* (= he hallowed, sanctified, consecrated; he went to Jerusalem), *quds* (= purity, holiness), *al-quds* (= Jerusalem; lit.: 'the holy place'), Akka. *quddushu* (= to cleanse, to hallow, sanctify,), Aram.–Syr. קְדָשָׁא (= ear or nose ring; orig. 'holy thing'). The orig. meaning of this base prob. was 'to separate'.] Derivatives: קֹדֶשׁ, קָדֵשׁ, קְדֵשָׁה, קָדְשָׁה, קָדְשָׁא, קָדוֹשׁ, קָדִישׁ, הֶקְדֵּשׁ, הַקְדָּשָׁה, אַקְדָּשָׁה, הִתְקַדְּשׁוּת, מִקְדָּשׁ, מְקֻדָּשׁ. cp. the second element in קַדְשְׁנוּן.

קֹדֶשׁ m.n. 1 holiness, sanctity. 2 a holy object. 3 a holy place. 4 the Holy Temple. [From קדש. cp. Aram. קוּדְשָׁא (= holiness), Syr. קוּדְשָׁא (= dedication, consecration), Ugar. *qdsh* (= holy place, sanctuary), *qdsh* (= a goddess), *qdsht* (name of a goddess).]

קַדְשָׁא m.n. PBH holiness, used in the phrase קֻדְשָׁא בְּרִיךְ הוּא, 'the Holy One Blessed be He' (= Heb. הַקָּדוֹשׁ בָּרוּךְ הוּא). In Aram. the abstr. n. קַדְשָׁא is used for the concrete קַדִּישָׁא. [Aram., from קדש. cp. Syr. קוּדְשָׁא (= sanctuary). cp. also קֹדֶשׁ.]

קְדֻשָּׁה f.n. PBH **1** holiness, sanctity. PBH **2** 'Kedushshah', name of the third of the 'eighteen benedictions' in the 'Amidah' (so called because it ends with the words הָאֵל הַקָּדוֹשׁ). MH **3** portion inserted in the 'Amidah' between the second and third benedictions (so called because it contains the verse beginning with the words קָדוֹשׁ קָדוֹשׁ קָדוֹשׁ (= 'Holy, holy, holy', etc.). [Formed from קדשׁ with first suff. ה. For the form cp. גְּאֻלָּה (= redemption), from גאל I (= to redeem).]

שֵׁשֶׁת (word 6, verse 6)

שֵׁשׁ I f. adj. six. [For שׁדשׁ, whence also Aram. שִׁית, Syr. שֵׁת (for shidt), אֶשְׁתָּא, Egypt.–Aram. שׁתה, Nab. שׁת, Palm. שׁתא, Ugar. tdt, tt (= six), Arab. sitt (f.), sitta (m.) (= six), sādis (= sixth), Ethiop. sessū (f.), sedestū (m.), OSArab. sdth, late sthth, stht, Akka. shishshit (f.), shishshi (m.) (= six), seshishu (= sixth), sudushu (= sixfold). cp. שִׁשָּׁה.] Derivatives: שִׁשָּׁה, שִׁשִּׁי, שִׁשִּׁים, שְׁתוּת, שְׁתִית, שְׁשָׁתַיִם. cp. שְׁתַיִם.

שִׁשָּׁה m. adj. six. [See שֵׁשׁ.]

שׁשׁה to divide by six; to multiply by six.
— **Pi.** - **1** שִׁשָּׁה he divided by six; NH **2** he multiplied by six; MH **3** he made a hexagon.
— **Pu.** - **1** שֻׁשָּׁה was divided by six; **2** was multiplied by six. [Denominated from שֵׁשׁ I or from שִׁשָּׁה.] Derivative: מְשֻׁשֶּׁה.

שִׁשִּׁי adj. **1** sixth. PBH **2** the sixth person called to the reading of the Torah in the synagogue. [Formed from שֵׁשׁ I with suff. י.] Derivative: שִׁשִּׁיָּה.

שִׁשִּׁיָּה f.n. NH **1** a set of six objects. **2** sextet (music). [Formed from שֵׁשׁ I or שִׁשָּׁה (= six), with suff. יָה.]

שִׁשִּׁית adj. & n. **1** sixth. **2** one sixth, sixth part. NH **3** sixth grade (in school). [f. of שִׁשִּׁי.]

שִׁשָׁתַיִם adv. NH sixfold. [Formed from שֵׁשׁ (= six), on the analogy of אַרְבַּעְתַיִם (= fourfold); q.v.]

יָמִים (word 7, verse 6)

יוֹם m.n. (pl. **1** יָמִים day. **2** time. **3** year. [Related to BAram., Aram., and Syr. יוֹמָא, Ugar. ym, Arab. yaum, Akka. ūmu (= day), Ethiop. yōm (= today), Aram. יְמָמָא, Syr. אִימָמָא (= day; in contradistinction to 'night'). cp. יְמָמָה. יוֹם.] Derivatives: יוֹמוֹן, יוֹמִי, יוֹמָם, יוֹמָן, יוֹמְיוֹמִי. cp. the second element in בַּרְיוֹם.

יוֹמָא m.n. PBH **1** day, the day. **2** name of a Mishnah, Tosephta and Talmud tractate in the order מוֹעֵד dealing with the laws referring to the Day of Atonement, hence lit. meaning 'the tractate dealing with the Day' by pre-eminence. [Aram., 'the day', i.e. 'the day by pre-eminence'. See יוֹם.]

יוֹמִי adj. MH daily. [Formed from יוֹם (= day), with suff. י.]

יוֹמְיוֹם adv. everyday, daily. [For [[illegible]] יוֹם־יוֹם (= day by day, every day, daily), repetition of יוֹם (= day).] Derivative: יוֹמְיוֹמִי.

יוֹמִית adv. daily. [Formed from יוֹם (= day), with adv. suff. ית.]

יוֹמָם adv. daily. [Formed from יוֹם (= day), with the adv. suff. ם. The same suff. appears in אָמְנָם. See אָמְנָם and words there referred to.]

תַעֲבֹד (word 8, verse 6)

עבד to work; to serve.

— Qal. - עָבַד v. **1** he worked, labored, tilled, cultivated (the soil); **2** he served. **3** he worshiped.

— Niph. - נֶעֱבַד. **1** was tilled, was cultivated; PBH **2** was worshiped; PBH **3** was dressed, was tanned (said of hides).

— Pi. - עִבֵּד **1** he cultivated; **2** he dressed, tanned (said of hides); he elaborated, adapted.

— Pu. - עֻבַּד **1** was worked; PBH **2** was dressed, was tanned (said of hides); NH **3** was elaborated, adapted.

— Nith. - נִתְעַבֵּד, הִתְעַבֵּד **1** was worked; **2** was dressed, was tanned (said of hides); NH **3** was adapted.

— Shiph. (see . - שִׁעְבֵּד).

— Hiph. - הֶעֱבִיד **1** he caused to work, made to serve; **2** he enslaved.

— Hoph. - הָעֳבַד was made to serve. [Aram. (also BAram.) and Syr. עֲבַד (= he worked, did, performed, made), whence BAram. עֲבַד, Aram. and Syr. עַבְדָּא (= slave, servant), Ugar. bd (= to work, serve, worship), Arab. 'abada (= he served, worshiped, obeyed), whence 'abd (= slave, worshiper),

OSArab. עבד (= servant), Ethiop. 'abbaṭa (= he imposed forced labor), Akka. abdu (= slave). Derivatives: עֶבֶד, עָבָד, עֲבָדָה, עִבְדָּן, עַבְדוּת, עָבְדָה, עָבוּד, עֲבוֹדָה, עוֹבֵד, הַעֲבָדָה, עָבַד, עַבְדָּא, עָבְדָּא. cp. מְעֻבָּד, מַעֲבָדָה, מַעֲבִיד, תַּעֲבוּד.

עֶבֶד m.n. 1 servant; 2 slave, bondman; 3 worshipper. [From עבד.]

עַבְדָּא m.n. PBH servant; slave. [Aram. and Syr., denominated from עָבַד (q.v.). cp. עֶבֶד.]

עָבְדָּא PBH, עָבְדָה NH 1 deed, act. 2 occurrence. 3 fact. [From Aram. עוֹבָדָא, Syr. עָבְדָּא (= work, fact, deed), from עָבַד (= he did).] Derivative: עָבְדָתִי.

עֲבָדָה f.n. household servants (occurring in the Bible only Gen. 26:14 and Job 1:3). [From עבד.]

עַבְדוּת f.n. slavery, servitude, bondage (in the Bible occurring only Ez. 9:8 following and Neh. 9:17). [Formed from עבד with suff. וּת. cp. Syr. עַבְדוּתָא (of s.m.).] Derivative: עַבְדוּתִי.

עַבְדוּתִי adj. NH slavish, servile. [Formed from עַבְדוּת with suff. י.]

עֲבוֹדָה f.n. 1 work, labor. 2 deed, action. 3 service. 4 divine service, worship. PBH 5 'abodah', the first of the last three benedictions of the 'Amidah'. MH 6 liturgy for the 'Musaph' service on the Day of Atonement. [From עבד.]

וְעָשִׂיתָ (word 9, verse 6)

עשה to do, make.

— Qal - עָשָׂה v. 1 he did, made; 2 he worked, labored; 3 he acted, dealt; 4 he produced, yielded, performed, accomplished; 5 he brought about, caused, effected; 6 he appointed; 7 he acquired, gained; 8 he spent (his time).

— Niph. - נַעֲשָׂה 1 was done, was made; 2 was produced, was performed, was accomplished; 3 was offered (as a sacrifice); 4 was observed; 5 was used.

— Pi. - עִשָּׂה PBH 1 he caused somebody to do; 2 he pressed, squeezed.

— Pu. - עֻשָּׂה 1 was made, was formed; PBH 2 was done by force, was forced.

— Hiph. - הֶעֱשָׂה he caused to be done, forced to do. [Moabite ואעש, עשתי, Ugar. 'shy (= he made), OSArab. עסו, Arab. sa'ā(y) (= he did, made, acted).] Derivatives: עָשֶׂה, עָשׂוּי, עָשׂוּי, עֲשִׂיָּה, הֵעָשׂוּת, מַעֲשֶׂה, מְעֻשֶּׂה, תַּעֲשִׂיָּה.

כָּל (word 10, verse 6)

כֹּל m.n. all, whole, the whole of. [From כלל I (= to comprehend, include). cp. Aram. (also BAram.) כֹּל, כָּל, Ugar. kl, Arab. kull, Ethiop. kellā, OSArab. כל, Akka. kullatu (= the whole of). See כְּלִי.]

עָשֵׂה m.n. PBH (pl. עָשִׂיִּין) positive command. [Shortened from מִצְוַת־עָשֵׂה (see מִצְוָה). Properly imper. of עָשָׂה (see עשה), used as a noun.]

מְלַאכְתֶּךָ (word 11, verse 6)

מְלָאכָה f.n. 1 work, occupation. 2 service, use. 3 goods, property. [Standing for מַלְאָכָה and derived from לאך (= to send), hence lit. meaning 'mission'.] Derivative: מְלַאכוּתִי, מְלַאכְתִּי. cp. מְלֶאכֶת.

מְלַאכְתִּי adj. NH pertaining to work; mechanical. [Formed from מְלָאכָה with suff. ־ִי.]

וְיוֹם (word 12, verse 6)

יוֹם m.n. (pl. **1** יָמִים) day. 2 time. 3 year. [Related to BAram., Aram., and Syr. יוֹמָא, יוֹם, Ugar. ym, Arab. yaum, Akka. ūmu (= day), Ethiop. yōm (= today), Aram. יָמָא, Syr. אִימָמָא (= day; in contradistinction to 'night'). cp. יוֹמָא, יָמָה.] Derivatives: יוֹמוֹן, יוֹמִי, יוֹמָם, יוֹמָן, יוֹמִיוֹמִי. cp. the second element in בַּרְיוֹם.

יוֹמָא m.n. PBH 1 day, the day. 2 name of a Mishnah, Tosephta and Talmud tractate in the order מוֹעֵד dealing with the laws referring to the Day of Atonement, hence lit. meaning 'the tractate dealing with the Day' by pre-eminence. [Aram., 'the day', i.e. 'the day by pre-eminence'. See יוֹם.]

יוֹמִי adj. MH daily. [Formed from יוֹם (= day), with suff. ־ִי.]

יוֹמְיוֹם adv. everyday, daily. [For [[illegible]] יוֹם־יוֹם (= day by day, every day, daily), repetition of יוֹם (= day).] Derivative: יוֹמְיוֹמִי.

יוֹמִית adv. daily. [Formed from יוֹם (= day), with adv. suff. ־ִית.]

יוֹמָם adv. daily. [Formed from יוֹם (= day), with the adv. suff. ־ָם. The same suff. appears in אָמְנָם. See אָמְנָם and words there referred to.]

הַשְּׁבִיעִי (word 13, verse 6)

שָׁבוּעַ m.n. (pl. שָׁבוּעוֹת, also שָׁבוּעִים) **1** period of seven days. **2** seven years heptad. [From שֶׁבַע (= seven). cp. Aram.

שְׁבוּעֲתָא, Arab. *usbū'*. For sense development cp. Late L. *septimāna* (= week); properly subst. use of the f. of the L. adj. *septimānus* (= pertaining to the number seven), and Hungarian *hét* (= week), from the numeral adj. *hét* (= seven).] Derivatives: שְׁבוּעוֹת, שְׁבוּעִי, שְׁבוּעוֹן.

שְׁבוּעִי adj. MH weekly, every week. [Formed from שָׁבוּעַ (= week), with suff. י.]

שבע I base of שֶׁבַע (= seven), and of words there referred to.

שבע III to do something seven times.

— Pi. - שִׁבַּע MH **1** he did something seven times; NH **2** he multiplied by seven.

— Pu. - שֻׁבַּע PBH **1** was done seven times; NH **2** was multiplied by seven. [Denominated from שִׁבְעָה, שֶׁבַע (= seven).] Derivatives: שִׁבַּע, מְשֻׁבָּע.

שֶׁבַע f. adj. (m. שִׁבְעָה) seven. [From שבע I, whence also Phoen. שבע (f.), Moabite שבעת (m.), Aram. and Syr. שְׁבַע, BAram. שִׁבְעָה, Aram.-Syr. שַׁבְעָא (m.), Ugar. *shb'* (f.), *shb't* (m.), Arab. *sab'* (f.), *sab'a* (f.), OSArab. שבעת (m.), Akka. *sibi* (f.), *sibitti* (m.).] Derivatives: שבע II, שבע III, שָׁבוּעַ, שְׁבִיעִי, שִׁבְעָנָה, שִׁבְעִים, שִׁבְעָתַיִם.

שִׁבְעָה adj. **1** seven. **2** 'shiv'a ʰ', short for שִׁבְעַת יְמֵי אֲבֵלוּת (the seven days of mourning held for a near relative). [See שֶׁבַע.]

שִׁבְעָנָה m. adj. seven (a hapax legomenon in the Bible, occurring Job 42:13). [A var. of שִׁבְעָה. The form שִׁבְעָנָה possibly arose from שִׁבְעָה through assimilation to שְׁמֹנָה (= eight).]

שִׁבְעָתַיִם adv. sevenfold, seven times. [Properly adv. use of the dual of שִׁבְעָה (= seven). The dual suff. added to certain numbers has the meaning '–fold'; see אַרְבַּעְתַיִם.]

שָׁבַת (word 14, verse 6)

שבת to cease, desist; to rest.

— Qal - **1** שָׁבַת he ceased, desisted; **2** he desisted from labor, rested; PBH **3** he observed the Sabbath, he spent the Sabbath; NH **4** he struck, was on strike (properly 'he stopped working').

— Niph. - נִשְׁבַּת ceased.

— Hiph. - **1** הִשְׁבִּית he caused to cease, put an end to; **2** he removed, exterminated, destroyed; NH **3** he locked out (workers).

— **Hoph.** - הָשְׁבַּת PBH **1** was made to cease, was stopped; PBH **2** he ceased, perished; NH **3** was locked out (from his work). [JAram. שְׁבַת (= he rested; he observed the Sabbath), Arab. *sabata* (= he cut off, interrupted, ceased, rested). Akka. *shabātu*, which prob. means 'to complete, cease, desist'. cp. שֶׁבֶת I.] Derivatives: שְׁבִיתָה, שׁוֹבֵת, מִשְׁבָּת, מִשְׁבֶּת II, שַׁבָּת. שְׁבוּת.

שַׁבָּת m.n. (pl. שַׁבָּתוֹת) **1** day of rest, Sabbath. **2** week, i.e. the seven days from Sunday to Sabbath (the JAram. and Syr. loan words also have both meanings: 'Sabbath', and 'week'; cp. also Gk. *sabbaton* and *sabbata*, which also have both these meanings). **3** feast, festival. **4** of years, i.e. a period of seven years. **5** the Sabbathical year, 'shemittah'. PBH **6** 'Sabbath', name of the first Mishnah and Talmud tractate of the order מוֹעֵד. [Derived from שבת and lit. meaning 'day of rest'. Aram.–Syr. שַׁבְּתָא, Arab. *sabt*, Ethiop. *sanbat*, are Heb. loan words. So are Gk. *sabbaton* (whence L. *sabbatum*, It. *sabato*, Old Provençal–Catalan *dissapte*, Spanish–Portuguese *sábado*, Serbo–Croatian *subota*, Czech and Slovak *sobota*, Russ. *subbóta*, etc.), and its Gk. vulgar var. *sambaton*, whence VL *sambatum*, Rumanian *sîmbătă*, Old Slavic *sǫbota*, Hungarian *szombat* (= Saturday), and *sambatīdiēs* (= the day of Sabbath), whence Old Fren. *sambe-di*, whence Fren. *samedi* (= Saturday), and prob. through the medium of the Gothic — the first element in Old High Ger. *sambaz-tac*, middle High Ger. *samez-tac*, Ger. *Samstag* (= Saturday). However, also Akka. *shabbatu, shappatu*, and Egypt. *smdt*, in the sense '15th day of the month' (but not in the meaning '7th day of the week', nor in that of '7th or 14th day of the month', as supposed by many scholars), are borrowed from ancient Hebrew. As shown by the above facts, the name שַׁבָּת and the idea it conveys are of Hebrew origin.] Derivatives: שַׁבְּתַאי, שַׁבָּתוֹן, שַׁבָּתִי, שַׁבְּתִין. cp. סַמְבַּטְיוֹן.

לַיהוָה (word 15, verse 6)

יְהֹוָה, יָהֶוֶה m.n. the proper name of God in the Bible, Tetragrammaton. [It prob. derives from הוה (= to be). The usual transliteration 'Jehovah' is based on the supposition that the Tetragrammaton is the imperfect Qal or Hiph'il of הוה and lit. means 'the one who is', 'the existing', resp. 'who calls into existence'. In reality, however, the pronunciation and literal meaning of the Tetragrammaton is unknown. cp. יָהּ I.]

אֱלֹהֶיךָ (word 16, verse 6)

אֱלֹהַּ, אֱלוֹהַּ m.n. 1 god. 2 God. [According to some scholars אֱלוֹהַּ is a back formation from the pl. אֱלוֹהִים, this latter being the plural of אֵל ᴵ with the infix ה, which has an analogy in Heb. אִמָּהוֹת, pl. of אֵם (= mother), in Aram. אֲבָהָת, pl. of אַב (= father), שְׁמָהָת, pl. of שְׁמָא (= name), to which may be added Ugar. 'mht, pl. of 'mt (= Heb. אָמָה, 'bondwoman'), bhtm, pl. of bt (= Heb. בַּיִת, 'house'), and 'lht, pl. of 'lt (= goddess), f. of 'l (= Heb. אֵל ᴵ, 'god'). Others see in אֱלוֹהַּ the orig. form from which the pl. אֱלוֹהִים was formed. The consideration of the fact that אֵל has the pl. אֵלִים, shows that the second view is surely preferable to the first. Fleischer sees in אֱלוֹהַּ the derivative of base אלה, which he connects with Arab. aliha (= he sought refuge in anxiety), whence אֱלוֹהַּ would have meant orig. 'fear', hence 'object of fear or reverence', 'the revered one'. However, Nöldeke and others are prob. right when they maintain that the verb aliha in the above sense is prob. denominated from 'ilāh (= god).]

לֹא (word 17, verse 6)

לֹא adv. no, not. [Related to Aram. (also BAram) and Syr. לָא, Ugar. l, Arab. lā, Akka. lā (= not, no). cp. לָאוּ, לָא, and the second element in אֶלָּא, אוּלַי, אִלּוּלֵא, לוּלֵא.]

לֹא combining form meaning 'non-'. [From לֹא (= no, not).]

לָא adv. PBH no, not. [Aram., related to Heb. לֹא (q.v.).]

תַּעֲשֶׂה (word 18, verse 6)

עשׂה to do, make.

— **Qal** - עָשָׂה v. **1** he did, made; **2** he worked, labored; **3** he acted, dealt; **4** he produced, yielded, performed, accomplished; **5** he brought about, caused, effected; **6** he appointed; **7** he acquired, gained; **8** he spent (his time).

— **Niph.** - נַעֲשָׂה **1** was done, was made; **2** was produced, was performed, was accomplished; **3** was offered (as a sacrifice); **4** was observed; **5** was used.

— **Pi.** - עִשָּׂה PBH **1** he caused somebody to do; **2** he pressed, squeezed.

— **Pu.** - עֻשָּׂה **1** was made, was formed; PBH **2** was done by force, was forced.

— **Hiph.** - הֶעֱשָׂה he caused to be done, forced to do.

[Moabite ואעש, עשתי, Ugar. 'shy (= he made), OSArab. עסו, Arab. sa'ā(y) (= he did, made, acted).] Derivatives: עָשָׂה, עָשׂוּי, עָשׂוּי, עָשִׂיָה, הֵעָשׂוּת, מַעֲשֶׂה, מִעֲשֶׂה, תַּעֲשִׂיָה.

עֲשֵׂה m.n. PBH (pl. עֲשִׂין) positive command. [Shortened from מִצְוַת־עֲשֵׂה (see מִצְוָה). Properly imper. of עָשָׂה (see עשה), used as a noun.]

כֹּל (word 19, verse 6)

כֹּל m.n. all, whole, the whole of. [From כלל I (= to comprehend, include). cp. Aram. (also BAram.) כָּל, כֹּל, Ugar. kl, Arab. kull, Ethiop. kellā, OSArab. כל, Akka. kullatu (= the whole of). See כְּלִי.]

מְלָאכָה (word 20, verse 6)

מְלָאכָה f.n. 1 work, occupation. 2 service, use. 3 goods, property. [Standing for מַלְאָכָה and derived from לאך (= to send), hence lit. meaning 'mission'.] Derivative: מְלַאכוּתִי, מְלַאכְתִּי. cp. מְלֶאכֶת.

מְלַאכְתִּי adj. NH pertaining to work; mechanical. [Formed from מְלָאכָה with suff. י.]

אַתָּה (word 21, verse 6)

אַתָּה m. personal pron. you, thou. [Related to BAram. אַנְתָּה, אַנְתְּ, Aram. אַנְתְּ, אַתְּ, Syr. אַנְתּ, Ugar. at, Arab. 'anta, Ethiop. 'anta, Akka. 'atta (= thou, you). The primitive form was prob. 'antā for the m. and 'antī for the f., which are perhaps compounded of the element 'an–, occurring also in אֲנִי (= I) and its correspondences, and – tā, resp. – tī, which appear also as suffixes, resp. prefixes, denoting the second person in the conjugation of the perfect and imperfect of the verbs. cp. אַתְּ, אַתָּה. cp. also אַנְתָּה.]

וּבִנְךָ (word 22, verse 6)

בֵּן m.n. 1 son; offspring. 2 branch, shoot. 3 inhabitant of. 4 worthy of, deserving. [Related to Moabite, Phoen., OSArab. בן, Ugar. bn, Arab. ibn, Akka. bin(= son), BAram. and Aram.–Syr. בַּר (pl. בְּנִין), Mehri ber (= son). All these words prob. derive from בנה I (= to build). The change of n to r in Aram., Syr. and Mehri is difficult to explain; it may be due to regressive dissimilation. cp. בנה II. cp. also בַּר and בַּת.] Derivatives: בְּנָיוֹת, בְּנִיּוּת.

The Real God Code

וּבִתֶּ֫ךָ (word 23, verse 6)

בַּת ᴵ f.n. (pl. **1 בָּנוֹת** daughter. **2** girl, maiden, young woman. **3** native, inhabitant of. **4** at the age of. **5** worthy of, deserving. **6** a village or a town situated near a large city. [**בַּת** is f. of **בֵּן** (= son), and developed from **בַּנְתְּ**, from orig. **בִּנְתְּ**. It is related to Ugar. bt, JAram. abs. state **ברת**, emphatic state **בְּרָתָא**, Syr. emphatic state **בְּרַתָּא**, c. st. **בַּת**, Arab. bint, OSArab. **בת, בנת** (= daughter), Ethiop. bent in benta 'ain (= pupil of the eye; cp. **בַּת־עַיִן**), Akka. bintu and buntu (= daughter). cp. the first element in the private name **בַּת־שֶׁבַע** (= Bath-sheba).]

עַבְדְּךָ (word 24, verse 6)

עבד to work; to serve.

— **Qal.** - **עָבַד** v. **1** he worked, labored, tilled, cultivated (the soil); **2** he served. **3** he worshiped.

— **Niph.** - **נֶעֱבַד**. **1** was tilled, was cultivated; PBH **2** was worshiped; PBH **3** was dressed, was tanned (said of hides).

— **Pi.** - **עִבֵּד 1** he cultivated; **2** he dressed, tanned (said of hides); he elaborated, adapted.

— **Pu.** - **עֻבַּד 1** was worked; PBH **2** was dressed, was tanned (said of hides); NH **3** was elaborated, adapted.

— **Nith.** - **נִתְעַבֵּד, הִתְעַבֵּד 1** was worked; **2** was dressed, was tanned (said of hides); NH **3** was adapted.

— **Shiph. (see** . - **שִׁעְבֵּד**).

— **Hiph.** - **הֶעֱבִיד 1** he caused to work, made to serve; **2** he enslaved.

— **Hoph.** - **הָעֳבַד** was made to serve. [Aram. (also BAram.) and Syr. **עֲבַד** (= he worked, did, performed, made), whence BAram. **עֲבַד**, Aram. and Syr. **עַבְדָּא** (= slave, servant), Ugar. bd (= to work, serve, worship), Arab. 'abada (= he served, worshiped, obeyed), whence 'abd (= slave, worshiper), OSArab. **עבד** (= servant), Ethiop. 'abbata (= he imposed forced labor), Akka. abdu (= slave). Derivatives: **עֶבֶד, עָבַד, עֲבָדָה, עַבְדָּן, עַבְדוּת, עָבוּד, עֲבוֹדָה, עוֹבֵד, הַעֲבָדָה, עֲבָד, עַבְדָּא, עֶבְדָּא**. cp. **מְעֻבָּד, מַעְבָּדָה, מַעֲבִיד, תַּעְבוּד**.

עֶבֶד m.n. **1** servant; **2** slave, bondman; **3** worshipper. [From **עבד**.]

עַבְדָּא m.n. PBH servant; slave. [Aram. and Syr., denominated from **עֲבַד** (q.v.). cp. **עֶבֶד**.]

עָבְדָּא PBH, עֲבָדָה NH **1** deed, act. **2** occurrence. **3** fact. [From Aram. עוֹבְדָא, Syr. עָבְדָא (= work, fact, deed), from עֲבַד (= he did).] Derivative: עָבְדָּתִי.

עֲבֻדָּה f.n. household servants (occurring in the Bible only Gen. 26:14 and Job 1:3). [From עבד.]

עַבְדוּת f.n. slavery, servitude, bondage (in the Bible occurring only Ez. 9:8 following and Neh. 9:17). [Formed from עבד with suff. וּת. cp. Syr. עַבְדוּתָא (of s.m.).] Derivative: עַבְדוּתִי.

עַבְדוּתִי adj. NH slavish, servile. [Formed from עַבְדוּת with suff. ־ִי.]

עֲבוֹדָה f.n. **1** work, labor. **2** deed, action. **3** service. **4** divine service, worship. PBH **5** 'abodah', the first of the last three benedictions of the 'Amidah'. MH **6** liturgy for the 'Musaph' service on the Day of Atonement. [From עבד.]

וַאֲמָתְךָ (word 25, verse 6)

אָמָה f.n. (pl. אֲמָהוֹת) maidservant, handmaid, female slave. [Related to Phoen. אמת. Aram.-Syr. אַמְתָא. Ugar. amt, Arab. 'amah, Ethiop. 'amat, Akka. amtu (= handmaid, female slave).]

וּבְהֶמְתֶּךָ (word 26, verse 6)

בְּהֵמָה f.n. animal, beast, cattle. [cp. Ugar. bhmt (= life stock, cattle), Aram. בהמיתה, בהמתה (= livestock), Mand. באהימא (= ass), Arab. bahīma (= beast, animal, cattle), bahma (= lamb, sheep), bahm (= small cattle). For the ending see suff. ה.] Derivatives: בהם, בָּהָם, בָּהֲמִי.

וְגֵרְךָ (word 27, verse 6)

גֵּר m.n. **1** foreigner, stranger, temporary dweller, newcomer. PBH **2** proselyte, convert. [Related to גֵּר, from גור (q.v.). cp. Arab. jara (= he went astray from), jawara (= he lived close by), Ugar. gr (= to dwell), Aram. גִּיּוֹרָא (= proselyte), Syr. גִּיּוֹרָא (= foreigner, temporary dweller, proselyte).] Derivative: גֵּרוּת

אֲשֶׁר (word 28, verse 6)

1 אֲשֶׁר who, which, that, that which. **2** in order that. [Related to Ugar. aṯr (= that which). cp. Moabite אשר. According to most scholars these words were originally nouns meaning 'trace, place', and are related to Arab. 'athira (= to leave traces), 'ithr (= trace, place), and to Aram. אֲתַר, אַתְרָא, Syr. אַתְרָא (= place). See אֲתַר.]

בִּשְׁעָרֶיךָ (word 29, verse 6)

שַׁעַר ᴵ m.n. 1 gate, entrance. MH 2 title page (of a book). MH 3 chapter, section of a book. NH 4 goal (in sports). [Related to Phoen. שער, Ugar. tgr, Arab. thagr (= crack, rift, opening of the mouth), OSArab. תֹעַר, BAram. תְּרַע, Aram.–Syr. תַּרְעָא, Egypt.–Aram., Nab., Palm., Modern Aram. and Modern Syr. תרעא; Samar, tera, Mand. תירא (= gate). cp. Arab. tur'aʰ (= door), which is an Aramaic loan word. cp. also תרע ᴵᴵ and its derivative תַּרְעָא (= gate, door).] Derivative: שׁוֹעֵר.

כִּי (word 30, verse 6)

כִּי ᴵ conj. 1 that. 2 because. 3 when, while, as. 4 if, in case. 5 although, though. [כִּי was orig. a demonstrative pron. meaning 'thus', 'therefore', 'then'. It is related to Phoen. כ, Moabite כי, Punic כא, כה, כע, Aram. כִּי (= as, like), Ugar. k (= as, when, that), Akka. kī (= as, like), prob. also to Arab. kay (= that, in order that), Syr. כִּי (= then). See prefix כְּ and כֹּה.]

שֵׁשֶׁת (word 31, verse 6)

שֵׁשׁ ᴵ f. adj. six. [For שדשׁ, whence also Aram. שִׁית, Syr. שֵׁת (for shidt), אֶשְׁתָּא, Egypt.–Aram. שתה, Nab. שת, Palm. שתא, Ugar. tdt, tt (= six), Arab. sitt (f.), sitta (m.) (= six), sādis (= sixth), Ethiop. sessū (f.), sedestū (m.), OSArab. sdth, late sthth, stht, Akka. shishshit (f.), shishshi (m.) (= six), seshishu (= sixth), sudushu (= sixfold). cp. שִׁשָּׁה.] Derivatives: שִׁשָּׁה, שִׁשִּׁי, שִׁשִּׁים, שְׁתוּת, שְׁתִית. cp. שִׁשָּׁתַיִם.

שִׁשָּׁה m. adj. six. [See שֵׁשׁ.]

ששה to divide by six; to multiply by six.
— Pi. - 1 שִׁשָּׁה he divided by six; NH 2 he multiplied by six; MH 3 he made a hexagon.
— Pu. - 1 שֻׁשָּׁה was divided by six; 2 was multiplied by six. [Denominated from שֵׁשׁ ᴵ or from שִׁשָּׁה.] Derivative: מְשֻׁשֶּׁה.

שִׁשִּׁי adj. 1 sixth. PBH 2 the sixth person called to the reading of the Torah in the synagogue. [Formed from שֵׁשׁ ᴵ with suff. ִי.] Derivative: שִׁשִּׁיָּה.

שִׁשִּׁיָּה f.n. NH 1 a set of six objects. 2 sextet (music). [Formed from שֵׁשׁ ᴵ or שִׁשָּׁה (= six), with suff. ִיָּה.]

שִׁשִּׁית adj. & n. 1 sixth. 2 one sixth, sixth part. NH 3 sixth grade (in school). [f. of שִׁשִּׁי.]

שִׁשְׁתַּיִם adv. NH sixfold. [Formed from שֵׁשׁ (= six), on the analogy of אַרְבַּעְתַּיִם (= fourfold); q.v.]

יָמִים (word 32, verse 6)

יוֹם m.n. (pl. יָמִים) **1** day. **2** time. **3** year. [Related to BAram., Aram., and Syr. יוֹם, יוֹמָא, Ugar. ym, Arab. yaum, Akka. ūmu (= day), Ethiop. yōm (= today), Aram. יְמָמָא, Syr. אִימָמָא (= day; in contradistinction to 'night'). cp. יוֹמָא. יְמָמָה.] Derivatives: יוֹמוֹן, יוֹמִי, יוֹמָם, יוֹמָן, יוֹמְיוֹמִי. cp. the second element in בְּרִיוֹם.

יוֹמָא m.n. PBH **1** day, the day. **2** name of a Mishnah, Tosephta and Talmud tractate in the order מוֹעֵד dealing with the laws referring to the Day of Atonement, hence lit. meaning 'the tractate dealing with the Day' by pre-eminence. [Aram., 'the day', i.e. 'the day by pre-eminence'. See יוֹם.]

יוֹמִי adj. MH daily. [Formed from יוֹם (= day), with suff. י.]

יוֹמְיוֹם adv. everyday, daily. [For [[illegible]] יוֹם־יוֹם (= day by day, every day, daily), repetition of יוֹם (= day).] Derivative: יוֹמְיוֹמִי.

יוֹמִית adv. daily. [Formed from יוֹם (= day), with adv. suff. ית.]

יוֹמָם adv. daily. [Formed from יוֹם (= day), with the adv. suff. ם. The same suff. appears in אָמְנָם. See אָמְנָם and words there referred to.]

עָשָׂה (word 33, verse 6)

עשׂה to do, make.

— **Qal** - עָשָׂה v. **1** he did, made; **2** he worked, labored; **3** he acted, dealt; **4** he produced, yielded, performed, accomplished; **5** he brought about, caused, effected; **6** he appointed; **7** he acquired, gained; **8** he spent (his time).

— **Niph.** - נַעֲשָׂה **1** was done, was made; **2** was produced, was performed, was accomplished; **3** was offered (as a sacrifice); **4** was observed; **5** was used.

— **Pi.** - עִשָּׂה PBH **1** he caused somebody to do; **2** he pressed, squeezed.

— **Pu.** - עֻשָּׂה **1** was made, was formed; PBH **2** was done by force, was forced.

— **Hiph.** - הֶעֱשָׂה he caused to be done, forced to do. [Moabite עשׂתי, ואעשׂ, Ugar. 'shy (= he made), OSArab. עסו, Arab. sa'ā(y) (= he did, made, acted).] Derivatives: עָשׂוּי, עָשׂוּי, עֲשִׂיָּה, הֵעָשׂוֹת, מַעֲשֶׂה, מְעֻשֶּׂה, תַּעֲשִׂיָּה.

עָשֶׂה m.n. PBH (pl. עָשִׂין) positive command. [Shortened from מִצְוַת־עֲשֵׂה (see מִצְוָה). Properly imper. of עָשָׂה (see עשׂה), used as a noun.]

יְהוָה (word 34, verse 6)

יְהוָה, יֱהוָֹה m.n. the proper name of God in the Bible, Tetragrammaton. [It prob. derives from הוה (= to be). The usual transliteration 'Jehovah' is based on the supposition that the Tetragrammaton is the imperfect Qal or Hiph'il of הוה and lit. means 'the one who is', 'the existing', resp. 'who calls into existence'. In reality, however, the pronunciation and literal meaning of the Tetragrammaton is unknown. cp. יָהּ ᴵ.]

אֵת (word 35, verse 6)

אֵת ᴵ, אֶת prep. the mark of the accusative. Usually prefixed only to a definite noun, as in אֶת־הָאִישׁ (= the man). [Related to Moabite את, Phoen. אית (to be read אַיָּת), Aram. (also BAram.) and Syr. יָת (this latter mostly used as a noun), Egypt.-Aram. ות, Arab. 'iyyā (only used with a suff. to emphasize the pron.) and possibly also to Ethiop. kīyā (also used only with a suff. for the sake of emphasis). Orig. — as Syr. יָתָא, יָת — a noun in the sense of 'being, essence, existence'. The orig. form prob. was 'iwyath (cp. the Phoen. form), which ultimately derives from base אוה (= to sign, mark), whence also אוֹת (= sign).]

הַשָּׁמַיִם (word 36, verse 6)

שָׁמַיִם m.n. pl. 1 visible heavens, sky. 2 Heaven, abode of God. 3 (fig.) God. [Related to Phoen. שממ, OAram. שמין, Aram. (also BAram.), Egypt. and Syr. שְׁמַיָּא, Samar. שומיא, Ugar. shmn (= heaven, sky), proper name בעלשממ (transliterated by Philo into Beelsamen), Arab. samā', OSArab. שמו, שמה, Ethiop. samay, Akka. shamū, pl. shamē, also shamāmu, shamai, TA shamūma, shamēma (= heaven, sky). The orig. meaning of these words is prob. 'high place, height'. cp. Aram. and Syr. שְׁמַיָּא, which besides 'heaven, sky', also mean 'height, highest part; ceiling, roof'; Arab. samā (= was high, was lofty; rose high), sumūw (= height, altitude); Akka. shamai in the meaning 'roof'; Talmudic Heb. שְׁמֵי קוֹרָה (= ceiling, roof).] Derivative: שְׁמֵימִי.

שְׁמֵימִי adj. MH heavenly, celestial. [Formed from שָׁמַיִם with suff. ־ִי.]

וְאֶת (word 37, verse 6)

אֵת ¹, אֶת prep. the mark of the accusative. Usually prefixed only to a definite noun, as in אֶת־הָאִישׁ (= the man). [Related to Moabite את, Phoen. אית (to be read אִיַת), Aram. (also BAram.) and Syr. יָת (this latter mostly used as a noun), Egypt.-Aram. ות, Arab. 'iyyā (only used with a suff. to emphasize the pron.) and possibly also to Ethiop. kīyā (also used only with a suff. for the sake of emphasis). Orig. — as Syr. יָת, יָתָא — a noun in the sense of 'being, essence, existence'. The orig. form prob. was 'iwyath (cp. the Phoen. form), which ultimately derives from base אוה (= to sign, mark), whence also אוֹת (= sign).]

הָאָרֶץ (word 38, verse 6)

אֶרֶץ f.n. (pl. **1** אֲרָצוֹת) earth. 2 land, country. 3 ground. [Related to BAram. אַרְקָא (for the change of צ to ק cp. Heb. קָטַר, 'he caused to smoke', with Aram. עֲטַר), Aram. אַרְעָה, אֲרַע, Ugar. arṣ, Arab. arḍ, Akka. erṣetu (= earth), Tigre 'ard. cp. Arakiel — name of the earth in the Book of Enoch 8:3. cp. אַרְעָה, ארק, אַרְקָה.] Derivatives: אַרְצִי, אַרְצָן.

אֶת (word 39, verse 6)

אֵת ¹, אֶת prep. the mark of the accusative. Usually prefixed only to a definite noun, as in אֶת־הָאִישׁ (= the man). [Related to Moabite את, Phoen. אית (to be read אִיַת), Aram. (also BAram.) and Syr. יָת (this latter mostly used as a noun), Egypt.-Aram. ות, Arab. 'iyyā (only used with a suff. to emphasize the pron.) and possibly also to Ethiop. kīyā (also used only with a suff. for the sake of emphasis). Orig. — as Syr. יָת, יָתָא — a noun in the sense of 'being, essence, existence'. The orig. form prob. was 'iwyath (cp. the Phoen. form), which ultimately derives from base אוה (= to sign, mark), whence also אוֹת (= sign).]

הַיָּם (word 40, verse 6)

יָם m.n. 1 sea. 2 lake. 3 large basin, reservoir. 4 West (lit.: 'the region of the Land of Israel situated toward the Mediterranean Sea'). [Related to Phoen. ים, Aram. יַמָּא (= sea), Ugar. ym, Akka. iāmu.] Derivatives: יַמַּאי, יָמָה, יַמִּי, יַמִּיָה.

וְאֵת (word 41, verse 6))

אֵת ᴵ, אֶת prep. the mark of the accusative. Usually prefixed only to a definite noun, as in אֶת־הָאִישׁ (= the man). [Related to Moabite את, Phoen. אית (to be read אֵיַת), Aram. (also BAram.) and Syr. יָת (this latter mostly used as a noun), Egypt.-Aram. ית, Arab. 'iyyā (only used with a suff. to emphasize the pron.) and possibly also to Ethiop. kīyā (also used only with a suff. for the sake of emphasis). Orig. — as Syr. יָת, יָתָא — a noun in the sense of 'being, essence, existence'. The orig. form prob. was 'iwyath (cp. the Phoen. form), which ultimately derives from base אוה (= to sign, mark), whence also אוֹת (= sign).]

כָּל (word 42, verse 6)

כֹּל m.n. all, whole, the whole of. [From כלל ᴵ (= to comprehend, include). cp. Aram. (also BAram.) כֹּל, כָּל, Ugar. kl, Arab. kull, Ethiop. kellā, OSArab. כל, Akka. kullatu (= the whole of). See כְּלִי.]

אֲשֶׁר (word 43, verse 6))

1 אֲשֶׁר who, which, that, that which. 2 in order that. [Related to Ugar. aṯr (= that which). cp. Moabite אשר. According to most scholars these words were originally nouns meaning 'trace, place', and are related to Arab. 'athira (= to leave traces), 'ithr (= trace, place), and to Aram. אַתְרָא, אֲתַר, Syr. אַתְרָא (= place). See אָתַר.]

בָּם (word 44, verse 6)

בָּם, בָּהֶם pron. in them (m.). [Inflected personal pron., formed from בְּ with suff. ם, resp. הֶם.]

וַיָּנַח (word 45, verse 6)

נוח to rest.

— Qal - נָח 1 he rested, settled down; 2 he was quiet.

— Niph. - נְנוֹחַ was given rest, was relieved.

— Hiph. - הֵנִיחַ 1 he caused to rest, gave rest; 2 he caused to alight, set down.

— Hiph. - הִנִּיחַ 1 he laid down, set down; 2 he deposited; 3 he let remain, left; 4 he abandoned; 5 he let alone; 6 he permitted; NH 7 he supposed; NH 8 he coined (words).

— Hoph. - הוּנַח was given rest.

— **Hoph.** - הֻנַּח was set down, was placed; NH **2** was supposed; NH **3** was coined (said of a word). [Phoen. נחת (= rest) n., Aram. נוּחַ (= to rest), Syr. נָח (= rested), Ugar. nḫ (= to rest), nḫt (= seat for resting, cushion, pillow), Ethiop. nōḫa (= was extended; rested), Akka. nāḫu (= to rest), Arab. 'anāḫa (= he made camels kneel down), munāḫ (= resting place of camel).] Derivatives: נָת, נוֹחַ, נוּחַ, נוֹחָה, נָיָת, גְיָת, נִיחָת, נִיחוֹחַ, מְנוּחָה, מַנַּת, מָנוֹחַ I, מָנוֹחַ II, הַנּוּחַ, הַנָּחָה, הַנָּחָת, הִתְנַחֲתָה, מָנוֹחַ I, נַחַת מְנָת I, מָנָּח II, מָנָּח, תְּנוּחָה, נְבוֹת, מנת, prob. also נַחַת III. cp. אֶתְנַחְתָּא, נִיחָא, הֲנִיחָא. cp. also ניח.

נוּחַ m.n. rest, repose (a hapax legomenon in the Bible, occurring Chron. II 6:41). [From נוח. cp. נוּחָה.]

נוּחָה f.n. PBH rest, repose. [Formed from נוח with first suff. ה.]

נָח adj. NH **1** restful. MH **2** quiescent (said of a 'shewa'). [Part. of נוּחַ (= to rest). See נוח.]

בַּיּוֹם (word 46, verse 6)

יוֹם m.n. (pl. יָמִים) **1** day. **2** time. **3** year. [Related to BAram., Aram., and Syr. יוֹמָא. יוֹם, Ugar. ym, Arab. yaum, Akka. ūmu (= day), Ethiop. yōm (= today), Aram. יְמָמָא, Syr. אִימָמָא (= day; in contradistinction to 'night'). cp. יוֹמָא. יְמָמָה.] Derivatives: יוֹמוֹן, יוֹמִי. יוֹמָם. יוֹמָן. יוֹמִיּוֹמִי. cp. the second element in בַּרְיוֹם.

יוֹמָא m.n. PBH **1** day, the day. **2** name of a Mishnah, Tosephta and Talmud tractate in the order מוֹעֵד dealing with the laws referring to the Day of Atonement, hence lit. meaning 'the tractate dealing with the Day' by pre-eminence. [Aram., 'the day', i.e. 'the day by pre-eminence'. See יוֹם.]

יוֹמִי adj. MH daily. [Formed from יוֹם (= day), with suff. י.]

יוֹמָיוֹם adv. everyday, daily. [For [[illegible]] יוֹם־יוֹם (= day by day, every day, daily), repetition of יוֹם (= day).] Derivative: יוֹמְיוֹמִי.

יוֹמִית adv. daily. [Formed from יוֹם (= day), with adv. suff. ית.]

יוֹמָם adv. daily. [Formed from יוֹם (= day), with the adv. suff. ם. The same suff. appears in אָמְנָם. See אָמְנָם and words there referred to.]

הַשְּׁבִיעִי (word 47, verse 6)

שָׁבוּעַ m.n. (pl. שָׁבוּעוֹת, also שְׁבוּעִים) **1** period of seven days. **2** seven years heptad. [From שֶׁבַע (= seven). cp. Aram. שְׁבוּעֲתָא, Arab. usbū'. For sense development cp. Late L.

septimāna (= week); properly subst. use of the f. of the L. adj. *septimānus* (= pertaining to the number seven), and Hungarian *hét* (= week), from the numeral adj. *hét* (= seven).] Derivatives: שְׁבוּעוֹן, שְׁבוּעִי, שָׁבוּעוֹת.

שְׁבוּעִי adj. MH weekly, every week. [Formed from שָׁבוּעַ (= week), with suff. ִי.]

שׁבע I base of שֶׁבַע (= seven), and of words there referred to.

שׁבע III to do something seven times.
— Pi. - שִׁבַּע MH **1** he did something seven times; NH **2** he multiplied by seven.
— Pu. - שֻׁבַּע PBH **1** was done seven times; NH **2** was multiplied by seven. [Denominated from שֶׁבַע, שִׁבְעָה (= seven).] Derivatives: שָׁבַע, מְשֻׁבָּע.

שֶׁבַע f. adj. (m. שִׁבְעָה) seven. [From שׁבע I, whence also Phoen. שבע (f.), Moabite שבעת (m.), Aram. and Syr. שְׁבַע, BAram. שִׁבְעָה, Aram.-Syr. שַׁבְעָא (m.), Ugar. *shb'* (f.), *shb't* (m.), Arab. *sab'* (f.), *sab'a* (f.), OSArab. שבעת (m.), Akka. *sibi* (f.), *sibitti* (m.).] Derivatives: שׁבע II, שׁבע III, שָׁבוּעַ, שְׁבִיעִי, שִׁבְעָנָה, שִׁבְעִים, שִׁבְעָתַיִם.

שִׁבְעָה adj. **1** seven. **2** 'shiv'a ʰ', short for שִׁבְעַת יְמֵי אֲבֵלוּת (the seven days of mourning held for a near relative). [See שֶׁבַע.]

שִׁבְעָנָה m. adj. seven (a hapax legomenon in the Bible, occurring Job 42:13). [A var. of שִׁבְעָה. The form שִׁבְעָנָה possibly arose from שִׁבְעָה through assimilation to שְׁמֹנָה (= eight).]

שִׁבְעָתַיִם adv. sevenfold, seven times. [Properly adv. use of the dual of שִׁבְעָה (= seven). The dual suff. added to certain numbers has the meaning '–fold'; see אַרְבַּעְתַּיִם.]

עַל (word 48, verse 6)

עַל I **1** height, upper part. **2** , above. [From עלה. See עַל II.]

עַל II prep. **1** on, upon, above. **2** at, beside. **3** toward(s). **4** against. **5** concerning, about. **6** because of, on account of. **7** together with. [Shortened from עֲלֵי, which is preserved in poetry (see אֱלֵי and עֲדֵי), from עלה. Related to Phoen. and Moabite על, עלת, Aram., BAram.) and Syr. עַל, Ugar. *'l*, Arab. *'alā*, OSArab. עלי, Ethiop. *lā'la*, Akka. *eli* (= on, upon). cp. עַל I. cp. also עָלֶיהָ II.] Derivative: עָל.

כֵּן (word 49, verse 6)

כֵּן I adv. 1 so, thus. MH 2 yes. [Related to Aram.-Syr. כֵּן, Phoen. כן (= so), Syr. הָכַן, הָכַנָּא (= so), Akka. akanna (= here, now) and prob. also to Arab. lākin, lākinna (= but), if formed from lā (= not), and kin (= Heb. כֵּן). These words prob. derive from the Semitic demonstrative base * kā-. cp. כֹּה, כִּי and אָכֵן. According to some scholars כֵּן derives from כון I, hence lit. means 'established, confirmed' and is related to כֵּן II. cp. לָכֵן.] Derivative: כנכן.

כֵּן II adj. right, truthful, honest. [Derived from כון I (= to be set up, be established, be firm), and lit. meaning 'firm'. cp. Syr. כֵּאנָא (= right, just), Akka. kēnu (= firm, strong), kettu (= truth, right). cp. כֵּן I.] Derivative: כֵּנוּת.

כֵּן III, כַּן m.n. BH, resp. PBH (pl. כַּנִּים) base, stand, pedestal. [From כון I (= to put, place). cp. Aram.-Syr. כַּנָּא (= base, stand). cp. also כַּנָּה II.]

בָּרֵךְ (word 50, verse 6)

ברך II to bless.
— Qal (occurs only in the pass. part. - בָּרוּךְ, q.v.).
— Niph. - נִבְרַךְ he blessed himself, wished himself a blessing.
— Pi. - 1 בֵּרַךְ the blessed; 2 he greeted; 3 (euphemistically) he cursed.
— Pu. - בֹּרַךְ was blessed.
— Hith. - 1 הִתְבָּרֵךְ he blessed himself; 2 (pl.) they blessed each other. [Phoen. ברך (= to bless), Aram. בָּרֵךְ, Syr. בָּרֵךְ (= he blessed), Ugar. brk (= to bless), Arab. bāraka (= he blessed), Akka. karābu (= to bless — a metathesis form), Ethiop. mekrāb (= temple). M.H. Goshen, referring to the fact that parallelism of the bases brk ‖ mrr is well established in Ugaritic and that mrr very prob. means 'to strengthen', suggests that the orig. meaning of ברך was 'to be strong', whence developed the meaning 'to bless'.] Derivatives: בָּרוּךְ, בְּרָכָה, הִתְבָּרְכוּת, מְבֹרָךְ.

יְהֹוָה (word 51, verse 6)

יְהֹוָה, יֱהֹוִה m.n. the proper name of God in the Bible, Tetragrammaton. [It prob. derives from הוה (= to be). The usual transliteration 'Jehovah' is based on the supposition that the Tetragrammaton is the imperfect Qal or Hiph'il of הוה and lit. means 'the one who is', 'the existing', resp. 'who calls into existence'. In reality, however, the pronunciation and literal meaning of the Tetragrammaton is unknown. cp. יָהּ I.]

אֵת (word 52, verse 6)

אֵת I, אֶת prep. the mark of the accusative. Usually prefixed only to a definite noun, as in אֶת־הָאִישׁ (= the man). [Related to Moabite את, Phoen. אית (to be read אַיַּת), Aram. (also BAram.) and Syr. יָת (this latter mostly used as a noun), Egypt.-Aram. ות, Arab. 'iyyā (only used with a suff. to emphasize the pron.) and possibly also to Ethiop. kīyā (also used only with a suff. for the sake of emphasis). Orig. — as Syr. יָתָא, יָת — a noun in the sense of 'being, essence, existence'. The orig. form prob. was 'iwyath (cp. the Phoen. form), which ultimately derives from base אוה (= to sign, mark), whence also אוֹת (= sign).]

יוֹם (word 53, verse 6)

יוֹם m.n. (pl. 1 (יָמִים day. 2 time. 3 year. [Related to BAram., Aram., and Syr. יוֹמָא. יוֹם, Ugar. ym, Arab. yaum, Akka. ūmu (= day), Ethiop. yōm (= today), Aram. יְמָמָא, Syr. אִימָמָא (= day; in contradistinction to 'night'). cp. יְמָמָה. יוֹמָא.] Derivatives: יוֹמוֹן, יוֹמִי, יוֹמָם. יוֹמָן. יוֹמִיוֹמִי. cp. the second element in בַּרְיוֹם.

יוֹמָא m.n. PBH 1 day, the day. 2 name of a Mishnah, Tosephta and Talmud tractate in the order מוֹעֵד dealing with the laws referring to the Day of Atonement, hence lit. meaning 'the tractate dealing with the Day' by pre-eminence. [Aram., 'the day', i.e. 'the day by pre-eminence'. See יוֹם.]

יוֹמִי adj. MH daily. [Formed from יוֹם (= day), with suff. י.]

יוֹמְיוֹם adv. everyday, daily. [For [[illegible]] יוֹם־יוֹם (= day by day, every day, daily), repetition of יוֹם (= day).] Derivative: יוֹמְיוֹמִי.

יוֹמִית adv. daily. [Formed from יוֹם (= day), with adv. suff. ית.]

יוֹמָם adv. daily. [Formed from יוֹם (= day), with the adv. suff. ם. The same suff. appears in אָמְנָם. See אָמְנָה and words there referred to.]

הַשַּׁבָּת (word 54, verse 6)

שבת to cease, desist; to rest.

— Qal - 1 שָׁבַת he ceased, desisted; 2 he desisted from labor, rested; PBH 3 he observed the Sabbath, he spent the

Sabbath; NH **4** he struck, was on strike (properly 'he stopped working').

— **Niph.** - נִשְׁבַּת ceased.

— **Hiph.** - **1** הִשְׁבִּית he caused to cease, put an end to; **2** he removed, exterminated, destroyed; NH **3** he locked out (workers).

— **Hoph.** - הָשְׁבַּת PBH **1** was made to cease, was stopped; PBH **2** he ceased, perished; NH **3** was locked out (from his work). [JAram. שְׁבַת (= he rested; he observed the Sabbath), Arab. *sabata* (= he cut off, interrupted, ceased, rested). Akka. *shabātu*, which prob. means 'to complete, cease, desist'. cp. שֶׁבֶת [.¹] Derivatives: שַׁבָּת, מִשְׁבָּת ᴵᴵ, שַׁבָּת, שׁוֹבֶת, שְׁבִיתָה.

שַׁבָּת m.n. (pl. שַׁבָּתוֹת) **1** day of rest, Sabbath. **2** week, i.e. the seven days from Sunday to Sabbath (the JAram. and Syr. loan words also have both meanings: 'Sabbath', and 'week'; cp. also Gk. *sabbaton* and *sabbata*, which also have both these meanings). **3** feast, festival. **4** of years, i.e. a period of seven years. **5** the Sabbathical year, 'shemittah'. PBH **6** 'Sabbath', name of the first Mishnah and Talmud tractate of the order מוֹעֵד. [Derived from שבת and lit. meaning 'day of rest'. Aram.–Syr. שַׁבְּתָא, Arab. *sabt*, Ethiop. *sanbat*, are Heb. loan words. So are Gk. *sabbaton* (whence L. *sabbatum*, It. *sabato*, Old Provençal–Catalan *dissapte*, Spanish–Portuguese *sábado*, Serbo-Croatian *subota*, Czech and Slovak *sobota*, Russ. *subbóta*, etc.), and its Gk. vulgar var. *sambaton*, whence VL *sambatum*, Rumanian *sîmbătă*, Old Slavic *sǫbota*, Hungarian *szombat* (= Saturday), and *sambatīdiēs* (= the day of Sabbath), whence Old Fren. *sambe-di*, whence Fren. *samedi* (= Saturday), and prob. through the medium of the Gothic — the first element in Old High Ger. *sambaz-tac*, middle High Ger. *samez-tac*, Ger. *Samstag* (= Saturday). However, also Akka. *shabbatu, shappatu*, and Egypt. *smdt*, in the sense '15th day of the month' (but not in the meaning '7th day of the week', nor in that of '7th or 14th day of the month', as supposed by many scholars), are borrowed from ancient Hebrew. As shown by the above facts, the name שַׁבָּת and the idea it conveys are of Hebrew origin.] Derivatives: שַׁבָּתַאי, שַׁבָּתוֹן, שַׁבַּתִּי, שַׁבָּתִין. cp. סַמְבַּטְיוֹן.

וַיְקַדְּשֵׁהוּ (word 55, verse 6)

קדשׁ to be holy, be sacred.

— **Qal** - **1** קָדַשׁ was set apart, was consecrated; **2** was forbidden.

— **Niph.** - 1 נִקְדַּשׁ was hallowed, was sanctified, 2 was consecrated, was dedicated.

— **Pi.** - 1 קִדֵּשׁ he hallowed, sanctified; 2 he dedicated; consecrated; 3 he declared holy; 4 he cleansed, purified; 5 he devoted, assigned; PBH 6 he sanctified the Sabbath or the festivals; PBH 7 he pronounced the benediction of Kiddush; PBH 8 he made something prohibited; PBH 9 he betrothed, wedded.

— **Pu.** - 1 קֻדַּשׁ was hallowed, was sanctified; 2 was dedicated was consecrated; PBH 3 was betrothed, was wedded.

— **Hith.** - 1 הִתְקַדֵּשׁ he kept himself separated, purified himself; 2 he became sanctified; 3 he prepared himself; PBH 4 it was forbidden (as food).

— **Hiph.** - 1 הִקְדִּישׁ he set apart as holy, devoted as holy; 2 he regarded as holy; 3 he designated, appointed; NH 4 he dedicated.

— **Hoph.** - 1 הֻקְדַּשׁ was set apart as holy, was devoted as holy; MH 2 was regarded as holy; NH 3 was designated, was appointed; NH 4 was dedicated. [Related to Ugar. *qdsh* (= sanctuary), Phoen. קדש (= holy), מקדש (= sanctuary, holy place), Aram.-Syr. קַדֵּשׁ (= he hallowed, sanctified, consecrated), Palm. קדש (= to sanctify, consecrate), Arab. *qadusa* (= was holy, was pure), *quaddasa* (= he hallowed, sanctified, consecrated; he went to Jerusalem), *quds* (= purity, holiness), *al-quds* (= Jerusalem; lit.: 'the holy place'), Akka. *quddushu* (= to cleanse, to hallow, sanctify,), Aram.–Syr. קְדָשָׁא (= ear or nose ring; orig. 'holy thing'). The orig. meaning of this base prob. was 'to separate'.] Derivatives: קֹדֶשׁ. קָדֵשׁ, קְדֵשָׁה, קָדְשָׁה, קַדְשָׁא, קָדוֹשׁ. קָדִישׁ. הֶקְדֵּשׁ. הַקְדָּשָׁה, אַקְדָּשָׁה, הִתְקַדְּשׁוּת. מִקְדָּשׁ. מְקֻדָּשׁ. cp. the second element in קִדָּשִׁנוּן.

קֹדֶשׁ m.n. 1 holiness, sanctity. 2 a holy object. 3 a holy place. 4 the Holy Temple. [From קדש. cp. Aram. קוּדְשָׁא (= holiness), Syr. קוּדְשָׁא (= dedication, consecration), Ugar. *qdsh* (= holy place, sanctuary), *qdsh* (= a goddess), *qdsht* (name of a goddess).]

קֻדְשָׁא m.n. PBH holiness, used in the phrase קֻדְשָׁא בְּרִיךְ הוּא, 'the Holy One Blessed be He' (= Heb. הַקָּדוֹשׁ בָּרוּךְ הוּא). In Aram. the abstr. n. קֻדְשָׁא is used for the concrete קַדִּישָׁא. [Aram., from קדש. cp. Syr. קוּדְשָׁא (= sanctuary). cp. also קְדֵשׁ.]

קָדְשָׁה f.n. PBH **1** holiness, sanctity. PBH **2** 'Kedushshah', name of the third of the 'eighteen benedictions' in the 'Amidah' (so called because it ends with the words הָאֵל הַקָּדוֹשׁ). MH **3** portion inserted in the 'Amidah' between the second and third benedictions (so called because it contains the verse beginning with the words קָדוֹשׁ קָדוֹשׁ קָדוֹשׁ (= 'Holy, holy, holy', etc.). [Formed from קדשׁ with first suff. ה. For the form cp. גְּאֻלָּה (= redemption), from גאל¹ (= to redeem).]

ז Verse 7

ז כַּבֵּד אֶת־אָבִיךָ וְאֶת־אִמֶּךָ לְמַעַן יַאֲרִכוּן יָמֶיךָ עַל הָאֲדָמָה אֲשֶׁר־יְהוָה אֱלֹהֶיךָ נֹתֵן לָךְ׃

7 Honour thy father and thy mother, that thy days may be long upon the land which Yehovah thy God giveth thee.

כַּבֵּד (word 1, verse 7)

כבד¹ to be heavy, be weighty; to be honored.

— **Qal** - כָּבֵד **1** was heavy; **2** was burdensome; **3** was honored, was respected.

— **Niph.** - נִכְבַּד was honored, was distinguished.

— **Pi.** - כִּבֵּד **1** he honored, he respected; PBH **2** he offered refreshments.

— **Pu.** - כֻּבַּד **1** he was honored, was respected; NH **2** he was offered refreshments.

— **Hith.** - הִתְכַּבֵּד **1** he honored himself, exalted himself; PBH **2** he was honored; NH **3** he was offered refreshments.

— **Hiph.** - הִכְבִּיד **1** he made heavy; **2** he made burdensome; PBH **3** it grew worse (said of illness).

— **Hoph.** - הֻכְבַּד MH **1** it was heavy, was burdensome; NH **2** it became heavier.

— **Shiph. see** . - שִׁכְבֵּד. [Ugar. kbd (= to honor), Arab. kabad (= difficulty), kābada (= he struggled with difficulties), Ethiop. kabda (= was heavy), Akka. kabta (= heavy, weighty), kubbutu (= to honor).] Derivatives: כָּבֵד (adj.), כָּבֵד (n.), כֹּבֶד,

הַכְּבָדָה, הַכְבָּרוֹת, ¹ כְּבֵדָה, כְּבֵדוּת, כָּבוֹד, כָּבוּד, כָּבוּר,
הִתְכַּבְּדוּת, מְכֻבָּד, נִכְבָּד.

כָּבֵד ¹ adj. 1 heavy, burdensome. 2 great. 3 hard, difficult. 4 numerous. [From כבד ¹.] Derivative: כְּבֵדָה.

כֹּבֶד m.n. 1 heaviness, weight, gravity. 2 abundance, multitude. [From כבד ¹.]

כְּבֻדָּה f.n. 1 abundance, riches, wealth (a hapax legomenon in the Bible, occurring Jud. 18:21). MH 2 heaviness. [From כבד ¹.]

אֵת (word 2, verse 7)

אֵת ¹, אֶת prep. the mark of the accusative. Usually prefixed only to a definite noun, as in אֶת־הָאִישׁ (= the man). [Related to Moabite את, Phoen. אית (to be read אַיָּת), Aram. (also BAram.) and Syr. יָת (this latter mostly used as a noun), Egypt.-Aram. ית, Arab. 'iyyā (only used with a suff. to emphasize the pron.) and possibly also to Ethiop. kīyā (also used only with a suff. for the sake of emphasis). Orig. — as Syr. יָתָא, יָת — a noun in the sense of 'being, essence, existence'. The orig. form prob. was 'iwyath (cp. the Phoen. form), which ultimately derives from base אוה (= to sign, mark), whence also אוֹת (= sign).]

אָבִיךָ (word 3, verse 7)

אָב ¹ m.n. (pl. 1 אָבוֹת) father. 2 forefather, patriarch. 3 ancestor, progenitor. 4 head (of a family), leader, chief. 5 God. 6 master, teacher. 7 important, great. PBH 8 parent (male). PBH 9 basic factor, origin, source. NH 10 Father (of the Christian Church). [cp. Aram. אַבָּא, Ugar. 'b, Akka. abu, Arab. abu.] Derivatives: אַבְהוּת, אַבְהִי, אָבוֹת.

אַבָּא m.n. PBH 1 father, daddy. PBH 2 'Abba' — title of ancient Rabbis. NH 3 reverend (father). [Aram., properly 'the father' (= הָאָב in Heb.).]

אָבוֹת m.n. pl. 1 pl. of אָב (= father). 2 parents, patriarchs.

אַבְהוּת f.n. MH fatherhood, paternity. [Formed with suff. ות from אָב (= father). cp. אַבְהוּת.]

וְאֵת (word 4, verse 7)

אֵת ¹, אֶת prep. the mark of the accusative. Usually prefixed only to a definite noun, as in אֶת־הָאִישׁ (= the man). [Related to Moabite את, Phoen. אית (to be read אַיָּת), Aram. (also BAram.) and Syr. יָת (this latter mostly used as a noun), Egypt.-Aram.

וֹת, Arab. 'iyyā (only used with a suff. to emphasize the pron.) and possibly also to Ethiop. kīyā (also used only with a suff. for the sake of emphasis). Orig. — as Syr. יָת, יָתָא — a noun in the sense of 'being, essence, existence'. The orig. form prob. was 'iwyath (cp. the Phoen. form), which ultimately derives from base אוה (= to sign, mark), whence also אוֹת (= sign).]

אִמֶּךָ (word 5, verse 7)

אֵם f.n. (pl. אִמּוֹת, in PBH 1 אִמָּהוֹת mother. 2 matriarch. 3 metropolis, large city. PBH 4 womb. [Related to Aram. אֵם, אִמָּא, Syr. אֵם, אִמָּא, Arab. imm, umm, Ugar. 'ụm, Ethiop. 'em, Akka. ummu (= mother). These words prob. go back to emm(a), umm(a), a child's word for 'mother'. cp. אִמָּא, אִמָּהִי, אִמָּהוֹת and first element in אַמְנוֹן. cp. also אֵם II. Like אָב (= father) אָב also prob. derives from child's word.]

אִמָּא f.n. PBH mother, mama, mummy. [Aram. 'the mother, my mother', emphatic state of אֵם (= mother). See אֵם.]

לְמַעַן (word 6, verse 7)

לְמַעַן 1 in order that. 2 for the sake of. [Formed with pref. לְ and the noun מַעַן (which occurs only in the conj. לְמַעַן), a derivative of ענה II (= to be occupied, to busy oneself with).]

ענה II to be occupied, busy oneself.
    — Qal - עָנָה was occupied with, busied. [Syr. עְנָא (= was occupied with), Arab. 'anā, 'aniya (= was concerned), OSArab. עני (= to be concerned).] Derivatives: עִנְיָן, לְמַעַן.

יַאֲרִכוּן (word 7, verse 7)

ארך to be long.
    — Qal - אָרַךְ was long, lasted, lasted long, was protracted.
    — Hiph. - הֶאֱרִיךְ he lengthened, prolonged, protracted; it became long.
    — Hoph. - הָאֳרַךְ was lengthened.
    — Hith. - הִתְאָרֵךְ was lengthened, became long. [Related to Phoen. ארך, Aram. אֲרַךְ, Syr. אֱרַךְ (= was long), Ugar. ạrk, Akka. arāku (= to be long), Arab. 'araka, 'arika (= he delayed), OSArab. ארכן (= enduring), Ethiop. 'arga (= became old).] Derivatives: אֲרוּכָה, אָרִיךְ, אֲרִיכָא, אָרֹךְ, אֹרֶךְ, אַרְכָּת, אַרְכִּי, אַרְכָּן, הַאֲרָכָה, הִתְאָרְכוּת, מַאֲרִיךְ, מַאֲרָךְ, מָאֳרָךְ, מַרְכָּא, מְרָכָה.

אָרֹךְ adj. long. [From ארך.]

אֲרָךְ c. st. of אֹרֶךְ (q.v.).
אֹרֶךְ m.n. length, longitude. [From ארך. cp. Aram.-Syr. אוֹרְכָּא (= length). Derivative: אָרְכִּי.]
אַרְכָה f.n. lengthening, prolonging. [BAram. אַרְכָה (Dan. 4:24), אַרְכָא (Dan. 7:12), from אֲרָךְ (= was long). See ארך and first suff. ה. As shown by the passages quoted from Dan., the form אֲרָכָה, given in most dictionaries, is wrong.]

יָמֶיךָ (word 8, verse 7)

יוֹם m.n. (pl. **1 (**יָמִים day. **2** time. **3** year. [Related to BAram., Aram., and Syr. יוֹם, יוֹמָא, Ugar. ym, Arab. yaum, Akka. ūmu (= day), Ethiop. yōm (= today), Aram. יָמָא, Syr. אִימָמָא (= day; in contradistinction to 'night'). cp. יוֹמָא, יָמָה.] Derivatives: יוֹמוֹן, יוֹמִי, יוֹמָם, יוֹמָן, יוֹמִיוֹמִי. cp. the second element in בַּרְיוֹם.
יוֹמָא m.n. PBH **1** day, the day. **2** name of a Mishnah, Tosephta and Talmud tractate in the order מוֹעֵד dealing with the laws referring to the Day of Atonement, hence lit. meaning 'the tractate dealing with the Day' by pre-eminence. [Aram., 'the day', i.e. 'the day by pre-eminence'. See יוֹם.]
יוֹמִי adj. MH daily. [Formed from יוֹם (= day), with suff. י.]
יוֹמיוֹם adv. everyday, daily. [For [[illegible]] יוֹם־יוֹם (= day by day, every day, daily), repetition of יוֹם (= day).] Derivative: יוֹמִיוֹמִי.
יוֹמִית adv. daily. [Formed from יוֹם (= day), with adv. suff. ית.]
יוֹמָם adv. daily. [Formed from יוֹם (= day), with the adv. suff. ם. The same suff. appears in אָמְנָם. See אָמְנָם and words there referred to.]

עַל (word 9, verse 7)

עַל I **1** height, upper part. **2** , above. [From עלה. See עַל II.]
עַל II prep. **1** on, upon, above. **2** at, beside. **3** toward(s). **4** against. **5** concerning, about. **6** because of, on account of. **7** together with. [Shortened from עֲלֵי, which is preserved in poetry (see אֱלֵי and עֲדֵי), from עלה. Related to Phoen. and Moabite על, עלת, Aram., BAram.) and Syr. עַל, Ugar. 'l, Arab. 'alā, OSArab. עלי, Ethiop. lā'la, Akka. eli (= on, upon). cp. עַל I. cp. also עֲלִיָּה II.] Derivative: עַל.

הָאֲדָמָה (word 10, verse 7)

אֲדָמָה f.n. ground; soil, earth, land. [Prob. derived from **אדם** (= to be red), and orig. denoting 'the red arable ground'. cp. Akka. adnāti (= pieces of land, places of residence), which is a loan word from Heb. **אֲדָמוֹת**, the change of m to n being due to the assimilation of the m to the d. For the ending of **אֲדָמָה** see suff. **ה**. cp. **אָדָם**.]

אֲשֶׁר (word 11, verse 7)

אֲשֶׁר 1 who, which, that, that which. 2 in order that. [Related to Ugar. aṭr (= that which). cp. Moabite **אשר**. According to most scholars these words were originally nouns meaning 'trace, place', and are related to Arab. 'athira (= to leave traces), 'ithr (= trace, place), and to Aram. **אֲתַר, אַתְרָא**, Syr. **אַתְרָא** (= place). See **אָתַר**.]

יְהוָה (word 12, verse 7)

יְהֹוָה, יֱהוִֹה m.n. the proper name of God in the Bible, Tetragrammaton. [It prob. derives from **הוה** (= to be). The usual transliteration 'Jehovah' is based on the supposition that the Tetragrammaton is the imperfect Qal or Hiph'il of **הוה** and lit. means 'the one who is', 'the existing', resp. 'who calls into existence'. In reality, however, the pronunciation and literal meaning of the Tetragrammaton is unknown. cp. **יָהּ** ¹.]

אֱלֹהֶיךָ (word 13, verse 7)

אֱלוֹהַּ, אֱלֹהַּ m.n. 1 god. 2 God. [According to some scholars **אֱלוֹהַּ** is a back formation from the pl. **אֱלוֹהִים**, this latter being the plural of **אֵל** ¹ with the infix **ה**, which has an analogy in Heb. **אִמָּהוֹת**, pl. of **אֵם** (= mother), in Aram. **אבהת**, pl. of **אַב** (= father), **שְׁמָהָת**, pl. of **שְׁמָא** (= name), to which may be added Ugar. 'mht, pl. of 'mt (= Heb. **אָמָה**, 'bondwoman'), bhtm, pl. of bt (= Heb. **בַּיִת**, 'house'), and 'lht, pl. of 'lt (= goddess), f. of 'l (= Heb. **אֵל** ¹, 'god'). Others see in **אֱלוֹהַּ** the orig. form from which the pl. **אֱלוֹהִים** was formed. The consideration of the fact that **אֵל** has the pl. **אֵלִים**, shows that the second view is surely preferable to the first. Fleischer sees in **אֱלוֹהַּ** the derivative of base **אלה**, which he connects with Arab. aliha (= he sought refuge in anxiety), whence **אֱלוֹהַּ** would have meant orig. 'fear', hence 'object of fear or reverence', 'the revered one'. However, Nöldeke and others are prob. right when they maintain that the verb aliha in the above sense is prob. denominated from 'ilāh (= god).]

נָתַן (word 14, verse 7)

נתן to give.

— **Qal** - נָתַן **1** he gave; **2** he granted; **3** he permitted; **4** he gave up, delivered; **5** he put, set; **6** he appointed, established; **7** he made.

— **Niph.** - נִתַּן **1** was given; **2** was granted; **3** was permitted; **4** was given up, was delivered; **5** was put, was set; **6** was appointed, was established.

— **Hoph. (or pass. of Qal) imperf.** - יֻתַּן **1** will be given; **2** will be given up, will be delivered; **3** will be put, will be set. [Aram. נְתַן (= he gave), BAram. יִנְתֵּן, Syr. נְתַל (= he will give), Ugar. ytn (= to give), Akka. nadānu (= to give). cp. גְּרָה, נָדָן II, גְּרָנְיָה, מְדָה II. cp. also תנה II.] Derivatives: נְתִינָה I, נָתוּן, נָתִין, מַתָּן, מַתָּנָה, מַתָּת, מַתָּן, אֶתְנַן, נְתִינָה II.

לְךָ (word 15, verse 7)

לְךָ (in pause לָךְ) inflected m. pers. pron. meaning 'to thee', 'to you'. [Formed from לְ with suff. ךָ. cp. לְכָה II and the second element in מַלְךְ.]

לָךְ inflected f. pers. pron. meaning 'to thee', 'to you'. [Formed from לְ with suff. ךְ.]

ח Verse 8

ח לֹא תִּרְצָח:

תִּרְצָח

8 Thou shalt not murder.

לֹא (word 1, verse 8)

לֹא adv. no, not. [Related to Aram. (also BAram) and Syr. לָא, Ugar. l, Arab. lā, Akka. lā (= not, no). cp. לָאו, לָא, and the second element in אֶלָּא, אוּלַי, אִלּוּלֵא, לוּלֵא.]

לֹא combining form meaning 'non-'. [From לֹא (= no, not).]

לָא adv. PBH no, not. [Aram., related to Heb. לֹא (q.v.).]

תִּרְצָֽח (word 2, verse 8)

רצח to murder, slay.
- **Qal** - רָצַח he murdered, slew, killed.
- **Niph.** - נִרְצַח was murdered, was slain, was killed.
- **Pi.** - רִצַּח he murdered, assassinated.
- **Pu.** - רֻצַּח was murdered, was assassinated.
- **Hith.** - הִתְרַצַּח he committed suicide, killed himself.

[Arab. *raḍaha, raḍaḥa* (= he broke, bruised, crushed).]
Derivatives: רֶצַח, רַצְחָן, רוֹצֵחַ, רְצִיחָה, הֵרָצְחוּת, מְרַצֵּחַ.

רֶצַח m.n. MH **1** murder, slaughter. **2** in the Bible used only figuratively in the sense of 'shattering' (Ps. 42:11).

רַצְחָן m.n. PBH murderer. [Formed from רֶצַח (see רצח) with agential suff. ן.] Derivatives: רַצְחָנוּת, רַצְחָנִי.

רַצְחָנוּת f.n. PBH murderousness. [Formed from רַצְחָן with suff. וּת.]

רַצְחָנִי adj. NH murderous. [Formed from רַצְחָן with suff. י.]

רְצִיחָה f.n. PBH **1** capital punishment, execution. **2** murder, assassination. [Verbal n. of רָצַח. See רצח and first suff. ה.]

ט Verse 9

ט לֹא תִּנְאָֽף׃

9 Thou shalt not commit adultery.

לֹא (word 1, verse 9)

לֹא adv. no, not. [Related to Aram. (also BAram) and Syr. לָא, Ugar. *l*, Arab. *lā*, Akka. *lā* (= not, no). cp. לָא, לָאו, and the second element in אֶלָּא אוּלַי, אִלּוּלֵא, לוּלֵא.]

לֹא combining form meaning 'non-'. [From לֹא (= no, not).]

לָא adv. PBH no, not. [Aram., related to Heb. לֹא (q.v.).]

תִּנְאָֽף (word 2, verse 9)

נִאוּף m.n. adultery, prostitution (in the Bible it occurs only in the pl.). [From נאף.]

נאף to commit adultery.
- Qal - נָאַף he committed adultery with.
- Pi. - נִאֵף he committed adultery.
- Hiph. - הִנְאִיף PBH he caused adultery. [Aram. נְאַף (= he committed adultery), Arab. nahaba (= he copulated). cp. Egypt. nhp (= he copulated).] Derivatives: נִאוּף, נַאֲפוּף, מְנָאֵף.

נַאֲפוּף m.n. adultery, prostitution (a hapax legomenon in the Bible, occurring Hos. 2:4 in the form נַאֲפוּפֶיהָ, 'her adulteries'). [From נאף.] Derivative: נַאֲפוּפִי.

נַאֲפוּפִי adj. NH adulterous. [Formed from נַאֲפוּף with suff. י.]

׳ Verse 10

י לֹא תִּגְנֹב׃

10 Thou shalt not steal.

לֹא (word 1, verse 10)

לֹא adv. no, not. [Related to Aram. (also BAram) and Syr. לָא, Ugar. l, Arab. lā, Akka. lā (= not, no). cp. לָא, לָאוּ, and the second element in אֶלָּא, אוּלַי, אִלּוּלֵא, לוּלֵא.]

לֹא combining form meaning 'non-'. [From לֹא (= no, not).]

לָא adv. PBH no, not. [Aram., related to Heb. לֹא (q.v.).]

תִּגְנֹב (word 2, verse 10)

גנב to steal, rob, cheat, delude.
- Qal - 1 גָּנַב he stole, he robbed; 2 he cheated, deceived, deluded.
- Niph. - נִגְנַב was stolen.
- Pi. - 1 גִּנֵּב he stole frequently, was a habitual thief; PBH 2 he slipped in, he slipped out.
- Pu. - גֻּנַּב he was stolen, it was stolen.
- Hith. - הִתְגַּנֵּב he slipped in.
- Hiph. - הִגְנִיב he passed on stealthily, he introduced surreptitiously, he smuggled in.

— Hoph. - הֻגְנַב he was passed on stealthily, he was smuggled in. [Aram. גְּנַב, Arab. janaba (= put aside), from janb (= side).] Derivatives: גֻּנָּב, גֶּנֶב, גְּנֵבָה, גַּנָּב.

גַּנָּב m.n. thief. [Derived from גנב, according to the pattern פַּעָל.] Derivatives: גַּנָּבוּת, גַּנָּבִי, and perhaps also גַּנְבְתָן.

גֶּנֶב m.n. PBH theft. [From גנב (q.v.).]

גְּנֵבָה f.n. theft, stolen goods, pilferage. [Formed from גנב with suff. ה.] Derivative: גְּנֵבוּת.

גְּנֵבוּת f.n. PBH theft. [Formed from גְּנֵבָה with suff. וּת.]

גַּנָּבוּת f.n. NH thievery. [Formed from גַּנָּב with suff. וּת.]

גַּנָּבִי adj. NH thievish. [Formed from גַּנָּב with suff. י.]

גַּנְבָן m.n. NH a thievish person, sneak thief. [Formed from גַּנָּב with suff. ן.] Derivatives: גַּנְבָנִי, גַּנְבָנוּת.

גַּנְבָנִי adj. NH thievish. [Formed from גַּנְבָן with suff. י.]

גַּנְבָנוּת f.n. NH thievery. [Formed from גַּנְבָן with suff. וּת.]

גְּנֻבְתִי adj. stolen (a hapax legomenon in the Bible, occurring Gen. 31:39). [Obsolete form of c. st. of גְּנוּבָה, f. of גָּנוּב (q.v.).]

גַּנְבְתָן adj. NH sneak thief, petty thief. [Formed from גַּנָּב or from גְּנֵבָה with adj. suff. ן or with dimin. suff. ן.]

יא Verse 11

יא לֹא־תַעֲנֶה בְרֵעֲךָ עֵד שָׁקֶר׃

11 Thou shalt not bear false witness against thy neighbour.

לֹא (word 1, verse 11)

לֹא adv. no, not. [Related to Aram. (also BAram) and Syr. לָא, Ugar. l, Arab. lā, Akka. lā (= not, no). cp. לָא, לָאוּ, and the second element in אֵלָא, אוּלַי, אִלּוּלֵא, לוּלֵא.]

לֹא combining form meaning 'non-'. [From לֹא (= no, not).]

לָא adv. PBH no, not. [Aram., related to Heb. לֹא (q.v.).]

תַּעֲנֶה (word 2, verse 11)

עֵנה ᴵ to answer, reply, respond.

— **Qal** - עָנָה v. **1** he answered, replied, responded; **2** he responded as a witness, testified.

— **Niph.** - נַעֲנָה **1** was answered, received an answer; **2** he made answer, replied. [BAram. עֲנָה, Aram. עֲנָא, Syr. עְנָא (= he answered; he heard), Ugar. ' ny (= to answer).] Derivatives: מַעֲנֶה, יַעַן ᴵ, הַעֲנוּת. יַעַן ᴵᴵ, עֲנָיָה, prob. also עֵת.

בְּרֵעֶךָ (word 3, verse 11)

רֵעַ ᴵ m.n. **1** friend, companion, associate. **2** fellowman. [Related to Akka. ru'u (= companion), ruttu (= female companion), Ugar. r', Bedouin rā'ī (= companion), and to Arab. ur'uwwa, Ethiop. 'ar'ūt (= yoke).] Derivative: רעה ᴵᴵ.

רעה ᴵᴵ to associate with, keep company with.

— **Qal** - רָעָה he associated with, kept company with (in the Bible occurring only in the form of the part.).

— **Pi.** - רֵעָה he associated with, kept company with.

— **Hith.** - הִתְרָעָה he made friendship with. [Prob. denominated from רֵעַ (= friend, companion). According to some scholars רעה ᴵᴵ represents a sense enlargement of רעה ᴵ.] Derivatives: הִתְרָעוּת, מֵרֵעַ ᴵ, רֵעָה, רַעְיָה, רֵעוּת רְעוּת.

רֵעָה m.n. friend, companion. [From רעה ᴵᴵ. According to some scholars the noun רֵעָה represents the orig. form qital; according to others the orig. form is qittal. cp. רֵעָה. cp. also רֵעַ.]

רֵעָה f.n. female friend, companion, fellow woman. [f. of רֵעֶה. cp. רְעוּת.]

רֵעוּת f.n. PBH friendship. [Formed from רֵעַ ᴵ with suff. וּת.]

רְעוּת ᴵ f.n. female friend, companion; fellow woman. [Formed from רעה ᴵᴵ. cp. the proper name רוּת (= Ruth), which is prob. a contraction of רְעוּת.]

רַעְיָה f.n. **1** female friend, beloved. NH **2** married woman, wife, spouse. [From רעה ᴵᴵ. For the ending see first suff. ה.]

עֵד (word 4, verse 11)

עֵד ᴵ m.n. **1** witness. **2** testimony. [From עוד.] Derivative: עֵדָה ᴵᴵ.

עֵדָה ᴵᴵ f.n. witness (f. of עֵד ᴵ).

עֵדָה III f.n. testimony. [From עוּד.]

עֵדוּת f.n. PBH **1** testimony. **2** the testimony of the Decalogue, the Decalogue. PBH **3** evidence. [Prob. from עוּד and lit. meaning 'exhorting sign', 'reminder'. Several other scholars derive עֵדוּת from יעד (= to appoint, to fix), and compare Akka. *adē* (= statements, commandments). cp. late L. *testimōnium* (= testimony of the Decalogue, the Decalogue), from L. *testimōnium* (= evidence, attestation, testimony), which is a loan translation of Heb. עֵדוּת. See 'testimony' in my CEDEL.]

שֶׁקֶר (word 5, verse 11)

שׁקר to lie, deal falsely.

— **Qal** - שָׁקַר he lied, dealt falsely.
— **Pi.** - שִׁקֵּר he lied, dealt falsely, swindled, defrauded.
— **Pu.** - שֻׁקַּר was proved a lie, was proved false.
— **Hith.** - הִשְׁתַּקֵּר was proved a liar. [Aram.–Syr. שְׁקַר, Pa. שַׁקֵּר (= he lied, deceived, dealt falsely), JAram., Mand. שִׁקְרָא, Syr. שׁוּקְרָא (= lie, falsehood), Arab. *suqar* and *shuqar*, Akka. *tashqirtu* (= lie). Arab. *suqar* and *shuqar* are Aram. loan words.] Derivatives: שֶׁקֶר, שַׁקָּר, שַׁקְרָן, שָׁקוּר, שְׁקִירָה, מְשַׁקֵּר. cp. שִׁקְרָא.

שֶׁקֶר m.n. lie, falsehood, deception (by words). [From שׁקר.] Derivatives: שִׁקְרָאִי, שִׁקְרוּת, שִׁקְרִי.

שַׁקָּר m.n. PBH liar. [Coined from שִׁקֵּר (= he lied), Pi. of שׁקר, according to the pattern פַּעָל, used to form nomina opificis. Accordingly שַׁקָּר denotes a habitual liar, i.e. one who is engaged in lying as if it were his profession. cp. שַׁקְרָן.]

שִׁקְרָא m.n. PBH lie. [JAram., corresponding to Heb. שֶׁקֶר (q.v.), more exactly to הַשֶּׁקֶר (= the lie), since שִׁקְרָא is the emphatic state although it is generally used in the sense of the abs. state.]

שִׁקְרָאִי m.n. PBH liar. [Formed from שֶׁקֶר with suff. ַאי.]

שִׁקְרוּת f.n. MH lying. [Formed from שֶׁקֶר with suff. וּת.]

שִׁקְרִי adj. MH based on a lie, false. [Formed from שֶׁקֶר with suff. ִי.]

שַׁקְרָן m.n. PBH liar. [Formed from שִׁקֵּר, Pi. of שׁקר. cp. שַׁקָּר. For the difference in meaning between these two nouns see second suff. ן.] Derivatives: שַׁקְרָנוּת, שַׁקְרָנִי.

שַׁקְרָנוּת f.n. MH mendacity. [Formed from שַׁקְרָן with suff. וּת.]

שַׁקְרָנִי adj. MH mendacious. [Formed from שַׁקְרָן with suff. ִי.]

יב Verse 12

יב לֹא תַחְמֹד בֵּית רֵעֶךָ לֹא־תַחְמֹד אֵשֶׁת רֵעֶךָ וְעַבְדּוֹ וַאֲמָתוֹ וְשׁוֹרוֹ וַחֲמֹרוֹ וְכֹל אֲשֶׁר לְרֵעֶךָ׃

12 Thou shalt not covet thy neighbour's house; thou shalt not covet thy neighbour's wife, nor his man-servant, nor his maid-servant, nor his ox, nor his ass, nor any thing that is thy neighbour's.

לֹא (word 1, verse 12)

לֹא adv. no, not. [Related to Aram. (also BAram) and Syr. לָא, Ugar. *l*, Arab. *lā*, Akka. *lā* (= not, no). cp. לָא, לָאו, and the second element in אֶלָּא, אוּלַי, אִלּוּלֵא, לוּלֵא.]

לֹא combining form meaning 'non-'. [From לֹא (= no, not).]

לָא adv. PBH no, not. [Aram., related to Heb. לֹא (q.v.).]

תַחְמֹד (word 2, verse 12)

חמד to desire.

— **Qal** - חָמַד he desired, took pleasure in, wished, coveted.
— **Niph.** - נֶחְמַד was desired, was desirable.
— **Pi.** - חִמֵּד 1 he desired greatly; MH 2 he pampered.
— **Nith.** - נִתְחַמֵּד he desired, longed for.
— **Hiph.** - הֶחְמִיד he caused to desire, made desirable.

[Aram. חֲמַד (= he desired), Ugar. *hmd* (= to be pleasant), Arab. *ḥamida* (= he praised).] Derivatives: חֶמֶד, חֹמֶד, חֶמְדָּה, חֶמְדּוֹן, חַמְדָּן, חָמוּד, תֶּמֶד, חֲמִידָה, מַחְמָד, מַחֲמַדִּים, נֶחְמָד, תַּחֲמוּד.

חֶמֶד m.n. desire, delight, grace, charm. [From חמד.]

חֹמֶד m.n. NH loveliness, grace; darling. [From חמד.]

חֶמְדָּה f.n. desire, a desirable thing, object of delight. [Formed from חמד with first suff. ה.]

חֶמְדּוֹן m.n. MH desire, delight, grace. [Formed from חמד with וֹן, suff. forming abstract nouns.]

חַמְדָן adj. MH lustful, covetous, greedy. [Formed from חמד with adj. suff. ן.] Derivatives: חַמְדָנוּת, חַמְדָנִי.

חַמְדָנוּת f.n. NH lustfulness, covetousness, greed. [Formed from חַמְדָן with suff. וּת.]

חַמְדָנִי adj. NH lustful, covetous, greedy. [Formed from חַמְדָן with adj. suff. י.]

חָמוּד adj. desirable, delightful, lovely. [Pass. part. of חָמַד. See חמד.] Derivative: חָמוּדוֹן.

חִמוּד m.n. PBH desire, lust. [Verbal n. of חִמֵּד (= he desired greatly), Pi. of חמד.]

חָמוּדוֹן adj. NH lovely, darling. [Formed from חָמוּד with dimin. suff. וֹן.]

חֲמוּדוֹת f.n. pl. precious articles, desired things. [Formally f. pl. of חָמוּד, pass. part. of חמד.]

חֲמִידָה f.n. MH desire, covetousness. [Verbal n. of חָמַד. See חמד and first suff. ה.]

בַּיִת (word 3, verse 12)

בֵּי m.n. house, home (occurring in numerous phrases quoted from Talmud or Midrash, as in בֵּי־כְנִשְׁתָּא, 'synagogue'; בֵּי־מַסּוּתָא, 'bath'; בֵּי־רַב, 'school'; בֵּי־שֻׁתָּפֵי, 'partnership'). Aram., c. st. of בֵּיתָא (= house). See בַּיִת.]

בַּיִת m.n. (pl. בָּתִּים) 1 house, home, family. 2 school. MH 3 stanza (of a poem). [Related to Akka. bītu, Ugar. bt, Phoen. בת, Aram. בֵּיתָא, Aram.–Syr. בַּת, Arab. bayt.] Derivatives: בֵּית, בית, בַּיָּת, בֵּיתִי, בֵּיתָנִי.

רֵעֶךָ (word 4, verse 12)

רֵעַ I m.n. 1 friend, companion, associate. 2 fellowman. [Related to Akka. ru'u (= companion), ruttu (= female companion), Ugar. r', Bedouin rā'ī (= companion), and to Arab. ur'uwwa, Ethiop. 'ar'ūt (= yoke).] Derivative: רעה II.

רעה II to associate with, keep company with.
— Qal - רָעָה he associated with, kept company with (in the Bible occurring only in the form of the part.).
— Pi. - רֵעָה he associated with, kept company with.
— Hith. - הִתְרָעָה he made friendship with. [Prob.

denominated from רֵעַ (= friend, companion). According to some scholars רעה II represents a sense enlargement of רעה I.] Derivatives: הִתְרָעוּת, מֵרֵעַ, רֵעַ I, רֵעָה, רַעְיָה, רְעוּת רֵעוּת.

רֵעָה m.n. friend, companion. [From רעה II. According to some scholars the noun רֵעֶה represents the orig. form *qital*; according to others the orig. form is *qittal*. cp. רֵעָה. cp. also רֵעַ.]

רֵעָה f.n. female friend, companion, fellow woman. [f. of רֵעֶה. cp. רְעוּת.]

רֵעוּת f.n. PBH friendship. [Formed from רֵעַ I with suff. וּת.]

רְעוּת I f.n. female friend, companion; fellow woman. [Formed from רעה II. cp. the proper name רוּת (= Ruth), which is prob. a contraction of רְעוּת.]

רַעְיָה f.n. **1** female friend, beloved. NH **2** married woman, wife, spouse. [From רעה II. For the ending see first suff. ה.]

לֹא (word 5, verse 12)

לֹא adv. no, not. [Related to Aram. (also BAram) and Syr. לָא, Ugar. *l*, Arab. *lā*, Akka. *lā* (= not, no). cp. לָאו, לָא, and the second element in אֶלָּא, אוּלַי, אֱלוּלֵא, לוּלֵא.]

לֹא combining form meaning 'non-'. [From לֹא (= no, not).]

לָא adv. PBH no, not. [Aram., related to Heb. לֹא (q.v.).]

תַחְמֹד (word 6, verse 12)

חמד to desire.

— **Qal** - חָמַד he desired, took pleasure in, wished, coveted.
— **Niph.** - נֶחְמַד was desired, was desirable.
— **Pi.** - חִמֵּד **1** he desired greatly; MH **2** he pampered.
— **Nith.** - נִתְחַמֵּד he desired, longed for.
— **Hiph.** - הֶחֱמִיד he caused to desire, made desirable.

[Aram. חֲמַד (= he desired), Ugar. *ḥmd* (= to be pleasant), Arab. *ḥamida* (= he praised).] Derivatives: חֶמֶד, חֹמֶד, חֶמְדָּה, חֶמְדּוֹן, חַמְדָּן, חָמוּד, חִמּוּד, חֲמִידָה, מַחְמָד, מַחֲמָדִים, נֶחְמָד, תַּחֲמוּד.

חֶמֶד m.n. desire, delight, grace, charm. [From חמד.]

חֹמֶד m.n. NH loveliness, grace; darling. [From חמד.]

חֶמְדָּה f.n. desire, a desirable thing, object of delight. [Formed from חמד with first suff. ה.]

חֶמְדּוֹן m.n. MH desire, delight, grace. [Formed from חמד with וֹן, suff. forming abstract nouns.]

חַמְדָן adj. MH lustful, covetous, greedy. [Formed from חמד with adj. suff. ן.] Derivatives: חַמְדָנוּת, חַמְדָנִי.

חַמְדָנוּת f.n. NH lustfulness, covetousness, greed. [Formed from חַמְדָן with suff. וּת.]

חַמְדָנִי adj. NH lustful, covetous, greedy. [Formed from חַמְדָן with adj. suff. י.]

חָמוּד adj. desirable, delightful, lovely. [Pass. part. of חָמַד. See חמד.] Derivative: חָמוּדוֹן.

חִמּוּד m.n. PBH desire, lust. [Verbal n. of חִמֵּד (= he desired greatly), Pi. of חמד.]

חָמוּדוֹן adj. NH lovely, darling. [Formed from חָמוּד with dimin. suff. וֹן.]

חֲמוּדוֹת f.n. pl. precious articles, desired things. [Formally f. pl. of חָמוּד, pass. part. of חמד.]

חֲמִידָה f.n. MH desire, covetousness. [Verbal n. of חָמַד. See חמד and first suff. ה.]

אֵשֶׁת (word 7, verse 12)

אִשָּׁה f.n. (pl. נָשִׁים, also, very rare, אִשּׁוֹת) woman, wife. [Related to Aram. אִנְתְּתָא, אִתְּתָא, Syr. אַתְּתָא, Nab. אתתה, Ugar. aṯṯ, Arab. 'unthā, Ethiop. 'anest, Akka. ashshatu, OSArab. אנתת (= woman, wife). The origin of these words is uncertain. They are not related to אִישׁ and אֱנוֹשׁ.]

רֵעֶךָ (word 8, verse 12)

רֵעַ I m.n. 1 friend, companion, associate. 2 fellowman. [Related to Akka. ru'u (= companion), ruttu (= female companion), Ugar. r', Bedouin rā'ī (= companion), and to Arab. ur'uwwa, Ethiop. 'ar'ūt (= yoke).] Derivative: רעה II.

רעה II to associate with, keep company with.

— Qal - רָעָה he associated with, kept company with (in the Bible occurring only in the form of the part.).

— Pi. - רֵעָה he associated with, kept company with.

— Hith. - הִתְרָעָה he made friendship with. [Prob. denominated from רֵעַ (= friend, companion). According to some scholars רעה II represents a sense enlargement of רעה I.] Derivatives: הִתְרָעוּת, מֵרֵעַ, רֵעָה, רֵעֶה, רַעְיָה, רֵעוּת, רְעוּת.

רֵעֶה m.n. friend, companion. [From רעה II. According to some scholars the noun רֵעֶה represents the orig. form *qital;* according to others the orig. form is *qittal.* cp. רֵעָה. cp. also רֵעַ.]

רֵעָה f.n. female friend, companion, fellow woman. [f. of רֵעֶה. cp. רְעוּת.]

רֵעוּת f.n. PBH friendship. [Formed from רֵעַ I with suff. וּת.]

רְעוּת I f.n. female friend, companion; fellow woman. [Formed from רעה II. cp. the proper name רוּת (= Ruth), which is prob. a contraction of רְעוּת.]

רַעְיָה f.n. 1 female friend, beloved. NH 2 married woman, wife, spouse. [From רעה II. For the ending see first suff. ה.]

וְעָבְדוּ (word 9, verse 12)

עבד to work; to serve.

— **Qal.** - עָבַד v. 1 he worked, labored, tilled, cultivated (the soil); 2 he served. 3 he worshiped.

— **Niph.** - נֶעֱבַד. 1 was tilled, was cultivated; PBH 2 was worshiped; PBH 3 was dressed, was tanned (said of hides).

— **Pi.** - עִבֵּד 1 he cultivated; 2 he dressed, tanned (said of hides); he elaborated, adapted.

— **Pu.** - עֻבַּד 1 was worked; PBH 2 was dressed, was tanned (said of hides); NH 3 was elaborated, adapted.

— **Nith.** - נִתְעַבֵּד, הִתְעַבֵּד 1 was worked; 2 was dressed, was tanned (said of hides); NH 3 was adapted.

— **Shiph. (see** - שִׁעְבֵּד**).**

— **Hiph.** - הֶעֱבִיד 1 he caused to work, made to serve; 2 he enslaved.

— **Hoph.** - הָעֳבַד was made to serve. [Aram. (also BAram.) and Syr. עֲבַד (= he worked, did, performed, made), whence BAram. עֲבַד, Aram. and Syr. עַבְדָּא (= slave, servant), Ugar. *bd* (= to work, serve, worship), Arab. *'abada* (= he served, worshiped, obeyed), whence *'abd* (= slave, worshiper), OSArab. עבד (= servant), Ethiop. *'abbata* (= he imposed forced labor), Akka. *abdu* (= slave). Derivatives: עָבַד, עֶבֶד, עֲבֻדָּה, עַבְדָן, עַבְדוּת, עָבוּד, עֲבוֹדָה, עוֹבֵד, הַעֲבָדָה, עָבַד, עַבְדָּא, עֶבְדָּא, cp. מַעֲבָד, מַעְבָּדָה, מַעֲבִיד, תַּעֲבוּד.

עֶבֶד m.n. 1 servant; 2 slave, bondman; 3 worshipper. [From עבד.]

עַבְדָּא m.n. PBH servant; slave. [Aram. and Syr., denominated from עֶבֶד (q.v.). cp. עֶבֶד.]

עֶבְדָּא PBH, עֲבָדָה NH 1 deed, act. 2 occurrence. 3 fact. [From Aram. עוֹבָדָא, Syr. עֲבָדָא (= work, fact, deed), from עֲבַד (= he did).] Derivative: עֶבְדָּתִי.

עֲבֻדָּה f.n. household servants (occurring in the Bible only Gen. 26:14 and Job 1:3). [From עבד.]

עַבְדוּת f.n. slavery, servitude, bondage (in the Bible occurring only Ez. 9:8 following and Neh. 9:17). [Formed from עבד with suff. וּת. cp. Syr. עַבְדּוּתָא (of s.m.).] Derivative: עַבְדוּתִי.

עַבְדוּתִי adj. NH slavish, servile. [Formed from עַבְדוּת with suff. י.]

עֲבוֹדָה f.n. 1 work, labor. 2 deed, action. 3 service. 4 divine service, worship. PBH 5 'abodah', the first of the last three benedictions of the 'Amidah'. MH 6 liturgy for the 'Musaph' service on the Day of Atonement. [From עבד.]

וַאֲמָתוֹ (word 10, verse 12)

אָמָה f.n. (pl. אֲמָהוֹת) maidservant, handmaid, female slave. [Related to Phoen. אמת. Aram.-Syr. אַמְתָא. Ugar. amt, Arab. 'amah, Ethiop. 'amat, Akka. amtu (= handmaid, female slave).]

אַמְהוּת f.n. PBH condition of a maid-servant or handmaid. [Formed from אָמָה with suff. וּת.]

אֲמָהוֹת f.n. pl. handmaids, slaves. [Pl. of אָמָה.]

וְשׁוֹרוֹ (word 11, verse 12)

שׁוֹר m.n. (pl. שְׁוָרִים) 1 ox, bull. PBH 2 Taurus (astronomy). [Related to Aram. תּוֹרָא (= ox, bull, steer), OSArab. תור, Arab. shaur, Ugar. tr (= ox, bull, steer), Phoen. thor (= the divine steer), Akka. shūru (of s.m.). cp. תּוֹרָא. Gk. tauros, L. taurus, Old Slavic turŭ (= bull), Lithuanian tawras (= aurochs), etc. are Sem. loan words. See 'Taurus' in my CEDEL and words there referred to.]

וַחֲמֹרוֹ (word 12, verse 12)

חֲמוֹר m. & f.n. ass, donkey. [Related to Aram.-Syr. חֲמָרָא, Ugar. ḥmr, Arab. ḥimār, Akka. imēru (= ass, donkey). These words prob. mean lit. 'the red animal', and derive from base חמר II. cp. יַחְמוּר (= roebuck) which is prob. of the same origin. For sense development cp. Spanish burro (= donkey), from Late L. burricus, būricus (= a small horse), from burrus (= red), from

Gk. *purros* (= flame-colored, yellowish red).] Derivatives:
חֲמוֹרָה, חֲמוֹרוֹן, חֲמוֹרִי, חמר, חַמֶּרֶת.

חֲמוֹרָה f.n. PBH a she-ass. [f. of חֲמוֹר. For the ending see first suff. ה.]

חֲמוֹרוֹן m.n. NH a little ass. [Formed from חֲמוֹר with dimin. suff. וֹן.]

חֲמוֹרִי adj. MH like an ass, asinine, foolish. [Formed from חֲמוֹר with adj. suff. י.] Derivative: חֲמוֹרִיּוּת.

חֲמוֹרִיּוּת f.n. NH the nature of an ass, asininity, foolishness. [Formed from חֲמוֹרִי with suff. וּת.]

וְכֹל (word 13, verse 12)

כֹּל m.n. all, whole, the whole of. [From כלל I (= to comprehend, include). cp. Aram. (also BAram.) כֹּל, כָּל, Ugar. *kl*, Arab. *kull*, Ethiop. *kellā*, OSArab. כל, Akka. *kullatu* (= the whole of). See כְּלִי.]

אֲשֶׁר (word 14, verse 12)

אֲשֶׁר 1 who, which, that, that which. 2 in order that. [Related to Ugar. a̱tr (= that which). cp. Moabite אשר. According to most scholars these words were originally nouns meaning 'trace, place', and are related to Arab. 'athira (= to leave traces), 'ithr (= trace, place), and to Aram. אֲתַר, אַתְרָא, Syr. אַתְרָא (= place). See אֲתַר.]

לְרֵעֶךָ (word 15, verse 12)

רֵעַ I m.n. 1 friend, companion, associate. 2 fellowman. [Related to Akka. *ru'u* (= companion), *ruttu* (= female companion), Ugar. *r'*, Bedouin *rā'ī* (= companion), and to Arab. *ur'uwwa*, Ethiop. *'ar'ūt* (= yoke).] Derivative: רעה II.

רעה II to associate with, keep company with.
— Qal - רָעָה he associated with, kept company with (in the Bible occurring only in the form of the part.).
— Pi. - רֵעָה he associated with, kept company with.
— Hith. - הִתְרָעָה he made friendship with. [Prob. denominated from רֵעַ (= friend, companion). According to some scholars רעה II represents a sense enlargement of רעה I.] Derivatives: הִתְרָעוּת, מֵרֵעַ, רֵעָה, רֵעֶה, רַעְיָה, רֵעוּת, רְעוּת.

רֵעֶה m.n. friend, companion. [From רעה II. According to some scholars the noun רֵעֶה represents the orig. form *qital;* according to others the orig. form is *qittal.* cp. רֵעָה. cp. also רֵעַ.]

רָעָה f.n. female friend, companion, fellow woman. [f. of רֵעֶה. cp. רְעוּת.]

רֵעוּת f.n. PBH friendship. [Formed from רֵעַ ᴵ with suff. וּת.]

רְעוּת ᴵ f.n. female friend, companion; fellow woman. [Formed from רעה ᴵᴵ. cp. the proper name רוּת (= Ruth), which is prob. a contraction of רְעוּת.]

רַעְיָה f.n. 1 female friend, beloved. NH 2 married woman, wife, spouse. [From רעה ᴵᴵ. For the ending see first suff. ה.

Epilogue

It has been my intention to present the Ten Commandments as rendered in the Leningrad Codex in such a way to be used as a reference as well to be able to help you to know and understand each word in its context.

I highly recommend that you consider having a daily reading and meditation on the Ten Commandments. I believe doing so will help enable you to truly come to know יְהֹוָה [Yehovah] in a very personal way, and, in doing so, you will have discovered "The Real God Code!"

I have provided a pdf downloadable link, on my website, so that you can print out "The Ten Commandments in the Leningrad Codex" to have for your own use.[42] That pdf page has the Leningrad Codex verse image on the right, the Hebrew font based verse to the left, and the modified English translation of the Jewish Publication Society of 1917 underneath the verse in the Hebrew font.

Of course, you can use this book as that reference as well!

I would be remiss if I did not mention a further discipline you could take upon yourself if you don't already have it. That is, I highly recommend that you regularly read the Hebrew–language based Jewish Scriptures such as those found on my website![43]

Believe it or not, I also recommend that you consider becoming familiar with the Christian New Testament, since Western Civilization has, historically, been so greatly influenced by it!

There is a Bible reading plan I use myself, which I gladly recommend to you.[44] By following that particular plan, you will read through the Hebrew–language based Jewish Scriptures (i.e. the Tanakh) once a year and the Christian New Testament twice.

---

[42] Robert Pill, 'The 10 Commandments In Exodus 20 In The Leningrad Codex', The-Iconoclast, last modified 24 Mar 2021, https://www.the-iconoclast.org/images/Exodus_20_LeningradCodex/Exodus20v1-12InLeningradCodex_Printable.pdf
[43] Robert Pill, 'Leningrad Codex Hebrew JPS 1917 English Tanakh', The-Iconoclast, last modified 17 May 2021, https://www.the-iconoclast.org/resources/tanakh/
[44] "Read / Hear Scripture in a Year," Congregation Sar Shalom, last modified 10 Oct 2010, http://sarshalom.us/resources/read_scripture.php
"Read / Hear Scripture In-A-Year," Congregation Sar Shalom, last modified 10 Oct 2010, http://sarshalom.us/resources/scripture/read_scripture-in-a-year.pdf

May יְהוָה [Yehovah] truly bless you as you seek Him with your whole heart!

I think the following passages found in Isaiah 55, beginning with "Seek Ye Yehovah while He may be found" is a fitting way to end this chapter.

Isaiah 55:6-13

ו דִּרְשׁוּ יְהוָה בְּהִמָּצְאוֹ קְרָאֻהוּ בִּהְיוֹתוֹ קָרוֹב:

6 Seek ye Yehovah while He may be found, call ye upon Him while He is near;

ז יַעֲזֹב רָשָׁע דַּרְכּוֹ וְאִישׁ אָוֶן מַחְשְׁבֹתָיו וְיָשֹׁב אֶל־יְהוָה וִירַחֲמֵהוּ וְאֶל־אֱלֹהֵינוּ כִּי־יַרְבֶּה לִסְלוֹחַ:

7 Let the wicked forsake his way, and the man of iniquity his thoughts; and let him return unto Yehovah, and He will have compassion upon him, and to our God, for He will abundantly pardon.

ח כִּי לֹא מַחְשְׁבוֹתַי מַחְשְׁבוֹתֵיכֶם וְלֹא דַרְכֵיכֶם דְּרָכָי נְאֻם יְהוָה:

8 For My thoughts are not your thoughts, neither are your ways My ways, saith Yehovah.

ט כִּי־גָבְהוּ שָׁמַיִם מֵאָרֶץ כֵּן גָּבְהוּ דְרָכַי מִדַּרְכֵיכֶם וּמַחְשְׁבֹתַי מִמַּחְשְׁבֹתֵיכֶם:

9 For as the heavens are higher than the earth, so are My ways higher than your ways, and My thoughts than your thoughts.

י כִּי כַּאֲשֶׁר יֵרֵד הַגֶּשֶׁם וְהַשֶּׁלֶג מִן־הַשָּׁמַיִם וְשָׁמָּה לֹא יָשׁוּב כִּי אִם־הִרְוָה אֶת־הָאָרֶץ וְהוֹלִידָהּ וְהִצְמִיחָהּ וְנָתַן זֶרַע לַזֹּרֵעַ וְלֶחֶם לָאֹכֵל:

10 For as the rain cometh down and the snow from heaven, and returneth not thither, except it water the earth, and make it bring forth and bud, and give seed to the sower and bread to the eater;

יא כֵּן יִהְיֶה דְבָרִי אֲשֶׁר יֵצֵא מִפִּי לֹא־יָשׁוּב אֵלַי רֵיקָם כִּי אִם־עָשָׂה אֶת־אֲשֶׁר חָפַצְתִּי וְהִצְלִיחַ אֲשֶׁר שְׁלַחְתִּיו׃

11 So shall My word be that goeth forth out of My mouth: it shall not return unto Me void, except it accomplish that which I please, and make the thing whereto I sent it prosper.

יב כִּי־בְשִׂמְחָה תֵצֵאוּ וּבְשָׁלוֹם תּוּבָלוּן הֶהָרִים וְהַגְּבָעוֹת יִפְצְחוּ לִפְנֵיכֶם רִנָּה וְכָל־עֲצֵי הַשָּׂדֶה יִמְחֲאוּ־כָף׃

12 For ye shall go out with joy, and be led forth with peace; the mountains and the hills shall break forth before you into singing, and all the trees of the field shall clap their hands.

יג תַּחַת הַנַּעֲצוּץ יַעֲלֶה בְרוֹשׁ וְתַחַת הַסִּרְפַּד יַעֲלֶה הֲדַס וְהָיָה לַיהוָה לְשֵׁם לְאוֹת עוֹלָם לֹא יִכָּרֵת׃

13 Instead of the thorn shall come up the cypress, and instead of the brier shall come up the myrtle; and it shall be to Yehovah for a memorial, for an everlasting sign that shall not be cut off.

Acknowledgements

I could not have written this book without the benefit of the efforts of many others.

First, I am so very thankful for those who allowed the Leningrad Codex to be photographed and put into a PDF format,[45] which made it possible to see the document without having to figure out how to have an audience in St. Petersburg, Russia, where, since the 1880s, it has been housed in the Russian National Library (Saltykov-Shchedrin).[46]

I am extremely blessed to also have found that same Leningrad Codex put into digital format by the Groves Center.[47] I used its digitally formatted source to "programmatically" convert to a web-Hebrew font for my website[48] (I modified the Hebrew in a couple of places; chiefly, I set the texts of both Exodus 20 and Deuteronomy 5 to actually conform to the Leningrad Codex verse separations, as well as corrected the last word in Deuteronomy 5:10 which I easily recognized did not match that of the Leningrad Codex itself: מִצְוֺתָו replaced מִצְוֺתָי).

Additionally, I am grateful to having had access to the JPS 1917 (in the public domain), which I modified for my online Tanakh.[49] I obtained the base JPS 1917 from Mechon Mamre.[50]

I owe a great debt to sefaria.org for digitizing and publishing Ernest Klein's 'A Comprehensive Etymological Dictionary Of The Hebrew Language For Readers Of English'.[51] Ernest Klein is a true, unsung hero, to me. His depth of knowledge in putting together his Etymological Dictionary of the Hebrew Language is a tremendous aid in understanding this ancient language of Hebrew Scripture.

---

[45] "Seforim Database," Seforim Online, accessed 13 May 2021, https://www.seforimonline.org/seforim-database/ (#264)
[46] "Leningrad Codex," USCDornsife, accessed 13 May 2021, https://dornsife.usc.edu/wsrp/leningrad-codex/
[47] "Home," J. Alan groves Center For Advanced Biblical Research, accessed 13 May 2021, https://www.grovescenter.org/
[48] "Tanach," Unicode/XML Leningrad Codex, accessed 13 May 2021, https://www.tanach.us
[49] Robert Pill, "Leningrad Codex Hebrew JPS 1917 English Tanakh," The-Iconoclast, last modified 17 May 2021, http://www.the-iconoclast.org/resources/tanakh/ (See notes at bottom)
[50] "A Hebrew - English Bible," Mechon Mamre, accessed 13 May 2021, https://www.mechon-mamre.org/p/pt/pt0.htm
[51] Ernest Klein, 'Klein Dictionary', Sefaria, accessed 13 May 2021, https://www.sefaria.org/Klein_Dictionary. See https://www.sefaria.org/Klein_Dictionary

Moreover, I would absolutely be remiss if I failed to mention my wife, Dana, who has "put up with me" for over 38 years. She has been a true rock of consistency which I needed to have in my life. She is also the mother of our two children, Rebekah and Joseph. When first Rebekah, and then Joseph were born, I used to say that my life didn't really begin until I had children; that is still true to this day!

I am so thankful to my entire family for their love and support, and am especially proud of the "better halves" my children have chosen (Sam and Shani, respectively). I want to mention both Sam's parents (Paul and Yehudit, aka Judy, Judith) and Shani's (Moises and Elizabeth) as all having had a very positive influence on me as well.

I am greatly indebted to Nehemia Gordon.[52] Even though we have yet to meet, he has been a true inspiration with his videos, podcasts and books which have helped me formulate my own ideas of how to live my life using Holy Scripture as the predominate guide.

My first exposure to Nehemia was from a video I saw titled "The Hebrew Yeshua vs. the Greek Jesus - NehemiasWall.com."[53] I highly recommend this very entertaining and informative resource. That link as well as other resources can be found on my website.[54]

Moreover, I have benefitted greatly by knowing when the new moon is sighted in Israel, from notifications by eyewitnesses. This work was formerly done by Nehemia Gordon, and has been continued by Devorah Gordon (not related).[55]

This work allows notifications of when to start a new month, allowing one to know when to begin the month for Passover as the barley is Aviv in Israel, of when to begin "counting the Omer"[56] – the fifty day

---

[52] Nehemia Gordon, "Nehemia's Wall," Nehemia's Wall, accessed 13 May 2021, https://www.nehemiaswall.com/
[53] Nehemia Gordon, " The Hebrew Yeshua vs. the Greek Jesus - NehemiasWall.com," YouTube, last modified 24 Apr 2011, https://www.youtube.com/watch?v=tddCNY6U77Y
[54] Robert Pill, "Resources," The-Iconoclast, last modified 25 Apr 2021, https://www.the-iconoclast.org/resources/
[55] Devorah Gordan, Devorah's Date Tree, last modified 13 May 2021, https://www.facebook.com/datetree
[56] Those of us who observe Shavuot based upon the starting of the counting of the Omer, begin that count starting "on the morrow after the sabbath," which is found in Leviticus 23:15-16. The "rabbis" interpret the passage to mean to start the Omer count on the day followng the day of the feast of Unleavened Bread, based upon the idea that it is a "High Sabbath" – a feast day where no work may be done (it can be noted that the Scripture does not say, from the morrow after the "Holy Convocation," or even specifically to say on first the day of the feast of unleavened bread!).

count to Shavuot (the feast of weeks), the new moon sighting to begin Rosh HaShanah, etc. To those of us who do not reside in Israel this is a true blessing, giving us the opportunity to observe these Biblically prescribed events at the right time! Devorah is a true inspiration and a great resource, along with all the many people who work with her in this endeavor.

I would further like to recognize a friend, Dr. Donald K. Burda, for helpful insight and particularly for his great assistance with grammar (or rather, for his insistence that I use proper grammar)!

Numbers 6:22-27

כב וַיְדַבֵּר יְהוָה אֶל־מֹשֶׁה לֵּאמֹר:

22 And Yehovah spoke unto Moses, saying:

כג דַּבֵּר אֶל־אַהֲרֹן וְאֶל־בָּנָיו לֵאמֹר כֹּה תְבָרֲכוּ אֶת־בְּנֵי יִשְׂרָאֵל אָמוֹר לָהֶם:

23 'Speak unto Aaron and unto his sons, saying: On this wise ye shall bless the children of Israel; ye shall say unto them:

כד יְבָרֶכְךָ יְהוָה וְיִשְׁמְרֶךָ:

24 Yehovah bless thee, and keep thee;

כה יָאֵר יְהוָה ׀ פָּנָיו אֵלֶיךָ וִיחֻנֶּךָּ:

25 Yehovah make His face to shine upon thee, and be gracious unto thee;

כו יִשָּׂא יְהוָה ׀ פָּנָיו אֵלֶיךָ וְיָשֵׂם לְךָ שָׁלוֹם:

26 Yehovah lift up His countenance upon thee, and give thee peace.

כז וְשָׂמוּ אֶת־שְׁמִי עַל־בְּנֵי יִשְׂרָאֵל וַאֲנִי אֲבָרֲכֵם:

27 So shall they put My name upon the children of Israel, and I will bless them.'

Leviticus 23:15-16 "15 And ye shall count unto you from the morrow after the sabbath, from the day that ye brought the sheaf of the waving; seven weeks shall there be complete; 16 even unto the morrow after the seventh week shall ye number fifty days; and ye shall present a new meal-offering unto Yehovah."

Acknowledgements

www.ingramcontent.com/pod-product-compliance
Lightning Source LLC
Chambersburg PA
CBHW070901080526
44589CB00013B/1161